KF
697
.F6
F57
2019

Fisher, Linda E., 1
author.
The foreclosure echo : how
the hardest hit have been
left out of the economic

P9-BEE-650

DATE DUE

WITHDRAWN

PRINTED IN U.S.A.

This book tells the ... t of ordinary people who experi... cated before now. The authors ... ding low- to moderate-income ... ng practices. They have a weal... Dream was shattered when the... xperiences – often examined th... science and legal research, *The* ... isis and how their lenders and p... he lingering effects of the crisis ... these effects have magnified in ... l help avoid another crisis.

LINDA E. FISHER ... teaches and litigates foreclosure ... nts. She has published in the a... hts. She has testified before the... at a Federal Trade Commission ... Safra Center for Ethics at Harva... Scholar. She was co-chair of the... urt Committee on the Reside... the Court's Committee on Mi... rsey AARP's Advocate of the Ye...

JUDITH FOX is Cl... l, where she teaches and practi... oject, a low-income clinic specializing in predatory lending and mortgage law. She has served on a number of committees and task forces including, most recently, the Indiana Mortgage Foreclosure Task Force and the Indiana Supreme Court's Coalition for Court Access. She was a member of the Consumer Financial Protection Bureau's Consumer Advisory Board until Acting Director Mulvaney disbanded it on June 6, 2018. Over the years, Professor Fox has been honored for her tireless work for low-income borrowers. She has received numerous awards, including the Rodney Ganey, Faculty Community Based Research Award, the Greenville Clark Award for service to the cause of peace and human rights and the St. Joseph Valley Project Community Achievement Award for Social Justice.

FASKEN LEARNING RESOURCE CENTER
9000090012

THE FORECLOSURE WHO

90012

The Foreclosure Echo

HOW THE HARDEST HIT HAVE BEEN LEFT OUT OF THE ECONOMIC RECOVERY

LINDA E. FISHER
Seton Hall University School of Law

JUDITH FOX
University of Notre Dame School of Law

CAMBRIDGE
UNIVERSITY PRESS

CAMBRIDGE
UNIVERSITY PRESS

University Printing House, Cambridge CB2 8BS, United Kingdom

One Liberty Plaza, 20th Floor, New York, NY 10006, USA

477 Williamstown Road, Port Melbourne, VIC 3207, Australia

314–321, 3rd Floor, Plot 3, Splendor Forum, Jasola District Centre, New Delhi – 110025, India

79 Anson Road, #06–04/06, Singapore 079906

Cambridge University Press is part of the University of Cambridge.

It furthers the University's mission by disseminating knowledge in the pursuit of
education, learning, and research at the highest international levels of excellence.

www.cambridge.org
Information on this title: www.cambridge.org/9781108415576
DOI: 10.1017/9781108234214

© Linda E. Fisher and Judith Fox 2019

This publication is in copyright. Subject to statutory exception
and to the provisions of relevant collective licensing agreements,
no reproduction of any part may take place without the written
permission of Cambridge University Press.

First published 2019

Printed and bound in Great Britain by Clays Ltd, Elcograf S.p.A.

A catalogue record for this publication is available from the British Library.

Library of Congress Cataloging-in-Publication Data
NAMES: Fisher, Linda E., 1953- author. | Fox, Judith L., author.
TITLE: The foreclosure echo : how the hardest hit have been left out of the economic recovery /
Linda E. Fisher, Seton Hall University School of Law; Judith Fox, University of
Notre Dame School of Law.
DESCRIPTION: Cambridge, United Kingdom ; New York, NY, USA : Cambridge University Press, 2019. |
Includes bibliographical references and index.
IDENTIFIERS: LCCN 2018056179 | ISBN 9781108415576 (hardback) | ISBN 9781108401616 (paperback)
SUBJECTS: LCSH: Foreclosure–Economic aspects–United States. | BISAC: LAW / Banking.
CLASSIFICATION: LCC KF697.F6 F57 2019 | DDC 332.7/20973–dc23
LC record available at https://lccn.loc.gov/2018056179

ISBN 978-1-108-41557-6 Hardback
ISBN 978-1-108-40161-6 Paperback

Cambridge University Press has no responsibility for the persistence or accuracy
of URLs for external or third-party internet websites referred to in this publication
and does not guarantee that any content on such websites is, or will remain,
accurate or appropriate.

90012

This book is dedicated to all of our foreclosure clients who have struggled to keep believing their American Dream.

Contents

Acknowledgments

As the dedication to this book demonstrates, our biggest debt of gratitude is to our clients, who bear their struggles with dignity and grace, despite the threat of losing their homes. We also acknowledge the many efforts made by concerned citizens and professionals in the Newark, New Jersey, and South Bend, Indiana areas to help prevent foreclosures, as well as mitigate their effects and rehabilitate neighborhoods. If only there were more such people, perhaps the crisis would not have been so deep and lasting.

More directly, Seton Hall Law School provided financial support and encouragement. We received extraordinarily helpful comments from the Progressive Property Scholars Conference, the Association for Law, Property and Society, the Safra Center for Ethics at Harvard, the Association of American Law Schools Bellows Scholars program and many others. We want to offer a special thanks to Kate Ravin for her wonderful assistance in editing. Our research assistants saved us many hours of investigation and their enthusiasm for the project was contagious. Not only were our academic colleagues helpful, our consumer lawyer colleagues were as well; together, they provided us with multiple perspectives on the issues. Peggy Jurow and Kevin Kelly have been enormously helpful in covering cases and classes while we wrote.

We also wish to thank our friends and families, and in particular our spouses Richard Gutman and Christopher Fox, for putting up with our preoccupation, obsessiveness and sometimes anxiety about ever finishing this book. Finally, we thank each other for simplifying the process of coauthoring.

Introduction

There is a neighborhood in South Bend, Indiana, a short distance from large, affluent homes and a major university. A school stands on the corner, yet no children play in the street. House after house is boarded up. Occasionally, through an open door, you can glimpse a bedroll on the floor, suggesting someone has claimed the house, at least for now. Newark, New Jersey – far away from South Bend – has similar blocks with jerry-rigged electrical wires strung to boarded-up homes next door to burnt-out husks of buildings. You probably have a neighborhood like this in your community. Scattered across America, they are the legacy of the great foreclosure crisis that began in 2008.

In *The Foreclosure Echo*, we examine the long-term consequences of this crisis through the eyes of our clients.[1] We are both law professors whose work includes supervising law students as they represent real people with real legal issues. The book includes historical and policy discussions, but it also recounts the stories of our clients, people who have experienced housing calamity firsthand. To really appreciate the upheaval our clients experienced – and continue to endure – readers need to follow the everyday lives of real people attempting to achieve stable housing arrangements for their families amid the chaos, both bureaucratic and personal.

Our clients are largely lower middle class, often the first in their families to have owned their own homes. They are black, white and Latino. They have worked hard at blue-, pink- or low-level white-collar jobs – at least until they were laid off, got sick or were scammed. Like many others, the bulk of their wealth was the equity in their homes. Many had mortgages, credit cards and car loans. In fact, immediately before the financial crisis, the poorest homeowners in America were highly leveraged, with

---

[1] Throughout the book, we will use the pronoun "we" or "our client" regardless of which one of us represented the client. All the narratives in this book are taken from real people, most of whom are our clients. Although we have permission to tell our clients' stories, we have opted to change many of their names to protect their privacy.

debt-to-income ratios of nearly 80 percent. At the other end of the spectrum, wealthy homeowners had very little debt – around 7 percent of their income.[2] Their wealth was diversified in stocks, bonds and other savings in addition to homes. "While the poor had $4 of home equity for every $1 of other assets, the rich were exactly the opposite with $1 of home equity for $4 of every other asset."[3]

The financial crisis wiped out the wealth of low- to moderate-income home-owners and ended their quest for the American dream. As Nobel Laureate Robert Shiller posited in his recent address to the National Economics Society, to truly understand what happens in an economic crisis, we need to "replicate in ourselves as best we can the feelings" of the people who experienced it.[4] In order to do this, we need to know and understand their stories. This book tells those stories, but it also helps explain the importance of narratives in understanding what happens after a financial crisis.

The long-term consequences of the financial crisis are only beginning to emerge. Even as certain higher-income, predominantly white neighborhoods across the country have largely recovered, other communities continue to suffer, with no end in sight. Communities of color, originally targeted for the worst loans, remain in crisis. The ever-increasing wealth inequality in this country is one obvious result. This book introduces you to the people who bore the brunt of the crisis and illustrates how the governmental response protected the assets of the wealthy while neglecting a newly emerging middle class. This version of A *Tale of Two Cities* has also exacerbated patterns of resegregation, as displaced homeowners tend to move to poorer, more segregated neighborhoods after foreclosure.

Economists have only recently begun to explore how narratives can influence and, as some suggest, affect economic fluctuations. While we are lawyers, not economists, our clients and their experiences can add to that understanding. By retelling the story of the housing crisis from the perspective of our clients who experienced it, we hope to better understand what happened and suggest ways to improve the response to the next crisis. More importantly, we hope to provide evidence that the lingering effects of that crisis remain for real people, even while the economic indicators tell us the crisis has passed. Those lingering effects, or the "foreclosure echo," as we have named it, continue to feel like a crisis to the individuals and communities that have been left behind.[5]

[2] Atif Mian & Amir Sufi, House of Debt: How They (and You) Caused the Great Recession, and How We Can Prevent It from Happening Again 20 (2015).

[3] *Id.*

[4] Robert J. Shiller, *Narrative Economics*, Cowles Foundation, Discussion Paper No. 2069 (2017), https://ssrn.com/abstract=2896857.

[5] The phrase "foreclosure echo" was derived from an early article on the subject written. Judith Fox, *Foreclosure Echo: How Abandoned Foreclosures Are Re-Entering the Market through Debt Buyers*, 26 Loy. Consumer L. Rev. 25 (2013). It later became the theme of the National Consumer Law Center's annual mortgage conference entitled, "The Foreclosure Echo: Addressing the Ongoing Consequences of the Foreclosure Crisis," July 10, 2015.

Prevailing narratives from previous financial crises, whether true or not, are also instructive. They drive not only the public's perceptions about the crisis but also, at times, the government's reaction to it. One of the most striking examples is the narrative of the bank runs of the Great Depression, so famously portrayed by Jimmy Stewart in *It's a Wonderful Life*. At the time, the government correctly determined that it had a responsibility to prevent such incidents in the future. In 1933, Congress passed the Glass-Steagall Act, which, among other things, created the Federal Deposit Insurance Corporation (FDIC). The FDIC insures deposits and thus removes the incentive to grab your money from the bank before it is gone. As added protection, the Federal Reserve was empowered to make low-interest loans to otherwise solvent banks to provide liquidity. These protections worked fairly well to shore up the banking industry. Between 1934 and 1980, only 243 banks failed.[6]

Despite all these efforts, 465 banks failed between 2008 and 2012.[7] Washington Mutual (WaMu) was one of the first and most public of these failures. Lines of people outside the bank brought back narratives of the Great Depression bank runs. In response, FDIC insurance on deposits was raised from $100,000, where it had been for nearly three decades, to $250,000.[8] In addition, the government took the unprecedented step of expanding deposit insurance to previously uninsured money market accounts for a year.[9] Economists have questioned the efficacy of these moves, but both are examples of how the response to the crisis of 2007–08 was driven not just by current realities but also by memories of previous crashes. Your bank deposits were never in real danger in 2008 – your house was.

Between the Great Depression of the 1930s and what is now called the Great Recession of 2007–09 was the Savings and Loan crisis of the 1980s. Three thousand banks or savings and loans failed, many more than had failed in any prior economic downturn. In fact, "[b]y 1994, one-sixth of federally insured depository institutions had either closed or required financial assistance, affecting 20% of the banking system's assets."[10] Why did an unprecedented number of savings and loan institutions and banks fail? In the years running up to the crisis, savings and loans and thrifts had moved away from their usual safe lending practices into riskier, higher-interest loans. A housing bubble developed, largely in the West and Southwest, and then it popped. The result was a crisis in the financial markets, but it was more localized than either the Great Depression or the recession that developed in 2008.[11]

---

[6] THE FIN. CRISIS INQUIRY REP.: FINAL REP. OF THE NAT'L COMMISSION ON THE CAUSES OF THE FIN. AND ECON. CRISIS IN THE UNITED STATES 36 (authorized ed. 2011).

[7] FED. DEPOSIT INS. CORP., FAILED BAN LIST, https://www.fdic.gov/bank/individual/failed/bank-list.html.

[8] *Id.*

[9] Shiller, *supra* note 4, at 44.

[10] FIN. CRISIS INQUIRY REP., *supra* note 6, at 36.

[11] *Id.* at 35–36; *see generally* Richard K. Green & Susan M. Wachter, *The American Mortgage in Historical and International Context*, 19 J. ECON. PERSP. 93 (2004).

The savings and loan crisis helped create the belief that housing crises are both caused by and preceded by a housing bubble. It follows that where there has been no bubble, there will be no crisis. Ironically, prior to 2008, policymakers spent a lot of time arguing that there was no bubble and, therefore, would be no crisis. Shortly before his nomination as chairman of the Federal Reserve in 2005, Ben Bernanke famously testified that rising house prices "reflect strong economic fundamentals" and not a housing bubble.[12] But advocates on the ground, including both of us, were seeing a very different picture and issuing warnings.

The noted economists Atif Mian and Amir Sufi make a very convincing argument in *House of Debt* that housing bubbles alone do not create financial crises. The debt burdens our clients were taking on, along with the predatory loan products targeting them, were warning signs of a problem to come. These warnings were ignored. Ben Bernanke eventually acknowledged that a housing bubble had preceded the crisis but insisted regulators bore no responsibility for it or the crisis that followed. He may be at least half right. We can see that burgeoning consumer debt combined with the housing bubble to foment the crisis.[13] By relying on the narrative of a market and culture that no longer existed, policymakers missed the warning signs. That narrative persists with some policymakers, making it likely they will miss the next crisis as well.

These prevailing narratives, as economists have named them, have a great deal of influence on decision-makers. Many new such narratives have been developed during the more recent financial crisis that is the subject of this book. Two of the most popular depicted as villains the irresponsible homebuyers who bought bigger homes than they could afford or who tried to benefit from the crisis by strategically defaulting on their mortgages. Neither narrative is based on fact. The poor and working-class neighborhoods of cities like South Bend, Indiana, and Newark, New Jersey went from credit deserts to credit oceans in the years running up to the crisis. As Mian and Sufi point out, the banking industry was deliberately targeting these areas for mortgages, but not for any altruistic reason or to satisfy community invest-ment obligations, as some have alleged.[14] They were fueling the securitization craze that will be discussed in more detail in Chapter 1 of this book. In a three-year period before the crisis, mortgages for new homes in zip codes with low credit scores grew by a remarkable "30 percent *per year*, compared to only 11 percent in high credit score areas."[15] Many naive buyers were pulled into the market by brokers and lenders bent on making a quick buck.[16]

Most of our clients did not lose their homes because they bought big and overly expensive properties. In fact, many of them did not buy properties at all. Instead,

[12] Neil Henderson, *Bernanke: There's No Housing Bubble to Go Bust*, WASH. POST, Oct. 27, 2005.

[13] Mian, *supra* note 2, at 76.

[14] *Id.* at 78–91.

[15] *Id.* at 77.

[16] *See*, RICHARD BITNER, CONFESSIONS OF A SUBPRIME LENDER: AN INSIDER'S TALE OF GREED, FRAUD AND IGNORANCE (2008).

they were convinced by slick and often very aggressive mortgage brokers to refinance their existing properties, sometimes for more than they were worth. It was common at that time to refinance for 100 or even 110 percent of home value, based on the belief that property values would perpetually rise. During the height of the subprime boom, mortgage brokers were literally going door to door in working-class neighborhoods. The plight of Eleanor Stames, an elderly client of the Notre Dame Clinical Law Center, was not uncommon. A broker knocked on her door, telling her he had "inspected her roof," which needed to be repaired. She was advised to take out a home equity loan. Initially, she refused, but he persisted. At one point, he stood on her porch, threatening her on his cell phone: "I know you are in there," and "You had better let me in." Eventually, she agreed to refinance her mortgage. The new loan was supposed to pay off her credit cards and give her money to fix the roof. Although she did receive the money to fix the roof – which arguably did not need fixing – the broker never paid off the credit cards. Instead, he pocketed the money and left town. Ms. Stames did not discover this until the credit card company began dunning her for unpaid bills.

Another elderly client of the clinic was in the process of moving to an assisted living facility when a mortgage broker drove her to his office to refinance her home, pulling $10,000 in equity out of the property. She was so obviously senile at the time that she kept asking anyone she encountered, included the judge in the resulting legal case, "Are you the dentist? I don't like dentists." Proving she was not competent to make the loan was easy; returning her money was not. As in the previous case, the money had disappeared along with the broker. The Notre Dame Clinical Law Center was able to rescind this obviously illegal loan, but the money was never recovered.

The Seton Hall Law Center for Social Justice represented many such clients in the greater Newark area. Some were victims of foreclosure rescue scams, which preyed on unwitting homeowners in foreclosure. The masterminds and their coconspirators – prominently including subprime mortgage brokers and appraisers – offered to take title to the home for a year or two while the homeowners improved their credit scores. The scammers explained that this would allow the borrowers to then refinance and retake title. In the meantime, the homeowners would pay "rent" to the fraudsters, who said they would use the money to make payments on a new mortgage. Of course, these schemes never worked out and the perpetrators always disappeared, leaving the original homeowners worse off than ever. One such client, Jim Colson, was even driven out of his home by five hammer-wielding thugs, associates of the mortgage broker. He remained homeless for some time thereafter, but we kept litigating for six years and eventually recovered a sizeable settlement. The primary defendant was an insurance company involved in securitizing mortgages, including the one taken out by the scammer's straw man. There were red flags indicating fraud that the company ignored. Eventually, the insurance company filed bankruptcy and the court discovered the debtor had defrauded thousands of elderly people who had invested their life savings in it.[17] After his case was resolved, Mr. Colson and his children were able to get back on their feet – his daughter even went to law school.

These are just a few examples of the millions of people unwittingly drawn into this crisis. Neither of the two women represented by Notre Dame lost their homes, but others were not so fortunate. Still, the purpose of this book is not to retell stories from the buildup to the crisis. Instead, we are telling the stories of those left behind after the government declared the recession over. Chapter 1 will provide some necessary background information about the boom in predatory and subprime lending that victimized moderate- and low-income homeowners and prospective homebuyers. To add perspective to the discussion, however, one must review the history of the government's role in and influence on housing markets.

HISTORICAL BACKGROUND OF HOUSING POLICY

Homeownership is built into the American psyche. President Franklin D. Roosevelt identified "the right to decent housing" as part of his Economic Bill of Rights.[18] For much of our history, however, only wealthy white men owned property. According to the United States Census Bureau, in 1900, fewer than half of all Americans owned their own homes. Homeownership peaked in 2005, right at the height of the subprime mortgage frenzy, at just under 70 percent. By the end of 2015, it had fallen to just under 64 percent, a number last seen in the 1980s. The numbers for African-American and Hispanic homeowners are much lower and fell much further. The rates of homeownership for these groups were just under 50 percent at the height of the bubble and have now fallen into the low 40s.[19]

As noted by Mechele Dickerson in her incisive book *Homeownership and America's Financial Underclass*, our culture has been saturated with the myth of the Happy Homeowner who has realized the promise of America. This narrative connected homeownership to the American dream, and made non-homeowners feel left behind.[20] As a country, we have come to believe that homeowners are more stable, and homes provide economic stability.[21] As a result, government policies have been developed to assist and encourage homeownership. While that is not

---

[17] *See*, Bert Caldwell, *'Loan to Own' Part of Met's Legacy*, THE SPOKESMAN-REV. (Feb. 17, 2005), http://www.spokesman.com/stories/2005/feb/17/loan-to-own-part-of-mets-legacy.

[18] UShistory.org, Economic Bill of Rights, http://www.ushistory.org/documents/economic_bill_of_rights.htm.

[19] U.S. CENSUS BUREAU, QUARTERLY RESIDENTIAL VACANCY AND HOMEOWNERSHIP, SECOND QUARTER 2018 (July 26, 2018), https://www.census.gov/housing/hvs/files/qtr416/hown416.png.

[20] A. Mechele Dickerson, HOMEOWNERSHIP AND AMERICA'S FINANCIAL UNDERCLASS (2014); *see also* Mechele Dickerson, *The Myth of Homeownership and Why Homeownership Is Not Always a Good Thing*, 84 IND. L. J. 189, 190 (2009).

[21] *Id.* at 190–91.

necessarily an imprudent policy, it did contribute to changes in the market, some of which have had unintended consequences.

Responses to the housing crisis of the late 1920s and 1930s formed the bedrock of United States housing policy for decades to come. Home loans before the Great Depression were very different than the loans available in the subprime boom of the early 2000s. The loans of the 1920s and 1930s were short term – usually less than ten years – and had variable interest rates. Loans were rarely given for more than 50 percent of a home's value. When they came due – or when borrowers experienced financial strain – they were often refinanced or renegotiated. The Great Depression changed all that. Home prices fell drastically, turning these once-safe loans into unsustainable liabilities. Homeowners found themselves owing more than their homes were worth and unable to refinance. As many as 250,000 foreclosures occurred per year between 1931 and 1935.[22] In the spring of 1933, up to 1,000 foreclosures were occurring per day.[23]

Across America, homeless people began building shantytowns, later known as Hoovervilles, in reference to then-President Hoover. After Franklin Roosevelt was elected, his administration moved quickly to respond to the high number of foreclosures and the resulting homelessness crisis by creating the Home Owners' Loan Corporation (HOLC).[24] The corporation purchased and refinanced defaulted mortgage loans as well as offering loans to homeowners who had been foreclosed upon. During its short tenure, the HOLC provided over a million mortgages to homeowners.[25] This model became the template for future governmental intervention including during the foreclosure crisis that is the subject of this book, with one significant difference: HOLC mortgages allowed principal reductions, something that was opposed at all levels of the government during the most recent crisis. We will discuss the implication of this decision at length throughout the book. HOLC not only set the narrative for interventions for distressed mortgages, it also changed the nature of the mortgage instrument itself. HOLC mortgages were fully amortized, fixed-rate, twenty-year loans as opposed to the shorter-term, non-amortizing loans they replaced. HOLC loans thus became the model for future mortgage lending until the subprime boom of the 2000s.[26]

Unfortunately, HOLC is also credited with creating the practice of redlining around African-American neighborhoods, a legacy that continues to afflict us today and is directly linked, decades later, to the crumbling communities we discuss herein. The highly descriptive term "redlining" refers to the lending industry's

---

[22] Richard K. Green & Susan M. Wachter, *The American Mortgage in Historical and International Context*, 19 J. ECON. PERSP. 93, 94(2004).

[23] Amy E. Hillier, *Redlining and the Home Owners' Loan Corporation*, 29 J. URB. HIST. 394, 416, note 1 (2009).

[24] *Id.* at 394.

[25] Green, *supra* note 22, at 94.

[26] Green, *supra* note 22, at 95.

refusal to provide mortgage loans to minorities, predominately African Americans. HOLC created the infamous color-coded maps that birthed the term "redlining" by coloring African-American neighborhoods red.[27]

After addressing the immediate need to stem foreclosures in the 1930s, the government moved to shore up mortgage markets and provide a means for Americans to realize the American dream of homeownership that Roosevelt had envisioned. The Federal Housing Administration (FHA) was created in 1936 to provide insurance backing for mortgage loans, thereby encouraging financial institutions to lend to prospective homeowners. FHA charges homeowners a small insurance premium payment in addition to the loan to provide this insurance. As we will discuss later, these premiums would become a problem for homeowners in the aftermath of the latest crisis.[28]

Having encouraged home lending, the government now needed to create a market for these loans to allow banks to continue lending beyond their immediate capital reserves. The Federal National Mortgage Association (Fannie Mae) was created in 1938 to fuel mortgage lending by developing the secondary market in mortgages. Now, a remote investor could readily purchase and trade in mortgages. Fannie Mae provided a cushion for bankers to comfortably offer longer-term mortgages in what was a relatively calm time for mortgage lending.

After World War II, things changed once again. The Servicemen's Readjustment Act of 1944, more commonly known as the Veteran's Bill of Rights, guaranteed returning soldiers an education and a home loan. The Veterans Administration (VA) loan was born.[29] A new American middle class followed. Returning vets, largely subsidized by low down payments offered with VA loans, helped stimulate a housing boom. "Vet villages," as they were often called, sprang up across America. Unfortunately, not all returning vets were able to avail themselves of these benefits. African-American veterans returned to discover that no one would sell a home to them. Racial covenants – clauses in deeds that prohibited sales to African Americans and sometimes Jews, and other race-based lending practices – locked racial and ethnic minorities out of the American dream of homeownership. Governmental policies also suppressed lending in minority neighborhoods.[30] The history of racial discrimination plays a significant role in the run up to our recent foreclosure crisis, a topic we will return to in a moment.

The FHA used this period of expanding ownership to further standardize the mortgage, extending terms out to thirty years. The secondary market for mortgages was further incentivized by the creation of the Mortgage Guarantee Insurance

---

[27] Richard Rothstein, The Color of Law: A Forgotten History of How Our Government Segregated America 64 (2017); *but see* Hillier, *supra* note 23, whose research disputes HOLC's responsibility for redlining.

[28] Green, *supra* note 22, at 96.

[29] *Id.*

[30] For a history of discriminatory governmental housing policies, *see*, Rothstein, *supra* note 27.

Corporation, which gave mortgage insurance guarantees outside of the strict FHA lending limits. To avail themselves of these insurance programs, lenders needed to standardize their products and their forms. The conventional American mortgage – the thirty-year, fixed-rate, fully amortized mortgage – would dominate the market for the next few decades.[31]

During this period, an investor in mortgage bonds could expect a healthy return of 5 to 6 percent. Treasury bonds, in contrast, paid only about 4 percent. Naturally, money flowed into the mortgage markets. When the rate on Treasury bonds increased, money began to flow out. The government sought to stimulate the mortgage markets again by splitting the Federal National Mortgage Association into the Government National Mortgage Association (Ginnie Mae) and Fannie Mae, which was now a private corporation. Ginnie Mae provided insurance and backing for FHA loans, while Fannie Mae provided backing for private mortgage loans made by banks. Freddie Mac, also private, was created several years later to insure loans made by the savings and loan industry.[32] These three – Ginnie Mae, Fannie Mae and Freddie Mac – are known as the GSEs, or Government Sponsored Entities. In 1970, Ginnie Mae became the first of the three to bundle loans into securitized loan pools, selling interests to investors.[33] Securitization, discussed at length in Chapter 1, is the process of putting hundreds or thousands of individual loans into a large pool, and then subdividing interests in the pool of loans into various grades of investment securities. Investors profit by receiving a stream of income each month from mortgage payments made by borrowers. Fannie Mae and Freddie Mac would play an important role in the foreclosure crisis to come, but securitization would play a larger one.

At first, only the GSEs securitized their loans. Private securitization began to develop in the period immediately before the savings and loan crisis of the early 1980s. As previously mentioned, this crisis caused a great number of financial institutions to fail. After the 1980s crisis, the federal government had a major problem to solve, having been left with "$402 billion in loans and real estate" from these failed institutions.[34] The Resolution Trust Corporation (RTC) was created to allow the government to sell these loans. Fannie Mae and Freddie Mac were able to buy a portion of them, but most did not meet their standards. Unable to sell them to the GSEs, the RTC instead securitized them, expanding the securitized mortgage market by some $25 billion. The marriage of subprime loan origination and private securitization had occurred, ironically, at the hand of the US government.[35]

---

[31] Green, *supra* note 22, at 99.

[32] Green, *supra* note 22, at 97–8.

[33] Judith Fox, *The Future of Foreclosure Law in the Wake of the Great Housing Crisis of 2007–2014*, 54 WASHBURN L. J. 496, 489–526 (2015).

[34] FIN. CRISIS INQUIRY REP., *supra* note 6, at 68.

[35] *Id.* at 69–70.

The negative impact of these emerging loan products and their subsequent private securitization will be a recurring theme throughout this book.

Securitization works well when people are able to make payments, but a brief history of the underlying loans begins to explain some of the problems that can occur when homeowners are unable to pay. As mentioned, prior to the Great Depression, a mortgage loan was generally of short duration. It was not uncommon for it to be renegotiated or refinanced at the end of that short term, because a large balloon (or lump-sum) payment remained. These negotiations also took place if a loan went into default. Prior to securitization, banks held their loans in their portfolio, so it was in their best interest to negotiate to continue to be paid after a loan defaulted. Selling a home in foreclosure virtually always results in further loss; holding and owning the property is an even bigger headache.

Once securitization became the norm, however, the situation changed dramatically. The originating mortgage lender had sold the loan to the securitized pool. It no longer had anything to lose if the loan failed. Renegotiating the loan was difficult due to the many parties and interests involved, the details of which we will discuss later in the book. The servicer of the loan – the entity taking payments – had no incentive to spend the time and money necessary to renegotiate. It was and is easier to simply foreclose. Or is it? The industry was never created with foreclosure in mind, and servicers lacked the expertise to do it right. The previous framework really did not provide much room for a homeowner to challenge a foreclosure. Securitization changed all that.

Unfortunately, the issues do not get any less complicated after foreclosure. When a lender sells a property at a foreclosure sale, the property generally sells for far less than the market value, resulting essentially in a fire sale. This is even more pronounced when many, many foreclosure sales are happening at once, as occurred in the financial crisis of 2008 and the Great Depression before it. When a property is sold, the proceeds are used to repay the mortgage debt. If the debt is larger than the selling price of the property, the homeowner is left with a "deficiency," a personal obligation that must be paid out of other assets or earnings if it is reduced to a judgment. During the Great Depression, policymakers became very concerned about the rise in foreclosures that was depressing sales prices and, as a result, dramatically increasing deficiencies.[36]

States reacted with a number of measures to stem the tide of foreclosures. The first was the foreclosure moratorium. California was an early adopter of this solution.[37] Many states enacted similar legislation that delayed foreclosures in ways ranging from extensions of the redemption period to delays in trials and sales. During the recent financial crisis, senators, congressmen and citizens called for a

---

[36] *See*, note, *Mortgage Relief during the Depression*, 47 HARVARD L. REV. 299 (1933).

[37] Stefan A. Riesenfeld, *California Legislation Curbing Deficiency Judgment*, 48 CAL. L. REV. 705, 706 (1960).

foreclosure moratorium, but the federal government refused.[38] A short-term halt to foreclosures eventually did occur in response to specific issues of faulty paperwork, but it only applied to those lenders implicated in the growing scandal.[39] This intervention was not intended to assist homeowners in any material way.

During the Great Depression, states also attempted to tackle the problem of sinking foreclosure sale prices and rising deficiency judgments with strategies ranging from regulating sale prices used to determine deficiencies to banning deficiencies outright.[40] New York was a leader in these reforms. It modified existing deficiency legislation to require that deficiencies be calculated based on the fair market value of the property, not the price at the foreclosure sale.[41] In 1914, the United States Supreme Court ruled in *Gelfert v. National City Bank of New York,* 313 US 212, that states can restrict the amount a lender can collect in a deficiency judgment. Other states followed suit. Some of these Depression-era fixes remained part of the legal landscape during the recent foreclosure crisis. Currently, twelve states ban deficiency judgments in most circumstances, though many of them have some exceptions. Fifteen states, including Indiana, allow deficiency judgments. New Jersey is among the remaining states that limit deficiencies but do not completely disallow them. In many states the lender can choose between a judicial or non-judicial foreclosure (explained in Chapter 6) but waive the ability to collect the deficiency if the lender uses a non-judicial process. In other states, the lender cannot seek a deficiency judgment if it repurchases the home in the foreclosure sale.[42]

What happens to someone whose home is sold in a foreclosure sale? As just discussed, some find themselves in collection actions due to their deficiency judgment. Others find that the house they thought they had lost is, in fact, not lost at all. Instead, the lender has failed to complete the foreclosure or, in even more bizarre situations, reversed the foreclosure, essentially "un-foreclosing" the home. These "zombie" mortgages have become significant problems for many urban areas. Abandoned properties and zombie mortgages are discussed at length in Chapter 3.

---

[38] Binyamin Applebaum, *A Foreclosure Tightrope for Democrats,* N.Y. TIMES (Oct. 11, 2010), http://www.nytimes.com/2010/10/12/business/economy/12foreclose.html; Ryan Haggerty & Andy Grimm, *Loop Marchers Call for Moratorium on Foreclosure,* CHICAGO TRIB., May 1, 2012; Randy Furst, *Ministers Call on Banks for Moratorium on Foreclosures,* STAR TRIB. (Dec. 13, 2011), http://www.startribune.com/ministers-call-on-banks-for-moratorium-on-foreclos ures/135532983; The American Presidency Project, press release, *Hilary Clinton Calls on Wall Street to Shoulder Responsibility for the Foreclosure Crisis* (Dec. 5, 2007), http://www.presi dency.ucsb.edu/ws/?pid=96442.

[39] David Streitfeld & Nelson D. Schwartz, *Largest U.S. Bank Halts Foreclosures in All States,* N.Y. TIMES (Oct. 8, 2010), https://www.nytimes.com/2010/10/09/business/09mortgage.html.

[40] Clifford C. Hynning, *Constitutionality of Moratory Legislation,* 12 CHICAGO-KENT L. REV. 182, 183–84 (1934).

[41] John L. Tierney, *"Fair Value" and the Deficiency Judgment,* 16 J. LAND PUB. UTILITY ECON. 181, 183–84 (1940).

[42] 12.2.2 State Statutory Restrictions on Deficiency Judgment, NAT'L. CONSUMER L. CTR, https:// library.nclc.org, downloaded Feb. 23, 2017.

While not all foreclosed homeowners face such horrors, they do all face one significant challenge – finding a new place to live. Homelessness has risen because of the crisis, but has not received nearly as much public recognition. Instead, the focus has been on the rental market as the foreclosure crisis morphed into a rental crisis. Stricter lending regulations, including larger down-payment requirements, have made it harder for new buyers to purchase homes. Homeowners displaced by the foreclosure crisis need places to live, yet are unable to purchase again until they have had time to regain their financial footing. Thus, more and more Americans are looking for rentals. Rental availability is at historically low levels, and prices have increased substantially since the crisis.[43]

Policymakers were once much more willing to intervene in stabilizing rental markets. Their reasons for doing so, however, were not altruistic. Most early rent-control legislation began in response to World War I, when governments needed workers for factories producing military equipment. Often, these factories were located outside of urban areas and lacked sufficient housing. Additionally, returning soldiers needed places to live. Both factors contributed to widespread rental short-ages and escalating prices. By war's end, every major Western nation had created rental legislation in response to this need.[44]

Early legislation largely aimed to maintain housing by barring or delaying evictions, especially for military personnel.[45] Congress reacted to the emergency of World War I by enacting rent control in the District of Columbia.[46] The Emergency Price Control Act of 1942 opened the door to widespread rent control that lasted throughout the war.[47] Rent controls now remain in very few locations, notably New York City. Interestingly, efforts to make rentals affordable were not repeated in the more recent crisis, even though we were also engaged in an overseas war. In an effort to protect the population needed to build arms during the World Wars, many states enacted laws providing due process protection for tenants. Most of these remain today. Ironically, this has resulted in a bizarre system in which renters being evicted from their rental units have more protection in many states than home-owners being foreclosed on.

Rentals did not garner the same attention in the most recent crisis. However, Congress did enact some short-term protections for tenants whose rental homes faced foreclosure. Since the crisis, eviction issues have gained more attention, partially because of the popularity of Matthew Desmond's book *Evicted: Poverty*

---

[43] Andrea J. Boyack, *Equitably Housing (Almost) Half a Nation of Renters*, 64 BUFFALO L. REV. 109, 119 (2017).

[44] Karl Borders, *Emergency Rent Control, Law & Contemporary Problems* 107, 109–10 (1943).

[45] Soldiers' and Sailors' Civil Relief Act of March 8, 1918, 40 Stat. 44; now known as Service-members Civil Relief, 50 U.S.C.A. §3932 (2008).

[46] John W. Willis, *Short History of Rent Control Laws*, 6 CORNELL L. REV. 54, 74–5 (1950), http://scholarship.law.cornell.edu/clr/vol36/iss1/3.

[47] *Id.* at 79.

and Profit in the American City. This book illustrates the realities for many low-income Americans who face the constant challenge of finding safe, affordable housing. Such common occurrences as flat tires or a child's illness can cause an hourly worker to lose the income needed to pay rent. In addition, many low-income clients do not have leases, or they rent properties with significant housing code defects. These conditions have grown considerably worse in the aftermath of the crisis. Many former rental properties have been foreclosed on, further reducing the available housing stock.

In 1944, President Franklin D. Roosevelt outlined his Economic Bill of Rights.[48] Among them was the right of every citizen to "a decent home." This is not law, but it does articulate a longstanding American ideal. This ideal has been translated into law through a few international agreements, beginning with Article 25 of the Universal Declaration of Human Rights.[49] "Decent" or even adequate housing has traditionally not been interpreted as a right to own a home or, similarly, the right to any particular kind of housing finance. Instead, in terms of homeownership, this right has more often been seen as a goal for assuring that markets allow nondiscriminatory access to credit and that consumers have some level of protection against deception.

THE RISE OF BEHAVIORAL ECONOMICS

Economists have been investigating issues relating to financial markets and housing policy for as long as there have been economic researchers. Because of this, economists faced quite a bit of criticism for failure to predict the financial crisis and resulting foreclosure crisis.[50] According to Ben Bernanke, this happened in part because academic economists simply did not believe that a "collapse of the financial system" would have a broad impact on the economy. After studying the depression of the 1930s, Bernanke claims to have disagreed.[51] This is why he believed it was so important for the government to prevent banks from failing. If the banks failed, he was convinced we would be facing another Great Depression. He also expected that saving Wall Street would save Main Street as well. This was his biggest

---

[48] Franklin D. Roosevelt Presidential Library and Museum, *State of the Union Message to Congress, President Franklin D. Roosevelt* (Jan. 11, 1944), fdrlibray.org, https://www.fdrlibrary .marist.edu/edu/archives/address_text.html.

[49] G. A. Res. 217 (III) Universal Declaration of Human Rights Art. 25, (Dec. 10, 1948); Convention on Economic, Social and Cultural Rights Art. 11, Dec. 16, 1966, 993 U.N.T.S. 3; Convention on the rights of the child Art. 27, Nov. 20, 1989, 1577 U.N.T.S.3; Convention on the elimination of all forms of racial discrimination Art. 5, Mar. 7, 1966, 660 U.N.T.S. 195; 5.

[50] David Colander, Hans Föllmer, Armin Haas, Michael Goldberg, Katarina Juselius, Alan Kirman, Thomas Lux & Brigitte Sloth, *The Financial Crisis and the Systemic Failure of Academic Economics*, 7 (Kiel Inst. for the World Econ., Working Papers No. 1489, 2009), https://pdfs.semanticscholar.org/22a9/5fc8524947c1b7f985bd75aee2ce604d6fea.pdf.

[51] Transcript, *Panic, Fear and Regret* (*Marketplace* radio broadcast Mar. 20, 2018), https://www .marketplace.org/topics/divideddecade.

miscalculation. The narrative of the past crisis played a significant role in shaping the response to the current crisis, despite vast differences between the financial worlds of 2008 and 1929.

We are still questioning how so many smart people got it wrong and missed the signs of the collapse. A paper that has come to be known as the Dahlmer report offers one explanation. The authors, all prominent economists, blame the fundamental assumptions underlying classic economic research, specifically challenging the notion of the "rational" actor.[52] Economists' models assume that consumers and lenders behave in ways they define as "rational." While there is no single definition of a rational actor, most definitions accept the basic idea that rational actors will make decisions that optimize their preferences, considering the costs and benefits of alternate decisions.[53] Of course, this definition naturally depends on having the necessary information about those costs and benefits. Under this theory of *constrained optimization*, consumers will make the best choices for their families based on the available options and their budgetary constraints.[54] One of the problems with classical economics, however, is that the economist, not the consumer, determines which decision is normatively considered *the best choice*. Behavioral economics emerged as economists began to realize that people's actual behavior "deviated systematically and predictably from the normative benchmark."[55] The crisis made it quite clear that neither banks nor their customers always make the best choices, nor do they possess all the necessary information in this complex world of financial decisions to make a so-called rational decision. People simply do not have the time or ability to evaluate all the variables when choosing a mortgage product. Mix this in with subjective preferences and hard-sell broker tactics and you've created a combustible mix.

During the crisis, many blamed borrowers for what appeared to be an irrational decision to borrow money they could not afford to repay. But this assumes a financial market where everyone is a "rational actor" who knows what is being offered and every product being offered is fair. During the crisis, all too many borrowers relied on the advice of brokers who owed them no legal duty and all too often gave advice that maximized their profit at the expense of their client's financial well-being. Borrowers were often sold inappropriate and complicated products that garnered high commissions for brokers but few advantages for borrowers. Mortgage documents are complex, and many people simply had no idea how to read and understand what they were signing, assuming they even had the opportunity to read the paperwork. Some have challenged the idea that people could not understand their mortgage paperwork and we acknowledge that there is no reliable

---

[52] *Id.*

[53] FLORES HEUKELOM, BEHAVIORAL ECONOMICS: A HISTORY 183 (2014).

[54] RICHARD THALER, MISBEHAVING: THE MAKING OF BEHAVIORAL ECONOMICS 5–7 (2015).

[55] Heukelon, *supra* note 53, at 170.

way to test now what people did or did not know years ago when they signed their mortgage papers. However, for many years we gave examples of variable rate mortgage documents to our law students, all highly educated graduates of some of America's best colleges and universities, and asked them to tell us what the loan payments would be when the rates reset. No one ever could. It is, therefore, no surprise to us that many Americans also had no idea what they had just agreed to.

Behavioral economics developed as a counter to the idea that all players in the market fit this ideal of the model "rational actor." It combines psychology with economics to explain how people behave in real life situations as opposed to how we hope they will behave in theory. Since the crisis, this approach for analyzing markets has gained prominence.[56] In fact, the 2017 Nobel Prize in Economics was awarded to Richard Thaler, a pioneer in behavioral economics. Behavioral economics also raises concerns about a second important tenet of classic economics, market equilibrium. Market equilibrium claims that when markets are left to their own devices, supply will always equal demand. A problem with this theory is that humans tend to be overly optimistic with predictions about markets and many other things.[57] In fact, some economists have used this understanding of behavior to explain away the industry's role in the financial crisis. To them, financial services were not flawed; it was the "overly optimistic beliefs about house prices" that caused a bubble and the resulting problems.[58] Others disagree, blaming the industry entirely for taking advantage of people. In actuality, it was both, which supports the idea that markets do not always reach an appropriate equilibrium. Sometimes, regulation is needed to help markets along. In *Phishing for Phools*, George Akerlof and Robert Shiller illustrate numerous ways in which markets fail because some people will always attempt to take advantage of others. As they point out, as long it is profitable to create what they dub "good-for-mes/bad-for-yous" – products that do harm – free markets will allow their creation.[59] Economic models fail, they suggest, because economics only looks to healthy markets and, as a result, "fails to grapple with deception and trickery."[60] They argue – and we agree – that financial markets need regulation to prevent the proliferation of these products meant only to deceive.

We understandably have to rely on the available economic research, some of which is cited throughout our book. However, we also need to acknowledge some of its weaknesses and urge a somewhat skeptical eye. It is always necessary to look behind the conclusions reached and into the assumptions that were made along the

[56] Colander, *supra* note 50.

[57] Thaler, *supra* note 54, at 5–6.

[58] Christopher L. Foote, Kristopher S. Gerardi & Paul S. Willen, *Why Did So Many People Make So Many Ex Post Bad Decisions? The Causes of the Foreclosure Crisis*, 2 (Fed. Res. of Atlanta, Working Paper 2012–17).

[59] GEORGE AKERLOF & ROBERT SHILLER, PHISHING FOR PHOOLS: THE ECONOMICS OF MANIPULATION AND DECEPTION 150 (2015).

[60] *Id.* at 164.

way. As we discovered, some researchers assume away all human behavior, while others base their findings on assumptions about how theoretical people behave or ideal court systems work, neither of which match our experiences with real clients. In a concrete example, one prominent study compares mortgages in communities that border judicial and nonjudicial states in order to see whether lenders are charging more for mortgages in judicial states than in nonjudicial. The study found that during the mid-1990s, mortgages in judicial states tended to be smaller than in bordering nonjudicial locations. In explaining the results, it suggests homebuyers may choose to buy in the judicial state despite these differences in order to afford themselves judicial protection.[61] Notre Dame is in just such a location: Indiana is a judicial state and Michigan, only a few miles away, is a nonjudicial state. We decided to try a very unsophisticated test of this theory. While presenting a draft of one of the chapters of this book, we asked the attending faculty how many of them had considered whether the foreclosure laws were judicial or nonjudicial when deciding where to purchase their home. The question was met with resounding laughter. Next, we asked how many knew whether the state they lived in had judicial or nonjudicial foreclosure. The answer was "no one." We suggest that if a room full of law professors from a well-respected law school do not know whether they live in a nonjudicial or judicial foreclosure state, most homeowners do not know either. More importantly, real people do not buy a home anticipating foreclosure. This was a nonconsequential assumption, but more significant and erroneous assumptions about how courts work, and the knowledge and behavior of homebuyers can be found in many studies.

We are also concerned with the underlying data sets often used. For instance, many studies use data from Lender Processing Services (LPS). During the crisis, LPS was notorious for its robo-signing and other bad behavior. In fact, Lorraine Brown, an LPS executive, was one of the very few people who went to jail.[62] Advocates across the county complain about the inaccurate record-keeping of the mortgage servicing industry and anyone who has ever obtained a loan history from LPS knows how inaccurate its records can be. We have no access to large LPS datasets, so perhaps those are more accurate. Nonetheless, relying on this data to make broad policy does give one pause.

On the other hand, academics and policymakers tend to disregard anecdotes – or "anecdata" – but often those stories create patterns and those patterns can tell us quite a bit about what is happening in the market. Economic data is fundamental to discerning broad trends. At the same time, we believe it is also important to drill

---

[61] Karen Pence, *Foreclosing on Opportunity: State Laws and Mortgage Credit*, 88 REV. OF ECON. & STATISTICS 177, 182 (2006). There are earlier version of this paper available online and, in fairness, in that version this suggestion is made and seems to be dismissed.

[62] Anna Louie Sussman, *Ex-Mortgage Document Exec Pleads Guilty in "Robo-Signing" Case*, REUTERS (Nov. 20, 2012), https://www.reuters.com/article/robosigning-plea/ex-mortgage-docu ment-exec-pleads-guilty-in-robo-signing-case-idUSL1E8MLoC120121121.

down to examine what is happening on a micro level to individual people. Ultimately, both types of data have begun to point to one inescapable conclusion: Foreclosure is bad for everyone involved.

In Chapter 8 we explore certain international law implications. Many covenants and treaties guarantee a certain security in the tenure of housing, though this guarantee traditionally has been thought to protect the homeless or tenants, not homeowners. It can ensure a measure of due process and the right not to be forcibly evicted. American law has not generally complied with these principles, nor, frankly, has it cared much for human rights norms. The prevailing wisdom is that owning is more secure than renting and for most people it probably is, though for many in America – especially lower-income groups – homeownership is not as secure as often believed. In many states, nonjudicial foreclosure makes it easier to evict homeowners than renters.[63] That said, the foreclosure crisis has caused a crisis in American rental markets as well. In fact, in 2017, more people were facing eviction than faced foreclosure at the height of the crisis.[64] Affordable housing is no longer something all Americans can expect.

We have been involved in this work for many years, witnessing the buildup to the crisis – which we could clearly foresee – as well as its aftermath. We continue to pick up the pieces. The foreclosure crisis has had an echo that, despite the deafness of policymakers, is still being heard and felt across America. We invite you to meet the participants and through their stories learn the true consequences. In the end, we hope to persuade you that it is time to revisit conventional thinking about housing in America. Universal homeownership was perhaps too ambitious a goal, but homeownership for only the wealthiest and most creditworthy is no more acceptable. All policy is grounded in history, but it must also consider the realities of current markets. The financial crisis has left us with vast expanses of abandoned and decaying houses, and thousands of people with no place to live. Clearly, something is wrong.

---

[63] Andrew Martin, *In a Sign of Foreclosure Flaws, Suit Claims Break-Ins by Banks*, N.Y. TIMES (Dec. 21, 2010), http://www.nytimes.com/2010/12/22/business/22lockout.htm; Gene Johnson, *Ruling: Lender Cannot Suddenly Change Your Locks if You Miss Mortgage Payments*, THE SEATTLE TIMES (July 17, 2016 at 5:43 PM), http://www.seattletimes.com/seattle-news/ruling-lender-cannot-suddenly-change-your-locks-if-you-miss-mortgage-payments.

[64] Evictionlab.org. webinar, Apr. 16, 2018. The project was introduced through this event.

1

The Housing Crisis

I believe that the root cause of any financial crisis,
the root cause, is flawed government policies.

Henry Paulson

Debates over the causes of the financial meltdown have swirled for years. Those on the left tend to assign primary responsibility to profiteering financial institutions using securitization practices to avoid responsibility for unprincipled lending, while the right zeroes in on the federal government's low-income homeowner policies. For their part, lenders blame dishonest mortgage brokers who used misrepresentations to originate and then sell poor quality loans, or the borrowers themselves for lying about their creditworthiness to obtain bigger mortgage loans. Our aim in this book is not to rehash investigations into these issues that have been well-documented elsewhere,[1] but rather to summarize what occurred in the buildup to the crisis to provide a context for its aftermath.

SECURITIZATION BASICS

The Introduction acquainted you with the term "securitization" but did not explain the intricacies of the process. Securitization involves pooling together bundles of debt – in our case, mortgages – converting them to financial instruments called "securities," and selling the securities to investors who collect the stream of income arising from monthly payments on each of the pooled mortgages. When the underlying loans are mortgages secured by residences, they are often called mortgage-backed securities (MBS) or

---

[1] For some of our favorite books about the causes of the crisis, *see* The Fin. Crisis Inquiry Rep.: Final Rep. of the Nat'l Commission on the Causes of the Fin. and Econ. Crisis in the United States 36 (authorized ed. 2011). Michael Lewis, The Big Short (W.W. Norton & Co. 2011); Atif Mian & Amir Sufi, House of Debt: How They (and you) Caused the Great Recession, and How We can Prevent It From Happening Again 20 (2015).

residential mortgage backed securities (RMBS). Thousands of mortgages can be contained in each securitization. The financial instruments backed by mortgages are generally sold in the form of a bond and held by a passive trust. The investors are usually large institutions such as pension funds, purchasing on behalf of their members. Investors do not own individual mortgages, but rather the right to the *pro rata* portion of the entire stream of income generated by the mortgages contained in the bond. As the Introduction explains, the Government Sponsored Entities (GSEs) established the securitization process to develop broader markets and incentivize lending. Private-label securitization didn't really take off until the 1990s, when investment banks began creating securitization vehicles for mortgages that did not conform to GSE standards, such as subprime mortgages. The GSEs would not purchase nonconforming mortgages and the private RMBS market filled in the gap, which turned out to be extremely profitable, at least in the short run.

Securitization trusts are governed by a lengthy, complex contract called a Pooling and Servicing Agreement (PSA). In order to be bankruptcy-remote – to have the trust assets protected from creditor claims in bankruptcy – trusts must comply with the complex requirements of the federal statutes for Real Estate Mortgage Investment Conduits (REMIC).[2] Thus, virtually all mortgage-backed securitizations follow a similar path: First, a lender originates the loan that is sold to another entity and the mortgages are bundled into a pool. The second entity is typically a special purpose vehicle, or issuer, that sells the accounts receivable on the secondary mortgage market. The mortgages act as collateral for the securities. Contracts called Pooling and Servicing Agreements mandate the path all mortgages must take from origination to final entry into the trust. Each step along the way must be documented to show that all transfers were handled properly. During the boom years of the aughts, these requirements frequently were not followed, leaving "orphan" mortgages in uncertain locations. As a result, when lenders needed to document their rights to foreclose, they were forced to became more and more creative in trying to present the foreclosure documentation, as will be recounted shortly.

A securitized bond normally is divided into "tranches," the French word for slice. Each tranche occupies its own level in a hierarchy of securities. The lower the quality of the tranche, the higher the interest it typically pays to investors; the inverse holds as well, so that the higher-ranked, higher-quality tranches pay significantly lower rates. Sometimes this structuring is referred to as "slicing and dicing" mortgages. Many of the

---

[2] REMICs were created by the Tax Reform Act of 1986. As a *Washington Post* article explained at the time, the law gave some favorable tax benefits to the REMIC issuer, including allowing it to "avoid paying taxes" by requiring "the holders of the securities to pay taxes on the income." In addition, the seller of these instruments could treat the underlying loans as assets, not debt. But the article also foretold the trouble to come. "[C]ritics of the REMICs say that in the long run they will only create 'junk' mortgage-backed securities." And so, they did. Cornelius F. Foote jr., "'REMICS' to Boost Mortgage Market," WASH. POST (Jan. 3, 1987), https://www.washingtonpost .com/archive/realestate/1987/01/03/remics-to-boost-mortgage-market/1e65de22-dedd-4fc2-a290-e5a94f54c397/?utm_term=.cf7926b3bcf1.

mortgages in lower tranches of private label RMBSs were subprime high-cost, high-interest rate loans made to borrowers with poor credit, often African Americans and Latinos who were targeted for the worst loans despite their credit scores.[3] Lower tranches carried higher interest rates because the mortgages they contained were the riskiest ones in the bond. As it turned out, they defaulted in huge numbers, overwhelming the system and ultimately causing even the highest tranches to pay out less. Pension funds – which are more risk-averse – typically purchased higher tranches, while hedge funds – risk-preferers – were more likely to buy low tranches. Adam McKay's film *The Big Short* does a fantastic and entertaining job of explaining this process to the uninitiated.

MORTGAGE-BACKED SECURITIES, FRAUD AND MISREPRESENTATIONS

Securitization was not the only cause of the problem – it was the quality of the underlying loans. Why were so many bad loans made in the first place? One reason is that they appeared to investors as much safer than they actually were. Securitization trusts paid ratings agencies, such as Standard & Poor's, Fitch or Moody's, to rate the credit quality of their offerings. These ratings were designed to help prospective investors obtain honest information about the nature of the underlying debt, but a major conflict of interest transformed them into something much different. The Financial Inquiry Report concluded that the "failures of credit ratings agencies were essential cogs in the wheel of financial destruction."[4] The ratings agencies proved incapable of providing an objective assessment of the mortgage pools created by paying clients for a variety of reasons. The pressure to maintain their market share by telling their customers what they wanted to hear proved too much to resist.[5] If Standard & Poor's gave an offering a subpar rating, for instance, the firm could simply take the offering over to Fitch or Moody's. As a result, mortgage-backed bonds received top ratings even when the underlying subprime mortgages were more likely than not to default, ending the investors' income stream and adding significant foreclosure costs to the bargain. Backed by these stellar ratings, mortgage-

---

[3] William C. Apgar Jr., Christopher E. Herbert, & Priti Mathur, *Risk or Race: An Assessment of Subprime Lending*, U.S. DEPT. OF HOUSING & URB. DEV. 6–8 (Aug. 2009), https://www.huduser.gov/portal/publications/pdf/risk_race_2011.pdf (finding "a racial and ethnic association with higher priced lending remains, even after entering a neighborhood credit metric and controlling for other neighborhood-level risk factors such as household incomes, housing prices, rental shares, share of the population with a college education, and housing turnover rate." *Id.* at iii; Debbie Gruenstein, Bocian, Keith S. Ernst & Wei Li, *Unfair Lending: The Effect of Race and Ethnicity on the Price of Subprime Mortgages*, CTR. FOR RESPONSIBLE LENDING. 5 (May 31, 2006) http://www.responsiblelending.org/mortgage-lending/research-analysis/rr011-Unfair_Lending-0506.pdf (finding that "for most types of subprime home loans, African-American and Latino borrowers are at greater risk of receiving higher-rate loans than white borrowers, even after controlling for legitimate risk factors"). *Id.* at 3.

[4] FIN. CRISIS REP., *supra* note 1, at xxv.

[5] *Id.*

backed securities were sold to investors with the promise of high yields (returns) and low risk. Yet the lower tranches were largely toxic, destined from origination to poison the rest of the pool. Fundamentally, investors were duped by false and misleading representations.[6]

Sophisticated investors were duped by false ratings, but borrowers, particularly lower-income borrowers, were duped by other misrepresentations. The rise of predatory and subprime lending in the 1990s coincided with the burgeoning of private label mortgage-backed securitized trusts. This is not a coincidence. Billions of dollars were pouring into securitized trusts, as they appeared to offer high yields with little risk, unlike other investments. The demand for loans to securitize exceeded the supply of available loans. The obvious response was to increase lending to meet this demand. Since there were not enough available borrowers to meet current underwriting standards, those criteria began to loosen. Loan underwriting is the process of determining the creditworthiness of borrowers based on such factors as their credit scores, income, assets, liabilities and whether they intend to occupy the property as their primary residence. Red flags, such as a lower-income borrower owning several investment properties while residing in a rental or a borrower with limited education purportedly making hundreds of thousands of dollars a year, should have signaled a fraudulent loan application. When such a red flag crops up, an underwriter is supposed to conduct a follow-up investigation, digging deeper for signs of veracity. But in the frenzy leading up to the recession, this step was often skipped. Many mortgage applications were full of false information, filled out by a mortgage broker whose only concern was making sure the loan closed, so she could get her commission.

The elderly client with dementia mentioned in the Introduction initially had her loan application rejected by the lender. The broker faxed the application to a lender and it was faxed back with a note indicating she needed more income. In less than half an hour, the loan was refaxed to the same lender with additional, imaginary and unexplained income. The lender did not inquire as to how the woman suddenly had a higher income. Instead, the loan was approved, and the broker pocketed $10,000.

A great many of the mortgages originated in this manner were subprime or Alt-A, a category in between subprime and prime. Prime loans are those with credit characteristics conforming to GSE standards, or "A" quality loans. These borrowers

---

[6] Goldman Sachs faced a lot of criticism and a subsequent lawsuit when an email was revealed in which one its employees characterized one of the offerings as a "sack of shit." Teri Buhl, *E-mails Suggest Bear Stearns Cheated Clients Out of Billions*, THE ATLANTIC (Jan. 25, 2011), https://www.theatlantic.com/business/archive/2011/01/e-mails-suggest-bear-stearns-cheated-clients-out-of-billions/70128. This comment came to dominate Senator Levin's questions to Goldman Sachs representatives during the hearings of the Governmental Affairs Subcommittee on investigations. For a video of the exchange see https://www.youtube.com/watch?v=1kCuQsMAIUI.

tend to have high credit scores and loan-to-value (LTV) ratios. The latter term refers to the percentage of the total market value of the home that the loan represents. For instance, an 80/20 LTV ratio indicates that the mortgage amount is 80 percent of the fair market value, while the remaining 20 percent is the homeowner's equity – or ownership share – in the home. Traditionally, borrowers had to make a down payment of 20 percent to qualify for any mortgages, but during the buildup to the crisis, LTV ratios of 90/10 or even over 100 percent were relatively common. Another type of loan called an 80/20 was also common. In this situation, the broker generally financed the down payment with one lender and the primary loan with another, not disclosing that the down payment had also been financed.

Prime borrowers also tend to have favorable debt-to-income ratios (DTI), meaning that their total level of indebtedness represents a relatively low percentage of their incomes. By contrast, subprime loans were designed for borrowers with low credits scores, and comparatively poor LTV and DTI ratios. Alt-A loans fell between the two categories. These were not A grade paper, but neither were they B or C grade subprime category loans.[7] Alt-A loans during the boom years were often "low-doc," or "stated income" or "no-doc," for which borrowers did not need to provide full documentation – or even any documentation at all – of their creditworthiness, as had routinely been required. Lenders would rely solely on credit reports, which often contain inaccuracies, if they relied on any external sources at all. New securitized trusts had to be filled within ninety days of creation to meet REMIC requirements; speed, not quality or accuracy, was of the essence.

We saw evidence of these abuses repeatedly while assisting our clients. One common abuse was the misstating of income. Years after obtaining loans, our clients were genuinely surprised by the numbers that appeared on their loan applications. To understand how this could have happened, you must first understand the process. Prospective clients typically filled out a loan application, often giving information over the phone to a mortgage broker or loan officer. The application was then retyped and included in the packet of closing documents. The packet was presented to homeowners to sign quickly, not in a manner that would allow them to read or review the paperwork. Therefore, they did not know that the income figures had been altered.

The brokers had developed a special trick, exposing only the bottom of pages to be signed, thereby blocking information about the loan itself. Closings were happening one on top of the other with very little time in between. We had clients closing loans in the backs of pickup trucks or at the 7-Eleven, and even in a hospital room. Two of our students – recent lawyers and now seasoned in the possibility of abuse – had this experience when trying to close their own mortgage loans. One student in California and another in Texas asked to read all the paperwork before signing. In both situations, the closing agent called the police. The student in California

7 *See*, *B/C Loans*, INVESTOPEDIA, http://www.investopedia.com/terms/b/bcloan.asp.

succumbed to the pressure and signed without reading. The student in Texas, a former law enforcement officer himself, waited for the police to arrive. He was very pleased when the officer looked at the closing agent and said, incredulously, "You want me to arrest him for reading his paperwork?" It is easy to see how people in that situation could sign paperwork they had not read, or generally even seen. Questions to a broker often went unanswered. Many clients never met the broker and had only spoken with him for about a minute on the phone. Afterwards, the broker would simply concoct the information in the application, sometimes listing the wrong race and gender for the client and inventing information about assets. Brokers even went so far as to forge some of our clients' signatures.

Some homeowners may have known that the information provided was false but did not understand the implications. Paula Trumbaugh was one such client. Ms. Trumbaugh had a mortgage that she was already struggling to pay when the city code enforcement office informed her that, in order to avoid fines, she needed to make major repairs to her home. Ms. Trumbaugh was disabled, with monthly income of approximately $650. She could not afford the repairs, and – despite her numerous requests – no social service agencies would assist her. She sought a second mortgage and was approved by a loan company but asked to sign a document at closing indicating that her income was $2,000 per month, with most coming from home care services she supposedly provided. She signed the documents, but imme-diately came to the Notre Dame Clinical Law Center with the paperwork because it just did not feel right. In addition, the loan payment was going to be over $700 per month, more than her entire monthly income. When we asked her why she had signed the paperwork, knowing that her income had been manufactured, she told us that the broker told her that they did this "on all their loans." According to the broker, she and her colleagues regularly advised people to falsify income by claiming that they were supplementing income by providing cleaning services, until lenders began to ask for verification. Now, they explained, homeowners like Ms. Trumbaugh were being encouraged to claim they ran a homecare service business, something apparently easier to falsify.

Federal law gives homeowners three days after signing a mortgage refinance to cancel the transaction. Paula was still within that time period when she came to our office. We filed a complaint with the Secretary of State regarding this broker's service and received a nasty call from the broker in return. She informed us that this was standard business practice in the industry and that there was nothing wrong. As far as we were able to ascertain, she did not suffer any negative consequences as the result of our complaint. Mortgage brokers generated upwards of 70 percent of all mortgages during the boom years preceding the Great Recession. A fair percentage of them engaged in these practices.[8] These brokers had no duty to borrowers,

---

[8] *See,* RICHARD BITNER, CONFESSIONS OF A SUBPRIME LENDER: AN INSIDER'S TALE OF GREED, FRAUD AND IGNORANCE (2008).

though many implied or claimed outright that they were taking care of them. No surprise that the situation blew up in the end.

These practices were either allowed or overlooked because securitizers were so hungry for loans. The industry all but abandoned serious underwriting. Brokers would search for borrowers, frequently seeking subprime borrowers through neighborhood contacts and word-of-mouth. As mentioned in the Introduction, some even went door to door. We saw recently arrived non-English-speaking immigrant day laborers inveigled into buying houses worth over $300,000 (or at least that's what an appraiser reported they were worth). A group of recent immigrants from Africa were convinced to buy "rental" homes, some as many as six in one day. The homes were supposed to have paying tenants, but in fact were in no condition for anyone to live in. Some of those brokers were prosecuted, but many carried on for years. These cases were aptly dubbed "loans in search of a borrower" and many said that anyone with a heartbeat could get a subprime loan. Those on the lender side spoke of "originate to distribute" lending, and lenders seemed to suck up everything like a vacuum cleaner. Ultimately, the entire situation was driven by the need for more supply, and not customer demand for new loans.

Why would lenders so eagerly provide the kind of loans we just described? Because they had nothing to lose from originating loans that were immediately sold into securitized trusts. They had few reasons to bother with the quality of their mortgages because they were paid at the time of origination. The brokers and lenders were not affected by what ultimately happened to those loans as they traveled upstream – or so they thought. There was one caveat. At the time of sale, originators signed warranties representing that their loans were of the quality listed in the PSA; if they were not, the originator was responsible for buying them back. Since the crisis, we have seen litigation on this issue and some loans are indeed being taken back by the originators,[9] but this did not occur before or during the crisis itself, when nobody seemed to have time to investigate the quality of the loans. Instead, the emphasis was on short-term profits. In any event, the representations and warranties were insufficient to mitigate the moral hazard of passing toxic mortgages upstream to an MBS issuer, which would in turn pass on a pool of mortgages to a trust. Fearing no consequences, entities at each link in the

---

[9] See, i.e., *Bank of America to Pay $16.65 Billion in Historic Justice Department Settlement for Financial Fraud Leading up to and during the Financial Crisis*, U.S. DEPT. OF JUST. (Aug. 21, 2014), https://www.justice.gov/opa/pr/bank-america-pay-1665-billion-historic-justice-department-settlement-financial-fraud-leading; Brendan Pierson, *Nomura, RBS Lose Bid to Overturn $839 Million Mortgage Bond Award*, REUTERS (Sept. 28, 2017, 3:53 PM), https://www.reuters.com/article/us-nomura-lawsuit/nomura-rbs-lose-bid-to-overturn-839-million-mortgage-bond-award-idUSKCN1C3305; Lawrence White & Makini Brice, *Barclays $2 Billion Fraud Fine Resolves Major U.S. Legal Issue*, REUTERS (Mar. 29, 2018, 9:29 AM), https://www.reuters.com/article/us-barclays-mortgages-fine/barclays-2-billion-fraud-fine-resolves-major-u-s-legal-issue-idUSKBN1H51WY.

securitization chain focused on short-term profits. Taking the time to properly underwrite loans meant losing money and market share to competitors.[10]

THE BORROWERS' ROLE

But what about the borrowers? Didn't they want to take out enormous refinance loans to gain cash for consumer spending? Weren't they aware of what they were doing, so that they should have known the full debt would come due, perhaps at an inopportune time? Some blame an unrealistic optimism that housing prices would forever rise.[11] Many others complained about borrowers using their homes as piggy banks or ATMs, exploiting the equity as collateral for refinance transactions so they could get cash back immediately upon closing.[12] These homeowners were perceived as being irresponsible and, therefore, undeserving of any assistance. This is the narrative that helped fuel the rise of the Tea Party, with an assumption that the entire country paid during the Great Recession for the greed of these irresponsible homebuyers who seemed to be getting away scot-free. Since then, however, it has become abundantly clear this was not the case.

Once again, a popular – though largely inaccurate – narrative contributed to a widespread misperception of borrowers, which fueled destructive political debates. At the same time, the crisis has given us some interesting insights into the concept of "deservingness." People, it seems, are less willing to assist a person in harm's way if they think he caused or contributed to his harm.[13] This is the narrative, for example, of the "underserving poor." We are more willing to assist a homeowner who lacks control over the "cause of the disadvantage," such as one laid off or seriously ill.[14] People react with anger if they see the person seeking assistance as somehow responsible, for example, a homeowner perceived to have taken out a risky loan or purchased an unaffordable home. The belief was that the government, by allowing some people to modify their mortgage loans, was encouraging others to "strategically default" on their mortgages. Borrowers who received assistance were seen in the same light as the "undeserving poor."

---

[10] *The Great Pool of Money*, THIS AMERICAN LIFE (May 9, 2008), https://www.thisamericanlife.org/355/the-giant-pool-of-money.

[11] Christopher L. Foote, Kristopher S. Gerardi & Paul S. Willen, *Why Did So Many People Make So Many Ex Post Bad Decisions? The Causes of the Foreclosure Crisis* 37 (Fed. Res. of Atlanta, Working Paper 2012–17).

[12] Jonathan Clements, *Here's the Downside of Using Your House as a Piggy Bank*, THE WALL STREET J. (Apr. 16, 2003, 1:06 AM), https://www.wsj.com/articles/SB105042947082936200.

[13] Mark J. Brandt, *Onset and Offset Deservingness: The Case of Home Foreclosures*, 34 POLITICAL PSYCHOL. 221, 221 (2013); *see also* Michael J. Seiler, Vicky L. Seiler, Mark A. Lane & David M. Harrison, *Fear, Shame and Guilt: Economic and Behavioral Motivations for Strategic Default*, 40 REAL ESTATE ECON. S199(2012).

[14] Brandt, *supra* note 13, at 221.

More interestingly, political leanings appear to influence one's perceptions about deservingness. Research has shown, for example, that "people who endorse conservatism prefer firm answers and search for less information."[15] As a result, they are more likely to make a deservingness decision based on their perception of whether the person in need of assistance has contributed to or caused their current situation, for instance by buying a home he or she cannot afford.[16] While the underlying values and norms people use to determine deservingness may differ by political leaning,[17] it is interesting to note that people of all political stripes are apparently willing to assist a homeowner in foreclosure whom they perceive to be the victim, such as someone who took out an affordable loan but lost her job due to the recession.[18] It will become apparent throughout this book that we believe the homeowners were the parties most deserving of assistance, while the institutions responsible for the crisis ultimately received it.

Returning to our borrowers, it is of course impossible to know what went on in other people's minds when they allowed themselves to be trapped by unsuitable mortgage loans – assuming there was no direct fraud involved – but we can attempt to imagine ourselves in their places as Robert Shiller suggests. Many borrowers were financially desperate and thus extra vulnerable to lending pitches from fast-talking mortgage brokers, who often upsold them into inappropriate loans when they merely needed enough money to, say, repair the roof.

Fraud permeated the subprime market. Brokers and loan officers almost universally told prospective borrowers that home prices would continually rise, and therefore they could refinance into a loan with better terms in a year or two. Many borrowers experienced remorse after closing. They couldn't believe they had entered into such bad deals and were ashamed of their naivete, but they also thought nothing could be done (often because the broker told them they would face serious penalties if they did not sign the loan documents they had agreed to). Once they signed, they felt stuck. Many of these loans contained large prepayment penalties. This served to trap the homeowner in the loan for, typically, three to five years.

If the loan is a refinance as opposed to a purchase, homeowners are legally permitted to cancel the loan, but many were not given legally prescribed information about how to do so. Others tried but were told that it was impossible. One couple came to us in this situation. After the closing, when they finally were able to review the loan paperwork, they realized to their horror that their new loan had a $50,000 balloon payment that would come due after both had reached retirement age. Knowing they would be in no position to pay such a large amount and not wanting to take on a new loan so late in life, they immediately returned to the lender to

---

[15] *Id.*

[16] *Id.* at 224.

[17] *Id.* at 222.

[18] *Id.* at 222–23, 232.

rescind the loan. They were chased from the office. We filed the necessary rescission paperwork, but it was refused again. We had to threaten litigation for the loan to be rescinded. Most people would have simply given in and given up. Many did.

Predatory foreclosure rescue scammers and property flippers made up the bottom of the subprime market. The Seton Hall Civil Litigation Clinic has represented at least a dozen clients victimized by one Newark, New Jersey flipper.[19] Maurice Bethea portrayed himself as a developer who rehabbed houses and then resold them either as primary residences or as small investment properties. He was extraordinarily charismatic. One client, a twenty-four-year-old teacher, sought to buy a small house, but Bethea somehow persuaded her to buy several small two-to-three unit rental buildings, saying she would make money on the rent for a few years, thus accruing enough to purchase her own home. She was assured property values would continue to rise and she could easily refinance to a better interest rate before selling.

Other clients fell prey to the same pitch. One couple we'll call the O'Neals, who originally sought a single-family house to live in, has been trying for years to get rid of the six-unit building they bought from one of Bethea's companies. Although Bethea had a contract with them to manage the building and keep it filled with tenants, it was a money-loser from the beginning, and units remained vacant. Then, Bethea's company stopped performing maintenance. Mrs. O'Neal was arrested and taken to the local police station because of the building's unsafe conditions. A real estate agent promised to arrange a short sale, a process where the bank allows you to sell the property for less than you owe, but after years of trying, he has been unable to find a buyer. The O'Neals continue to pay someone to guard the building, which is in Irvington, New Jersey, next to Newark and suffering from urban blight and low property values. There is not much of a market for decrepit buildings in Irvington. It did not take long for the O'Neals to realize they had been taken advantage of and would be stuck with the consequences for years. They are not even able to give the building away because any recipient would be subject to the $300,000 plus mortgage on a building that in late 2016 was worth $75,000.

Shiller's recent work on Narrative Economics describes the flipping phenomenon executed by actors like Bethea:[20]

> [D]uring the 1997 to 2005 boom there were multitudes of narratives about smart investors who were bold enough to take a position in the market. To single out one strand, recall the stories of flippers who would buy a house, fix it up, and resell it within months at a huge profit. These stories appear to have been broadly exciting to people

---

[19] *See*, e.g., Laura Craven, *Newark Man Admits Guilt in Million-Dollar Mortgage Scam*, The Star-Ledger (June 3, 2008), https://www.nj.com/news/index.ssf/2008/06/newark_man_admits_guilt_in_mil.html; complaint in Gibson v. Bethea, https://law.shu.edu/Programs Centers/PublicIntGovServ/upload/complaint_predatory_lending-2.pdf.

[20] Robert J. Shiller, op-ed, *How Tales of 'Flippers' Led to a Housing Bubble*, N.Y. Times (May 21, 2017), https://www.nytimes.com/2017/05/18/upshot/how-tales-of-flippers-led-to-a-housing-bubble.html; *See also* Robert J. Shiller, *Narrative Economics*, Cowles Foundation, Discussion Paper No. 2069, (2017), *available at* SSRN: *https://ssrn.com/abstract=2896857*.

who didn't flip houses themselves but who appear to have begun to think that stretching a little and buying a house with a large mortgage would make them wise investors.[21]

Bethea's pitch to purchasers incorporated this narrative, encouraging them to think boldly and stretch a little to buy investment properties. In the end, he assured them, it would pay off handsomely. Of course, things did not turn out that way. He arranged for a coconspirator to appraise the distressed buildings at amounts greatly exceeding their actual market value – buildings Bethea had bought for a song and only partially renovated.[22] Working with unscrupulous mortgage brokers and lenders, Bethea obtained mortgages for his customers that matched the inflated appraised values, leaving them owing more than the home was worth right from the start. Almost inevitably, the buildings ended up in foreclosure. Bethea recently served a federal sentence after pleading guilty to wire fraud in connection with his businesses. We continue to litigate a case involving a senior citizen who purchased a home from him for almost $300,000 that he had bought for a little over $10,000 with only a few renovations done. The home is full of defects and problems and not worth anything close to the purchase price.

Why didn't Bethea's victims recognize what was going on? Like many successful con artists, he made an extremely positive and trustworthy impression. The customers were also financially unsophisticated and believed the common narrative that housing prices would always rise. This myth justified their decision to take out a large mortgage loan for a short period. In retrospect, their actions seem extremely unwise; however, we need to remember that, before the housing bubble burst, even the most sophisticated economists and Wall Street financiers believed that home prices would continue to rise.[23] Virtually all of Bethea's customer-victims are African Americans whom Bethea – who is also black – targeted for a race-based confidence pitch. Affinity fraud, or fraud by one member of a close-knit community against another, flourished during the crisis. Prospective borrowers, especially those in communities historically discriminated against, tended to trust members of their own community not to defraud them. They were wrong. Ultimately, the entire context within which Bethea operated contributed to the customers' credulity. Professor Igor Grossman, a noted researcher on wise decision-making notes:

---

[21] Robert J. Shiller, op-ed, *supra* note 20.

[22] The role of appraisers is similar to that of credit rating agencies. Some were coconspirators, but others simply succumbed to the pressures of the market. Failing to provide the appraisal the broker wanted could mean a loss of further referrals. *See*, i.e., Joe Eaton, *The Appraisal Bubble: In Run up to Real Estate Bust, Lenders Pushed Appraiser to Inflate Values*, THE CTR. FOR PUBLIC INTEGRITY (Apr. 14, 2009, 3:13 PM), https://www.publicintegrity.org/2009/04/14/2895/appraisal-bubble.

[23] Kristopher S. Gerardi, Christopher L. Foote & Paul S. Willen, *Reasonable People Did Disagree: Optimism and Pessimism about the U.S. Housing Market before the Crash*, 2 (Fed. Reserve Bank of Boston, Public Policy Discussion Paper, No. 10–5). (pointing out that those who thought that housing prices would fall was a "distinctly minority view, especially among professional economists" in the run up to the financial crisis).

Recent empirical findings from cognitive, developmental, social, and personality psychology cumulatively suggest that people's ability to reason wisely varies dramatically across experiential and situational contexts.[24]

What in hindsight appears to be bad judgment, is more easily understood in the context of the relationships involved and the conventional wisdom of the moment. Unsuspecting moderate-income first-time property buyers and Wall Street financiers were not the only ones to believe the rising property value narrative: Much of the vast American middle class did as well. People thought of their homes as good investments and believed that owning a home – along with having a 401(k) – would ensure their retirements. As we now know, that has not turned out to be the case.[25]

PAYMENT OPTION ARMS: THE WORST OF THE WORST

The housing bubble continued to inflate in the early 2000s, reaching a peak from 2004 to 2006. We were watching the process from the sidelines. Every time we thought that the bubble would burst, and subprime lending would cease generating ever more toxic and fraudulent mortgages, cases would hit a new high. The primary problems were not only that financial institutions – both banks and nonbanks – were lending to people who could never afford to repay their loans, but also that the loans themselves contained toxic features destined to blow up in the faces of borrowers. The very worst loans were the payment option Adjustable Rate Mortgages (ARMs), a mouthful to pronounce and much more difficult to understand.[26] The initial payments of these mortgages were generally at a teaser rate as low as 1 percent, but the rate would float upwards soon thereafter, based on adding a fixed percentage to a market index. The rate would also readjust at designated intervals. An option ARM permits a borrower to choose one of "four payments: the minimum payment, the interest-only payment, the thirty-year fully amortized payment and the fifteen-year fully amortized payment."[27] People routinely only made the minimum payment, which rarely covered both the interest and principal amounts due.[28] As a result, the additional amount owed under the actual interest rate is capitalized or tacked onto

---

[24] Igor Grossman, *Wisdom in Context*, 12 PERSP. ON PSYCOL. SCI. 233, 249 (2017).

[25] *See*, Noah Smith, How Middle-Class America Got Fleeced, BLOOMBERG VIEW (Apr. 7, 2017, 8:00 AM), https://www.bloomberg.com/view/articles/2017-04-07/how-middle-class-america-got-fleeced.

[26] Allen J. Fishbein & Patrick Woodall, *Exotic or Toxic? An Examination of the Non-Traditional Mortgage Markets for Consumers and Lenders*, CONSUMER FED'N OF AM, May 2006, https://consumerfed.org/pdfs/Exotic_Toxic_Mortgage_Report0506.pdf.

[27] ANDREW G. PIZOR, CAROLYN L. CARTER, DIANE E. THOMPSON, ALYS I. COHEN, ELIZABETH RENAURT, MARGOT SAUNDERS, JONATHAN SHELDON & TARA TWOOMEY, MORTGAGE LENDING §6.2.5.1.4 (2018), https://library.nclc.org/ml/0602050104.

[28] *The State of the Nation's Housing*, JOINT CTR. FOR HOUSING STUDIES OF HARVARD UNIVERSITY 17 (2007), http://www.jchs.harvard.edu/sites/default/files/son2007.pdf.

the principal balance. The loan was negatively amortizing or, in layman's terms – the balance owed went up, not down, each month.[29]

According to the National Consumer Law Center, most loans automatically reset after five or ten years, but many also reset if the principal became too large, generally between 100 and 125 percent of the original loan balance. Homeowners were unaware that the interest rate was increasing because the "minimum payment would remain fixed for a year and, after that year, until either of the two triggers was hit, would increase only gradually from year to year, at a far lower rate than the increase in interest."[30] After reset, however, "borrowers' payments could double or triple with no more than thirty days' notice."[31] The term "payment shock" truly applies here. To be clear, there is nothing wrong with adjustable rate mortgages *per se*; in fact, one of us had one for a short period. But payment option ARMs are only suitable for a small number of educated borrowers who can understand their mechanics and calculate the risks. For example, an option ARM could be appropriate for borrowers who know that their income will soon be rising substantially or those who plan to resell soon.

As mentioned, paying less than what is owed each month increases the principal balance over time, so that the loan negatively amortizes. Instead of the principal balance reducing with each monthly payment, as with a regular amortizing mortgage whose principal balance is completely paid off at the end of the term, the principal keeps growing over time until reset. Paying what you choose, rather than what you owe, is a terrible financial strategy, but most of these loans went to unsophisticated borrowers in straitened and even desperate circumstances. The mechanics of the loan are virtually impossible for an average person to understand. In fact, they are challenging even to highly educated people. For years, we would give one such loan document to our third-year law students and ask them to figure out the proper payment. Only one student was ever able to do so, and she was a former mortgage loan officer.

The Wilsons, an elderly couple with only high school educations, were duped into signing one of these loans. The broker handled all aspects of the transaction with the lending bank, World Savings, and failed to explain the terms to them. The broker made thousands of dollars on the transaction, and the Wilsons almost lost their multigenerational family home. The couple was unable to comprehend the loan documents, which was entirely understandable, given the terms: A yearly interest rate was listed on the note, but it could change monthly after a few months,

---

[29] Fin. Crisis Rep., *supra* note 1 at 106–7. Golden West Savings was the first institution to originate option arms, called "pick a pay." They were structured in a way to be successful and they were. Washington Mutual and Countrywide began offering a similar product, but they created a product more likely to reset sooner and at a higher interest rate. Even though their own brokers thought it was a bad product, employees were encouraged to sell it.

[30] Pizor, *supra* note 27.

[31] Id.

up to a cap of over 11 percent. A margin (additional) rate would be added to the applicable index at each interest change date. The index was identified as an average of the interest rates of a certain bank. Nonetheless, the borrowers were to make initial monthly payments that were apparently based on the minimum payment allowed. Monthly payments would change annually, though the increase was capped. If the monthly payments were insufficient to pay all interest due, the remaining interest would be added onto the principal and accrue interest at the same rate. The unpaid principal balance was capped at 125 percent of the original loan amount; if the cap was exceeded, monthly payments would immediately increase to fully amortized payments. In addition, the payment cap limitation would not apply on the tenth payment change date and every fifth change date after that. A prepayment fee would be charged if the borrowers attempted to prepay the loan. How comprehensible is this?

Two years later, a World Savings loan officer contacted the Wilsons, encouraging them to refinance into another of these loans. This sort of churning was quite lucrative for loan officers and mortgage brokers. The couple agreed to refinance their loan, in part because they had not yet had any issues with the earlier loan. Interest rates had not yet reset. They were persuaded to refinance for a larger loan, taking additional cash out to meet family needs. At the time, property values were still rising astronomically. Their home had appreciated, giving them the equity to take out extra cash, which they were able to use for home repairs. The terms of this mortgage note were similar to those in the first note, but the yearly interest rate was a little lower, a different index was used and the margin rate was a little lower. Initial monthly payments, however, were hundreds of dollars higher. This time, an escrow account for taxes and insurance was *not* set up, which meant the family would also have additional expenses for taxes and insurance payments. The Wilsons borrowed considerably more money this time and had to pay a prepayment fee, as well as additional commitment and funding fees to the bank. Mr. Wilson explained to the loan officer that he and his wife were retired and living almost solely on Social Security, but the officer filled out the application falsely, indicating that the couple had a combined monthly pension income of close to $12,000 (a significant increase from the false income of almost $10,000 listed in the prior application). The underwriter apparently failed to see a problem with this sudden increase in income for retired senior citizens or the fact that they were refinancing their home with a loan for hundreds of thousands of dollars. The Wilsons defaulted on the second loan after making payments for over two years. After that, they engaged in numerous futile attempts to have the mortgage modified.

This kind of loan flipping was common during the run-up to the crisis. One of the tools used by brokers when selling these loan products was to assure buyers that they could easily refinance before their interest rate reset to a higher level. This may have worked out for some, but for many the result of multiple refinances was an increasing principal loan amount and the payout of multiple fees. By the time many homeowners realized they could not afford the loan payments, it was too late to refinance. The crash had come, and no one would give them a loan.

The Consumer Financial Protection Bureau has now promulgated rules, pursuant to the Dodd-Frank Act, requiring lenders to determine borrowers' ability to repay mortgage loans that are not considered "Qualified Mortgages."[32] These rules, as well as some of the unintended consequences of them, will be discussed in further detail in Chapter 4. The two Pick-A-Payment Option ARM loans the Wilsons were influenced to sign would be prohibited under the new regulations. After reset, the Wilsons' monthly payments could easily have exceeded their entire monthly income. In addition, World Savings did not escrow payments for the Wilsons' taxes and insurance, something also required by the new regulations. The entire loan package was clearly unaffordable from the outset.

Several other clients were driven to foreclosure because escrow accounts had not been set up. One particular nonbank lender we encountered on a regular basis gave the clients paperwork indicating taxes were being escrowed but slipped a paper in at closing that waived the account. The homeowners were left believing their taxes were being paid until they found themselves facing a tax foreclosure. While saving your home from a tax sale is easier than from a standard foreclosure, it is still stressful, and some homeowners simply did not have the available funds to recover.

The Wilsons' Option ARM was predatory, though not illegal at the time. Predatory mortgage brokers and loan officers frequently steered members of vulnerable populations into the worst loans. Seniors on fixed incomes were common targets for these unscrupulous practices if for no other reason than their reliable source of income: Social Security. Both the mortgage broker on the first loan and the loan officer on the second had identified the Wilsons as appropriate candidates for long-term loans with increasingly higher payments. The Wilsons clearly could not afford to repay the mortgages once the interest rates reset, suggesting that the bank was engaging in "equity-based lending," a practice common during the subprime housing bubble. Lenders based the size of a loan on the value of the secured real estate as opposed to the borrower's income. When it became clear the Wilsons would be unable to make their loan payments, the lender was unwilling to negotiate

---

[32] *See, Protecting Consumers from Irresponsible Mortgage Lending*, CONSUMER FIN. PROTECTION BUREAU (Jan. 10, 2013), https://files.consumerfinance.gov/f/201301_cfpb_ability-to-repay-factsheet.pdf.

These rules were not in effect when these borrowers took out their loans, but they provide useful guidance on loan terms and features that are considered predatory:

In the lead up to the financial crisis, certain lending practices set consumers up to fail with mortgages they could not afford. Lenders sold no-doc and low-doc loans where consumers were "qualifying" for loans beyond their means. Lenders also sold risky and complicated mortgages like interest-only loans, negative-amortization loans where the principal and eventually the monthly payment increases ... and option adjustable-rate mortgages where the consumer could "pick a payment" which might result in negative amortization and eventually higher monthly payments. *Id.*

a workout. Lenders are not obligated to do so, but they should have been, considering their role in creating the problem.

A common, though simplistic, narrative heard after the crash claimed that borrowers like the Wilsons chose to live beyond their means. As we have seen, research indicates that others will therefore feel less sympathy for them and be less willing for the government to help. Some borrowers were eager to take advantage of their increased home equity, and some did buy larger homes than they could afford, but many other situations were considerably more complicated. For most of us, homes represent more than just assets. Several generations of the Wilsons' family had lived in their home for decades. Losing it also meant losing this family connection and required them to not only move themselves, but also to evict their children and grandchildren. Things might have worked out financially if several family members had been able to work steadily. But the couple had retired, and a son lost his job. Refinancing with a good loan that would have allowed them to take advantage of their increased equity could have been worthwhile. Better alternatives were available, given the borrowers' credit status. But none were offered.

PREDATORY LENDING, RACIAL TARGETING AND REVERSE REDLINING

One of the most pernicious features of predatory lending was the targeting of African Americans and Latinos for the worst loans.[33] This practice becomes abundantly clear when superimposing a map of the geographic distribution of subprime lending over a map of minority census tracts. Lenders argue that African Americans and Latinos overall have worse credit scores than their white counterparts, which could legitimately account for the correlation. Numerous studies counter this argument. A study by the US Department of Housing and Urban Development found that these minorities received higher-priced loans "even after entering a neighborhood credit metric and controlling for other neighborhood-level risk factors such as household incomes, housing prices, rental shares, share of the population with a college education, and housing turnover rate."[34] Researchers have been able to obtain credit score data for individual subprime loans in order to correlate credit scores and race. The results demonstrate that African Americans with credit profiles equivalent to those of whites were nonetheless disproportionately given subprime loans even when they fully qualified for prime loans.[35] That is the essence of predatory lending as it occurred from the late 1990s until the housing market started to crash in 2007.

[33] Apgar, *supra* note 3, at 44.
[34] *Id.* at iii.
[35] Gruenstein, *supra* note 3, at 3.

If acknowledging that a loan could be predatory was controversial at the beginning of the crisis, agreeing on a definition was even more so. In *Associates Home Equity Services v. Troup*, the New Jersey Appellate Division became a leader in this area when it recognized the existence of predatory lending and causes of action to combat it.[36] The court recognized predatory lending as, "'[A] mismatch between the needs and capacity of the borrower ... In essence, the loan does not fit the borrower, either because the borrower's underlying needs for the loan are not being met or the terms of the loan are so disadvantageous to that particular borrower that there is little likelihood that the borrower has the capability to repay the loan.'"[37] This was surely the case when the 1995 application of long-time Newark residents Beatrice Troup and her son Curtis "provided for a $46,500 loan at an annual interest rate of 11.65 percent, adjustable after six months ... [T]he loan was a 'balloon' type, payable in fifteen years, with the last payment being $41,603.58. The Troups were also charged four points, or four percent of the total loan amount."[38]

The court also recognized that racial targeting is frequently an element of predatory lending, allowing the Troups to sue for "reverse redlining." Redlining, the court explained, consistent with our aforementioned definition, is "the practice of denying the extension of credit to specific geographic areas due to the income, race or ethnicity of its residents."[39] Redlining comes from "the actual practice of drawing a red line around designated areas in which credit is to be denied" and "[r]everse redlining is the practice of extending credit on unfair terms to those same communities."[40] A borrower may be able to claim damages for reverse redlining by demonstrating that "defendants' lending practices and loan terms were 'unfair' and 'predatory,' and that the defendants were either intentionally targeted on the basis of race, or that there is a disparate impact on the basis of race."[41] The Troups therefore were able to claim a predatory lending violation under the New Jersey Consumer Fraud Act and claim reverse redlining under both state and federal fair housing laws.

Many were initially skeptical of this kind of action. However, in 2017, the US Supreme Court endorsed this approach when it held that the City of Miami was also an "aggrieved person" under the Fair Housing Act and, as such, it could proceed with its claims against both Bank of America and Wells Fargo for discriminatory predatory lending practices.[42] The City had alleged that the banks

---

[36] 778 A.2d 529 (N.J. Sup. Ct., App. Div. 2001).

[37] *Id.* at 536–37, quoting Daniel S. Ehrenberg, *If the Loan Don't Fit, Don't Take It: Applying the Suitability Doctrine to the Mortgage Industry to Eliminate Predatory Lending*, 10 J. Afford-able Housing Cmty Dev. L. 117, 119–20 (2001).

[38] Associates Home Equity Services, 778 A.2d at 535.

[39] Associates Home Equity Services, 778 A.2d at 537 (citations omitted).

[40] *Id.*

[41] Associates Home Equity Services, 778 A.2d at 537–38 (citations omitted).

[42] Bank of America and Wells Fargo & Co. v. City of Miami, 137 S. Ct. 1296, 1298 (2017).

discriminatorily imposed more onerous, and indeed "predatory," conditions on loans made to minority borrowers than to similarly situated nonminority borrowers. Those "predatory" practices included, among others, excessively high interest rates, unjustified fees, teaser low-rate loans that overstated refinancing opportunities, large prepayment penalties, and—when default loomed—unjustified refusals to refinance or modify the loans.[43]

In future chapters, we will discuss the impact of this kind of lending on communities of color. It is one of the most significant aftereffects of the crisis.

DEREGULATION'S CONTRIBUTION TO THE CRISIS

By now, you may be wondering why such egregious lending practices were legal. Answering this question involves looking back to the 1980s, when the federal government began deregulating financial institutions. Patricia McCoy and Kathleen Engel provide an incisive analysis in their book *The Subprime Virus*. They explain the regulatory failure thus:

> Federal regulators acted in time to stop a complete collapse of the world economy, but where were they when consumers and their advocates, researchers, cities, and states were warning about the growing abuses in the subprime market? Even when the chorus reached a deafening crescendo in 2006, regulators continued to shrug their shoulders at the problems in subprime. Their indifference was part and parcel of the same deregulatory agenda that prompted Congress to abolish substantive controls on home mortgages in the early 1980s. From then on, the federal government embraced the credo that the market, not the government, was the one to fix problems in the mortgage market.
>
> Federal regulators gave subprime lending their blessing by leaving subprime loans untouched, even though many of the loans violated the most basic tenet of lending: that no loan should be made unless the borrower could repay. Worse yet, federal regulators actively resisted using their substantial powers of rulemaking, examination, and sanctions to crack down on the proliferation of virulent loans. At the same time, they gave banks the green light to invest in subprime mortgage-backed securities and CDOs, leaving the nation's largest financial institutions awash in toxic assets.[44]

When states such as North Carolina, Georgia and New Jersey passed antipredatory lending legislation that was considerably stronger than any federal statute, the federal Office of the Comptroller of the Currency (OCC) stepped in, claiming that state laws could not be applied to federally regulated banks.[45] For consumer advocates in New Jersey, it was a disappointing roller-coaster ride. A coalition of

---

[43] Bank of America, 137 S. Ct. at 1301.
[44] Kathleen C. Engel & Patricia A. McCoy, The Subprime Virus: Reckless Credit, Regulatory Failure, and Next Steps 149 (2011).
[45] Bank Activities and Operations, 69 Fed. Reg. 1904 (Jan. 13, 2004).

consumer groups had worked tirelessly, facing intense lobbying efforts, to pass an effective statute, only to have the federal government nullify all their efforts.

Still, not all the news was bad. Nonbank lenders (such as Countrywide), which were responsible for so many of the worst loans, were not federally regulated, so state laws did apply to them. However, few states had such laws. Nonbank lenders did not become subject to federal regulation until the Consumer Financial Protection Bureau acquired regulatory power in 2011. The complex derivatives and other securities derived from subprime mortgages were generally not regulated either. The pressures to profit and remain competitive led to a sort of doomed arms race of financial products. Viewing the aftermath is especially painful. The people who created these risky products did not suffer during the meltdown; instead, our clients and millions like them paid the price.

FORECLOSURE BASICS AND THE EXPLOSION OF 2006–10

While the crisis officially began in 2008, foreclosures resulting from these predatory products had begun to increase in places like Indiana and Ohio several years prior. By 2006, many subprime loans were defaulting within the first few months after origination – with some borrowers unable to make even the first payment. By 2007, the number of completed foreclosures exceeded half a million homes, and things would only get worse.[46] The economy reacted like a stack of dominoes. Once the housing market began to fail, so did affiliated housing businesses such as construction firms and purveyors of consumer goods related to home ownership. Outside of the US Department of Housing and Urban Development (HUD), most lenders had no established system for engaging in meaningful loss mitigation, a fact we will address in Chapter 2. Our clients and thousands of other Americans were being squeezed from all sides. If they became delinquent on their mortgages, their credit scores fell, rendering them unable to refinance. If they sought to modify their mortgages, they encountered endless runarounds from their servicers. Capital for new lending shut down. Homeowners who had been assured they could refinance when their interest rates reset discovered the emptiness of these promises. Millions of people fell into foreclosure.

If not for the foreclosure crisis we would not be writing this book and you would not be reading it. We therefore will be discussing aspects of foreclosure throughout the book and to understand the fallout of a foreclosure, it is first necessary to understand the process itself. There are two main types of foreclosure in this country: judicial and nonjudicial. Approximately twenty states have some form of judicial foreclosure, which generally requires filing a complaint in court, having an opportunity to raise and litigate defenses and entering a judgment before a home

---

[46] *United States Residential Foreclosure Crisis: Ten Years Later*, CoreLogic 4 (Mar., 2017), https://www.corelogic.com/research/foreclosure-report/national-foreclosure-report-10-year.pdf.

can be sold at auction. The remaining states have primarily nonjudicial foreclosure regimes, which ordinarily permit a home to be foreclosed on and sold without a court proceeding, though homeowners may file an affirmative lawsuit to contest the foreclosure. Even in judicial-foreclosure states, cases may proceed to default judgment via a largely administrative process because borrowers are rarely able to contest or defend against foreclosure.

Both Indiana and New Jersey have judicial foreclosure systems. Both also developed additional procedural protections as a result of the crisis.[47] For instance, New Jersey requires lenders to file a notice of intention to foreclose containing information about the lender, servicer and amount required to cure, before filing a foreclosure complaint in court.[48] Indiana's provisions are similar, though not quite as comprehensive. In judicial foreclosure states, once a lender files a complaint, the homeowner files an answer and then proceeds to litigate the matter, as they would any other civil case. Most homeowners never file an answer. For example, in a typical year, nineteen out of twenty New Jersey foreclosures are not contested. The process is largely administrative and handled through a statewide Office of Foreclosure. Court personnel scrutinize bank evidence in support of default judgments. Until the time of judgment, borrowers can pay the mortgage arrearages and foreclosure fees to end the foreclosure. After a chancery judge enters judgment and a writ of execution (equivalent to an eviction order), authority to sell the property at auction is transferred to the sheriff's office. Borrowers are entitled by statute to two fourteen-day extensions of the sale and may seek judicial approval of additional extensions; lenders, on the other hand, are statutorily entitled to an indefinite number of extensions. In New Jersey, the borrower's right to redeem the property continues for ten days following sale, though very few borrowers are able to refinance at this point.

Indiana homeowners have no right of redemption post foreclosure. The process is more streamlined and, in many ways, more localized. While the state law remains consistent, there are considerable differences between counties and even between courts within a county, as to how long a foreclosure will take and the procedures for the sale. One example can be seen in the state's settlement conference program. While state law gives all homeowners the right to a settlement conference, only some counties facilitate those conferences and even fewer provide neutral mediators. When you look at judicial foreclosures at a national level, the process becomes far less consistent.

By contrast, a little more than half of the states have a primarily nonjudicial foreclosure system. Nonjudicial foreclosure seldom provides an opportunity for a hearing prior to a public sale of the property. The homeowner gets a notice and the home is sold, usually by a trustee. The process can happen very quickly, sometimes in a matter of days, not weeks. A borrower can take the initiative and file an

---

[47] N.J. STAT. ANN. § 2A:50–53 (West 2011); IND. CODE § 32–30-10.5–1 (Burns 2009).
[48] N.J. STAT. ANN. § 2A:50–53 (West 2011).

injunction suit to stop a pending sale, a suit to set aside the sale after it occurs, or a damages action. These suits are uncommon and costly. It should come as no surprise that homeowners unable to pay a mortgage are unable to hire an attorney.

The multiple state and federal interventions intended to stem the tide of foreclosures will be discussed in subsequent chapters. The federal government's efforts to prevent foreclosures proved insufficient to the task. Chief among them was the Making Home Affordable Program (MHA), launched in March 2009, and cosponsored by the Treasury Department and HUD. Previous loss mitigation programs existed – most of them private – but many of those modified mortgages redefaulted, often because monthly payments increased or went unchanged. Few borrowers in default can afford to keep paying their mortgages under these circumstances – after all, many already found the monthly payments unaffordable. Although payment reductions began to appear as the crisis deepened in 2008, the reductions generally were insufficient to prevent redefault. We will discuss later the multiple reasons for these failures, but at this point it is only necessary to say these efforts had little effect in stemming the tide of foreclosures.

THE MORTGAGE NOTE, ROBO-SIGNING AND MERS

In 2010, Thomas Cox, a retired banking attorney volunteering for Pine Tree Legal Services in Maine, was representing a foreclosure client. As part of that representation he conducted a deposition of Jeffrey Stevens, an employee of GMAC. During the questioning he discovered that Mr. Stevens had been signing thousands of affidavits a month to be used in mortgage foreclosures without ever verifying any of the information in the documents. Attorney Cox was incensed and went public. He was subsequently awarded AARP's Purpose Prize for his part in uncovering this nationwide scandal. Later, many of the foreclosure processing firms' employees were also revealed to have signed affidavits claiming personal knowledge of critical facts they did not verify. Not only were the signers completely ignorant about individual cases, many never even read the affidavits before signing them! Later estimates found that each employee had about three seconds per affidavit to sign, given the volume of documents they were responsible for each day. The term "robo-signing" was born.

One of these employees, Linda Green, appeared on *60 Minutes* to speak further about robo-signing. It turned out that many other employees in her office typically forged her signature if she wasn't available. Multiple versions of her "signature" on affidavits are available online; it is quite evident that most have been forged.[49] Ms. Green was far from the only robo-signer – hundreds, if not thousands, existed. We discovered a robo-signer early in the crisis, but at the time failed to realize the

---

[49] 60 MINUTES: *Mortgage Paperwork Crisis: Next Housing Shock?* (CBS television broadcast Apr. 23, 2011). Scott Pelley interviewed Linda Green and others about the robo-signing issues. The episode received a Loeb award for business journalism.

practice was widespread. Ester and David Bellows took out a mortgage with Alliance Funding, a division of Superior Bank. Days after they signed the mortgage, the bank failed and was closed by the Office of Thrift Supervision. After the death of her husband, Ester fell behind on her payments. Ocwen, the loan servicer, filed to foreclose using documents allegedly signed by Susan Augienello, a former Alliance Funding employee. We located Ms. Augienello, who signed an affidavit attesting to the fact that, although her name appeared on the documents, she had not signed any of them. She went on to tell us that a room full of people sat in her office signing her name. The foreclosure was subsequently settled, but not before we learned an important lesson: Trust nothing that a lending institution claims.

Robo-signing graphically called into question the veracity of evidence used to establish grounds to foreclose in hundreds of thousands of cases. In order to foreclose, a lender must prove that it has the right to foreclose, that the borrower has failed to make payments and now owes it a certain amount of money. Therefore, if the lender cannot prove itself the party entitled to enforce the mortgage note, it cannot obtain a judgment or sell the house. The rules for foreclosing are set out in Article III of the Uniform Commercial Code (UCC), which has been adopted by all fifty states.[50] It governs what are called "negotiable instruments," such as checks and most mortgage notes, which, when endorsed, may become fungible like cash.

All mortgage transactions involve both a note and a mortgage: The note reflects the debt obligation, while the mortgage is security – or collateral – for the loan. Acquiring a mortgage on a property to secure the obligation makes lending much more attractive because lenders know that if the borrower defaults, they can foreclose and acquire the property at sale. This is typically a more reliable way to recover the amount owed than suing on the loan contract itself. The note is the main driver of the transaction, which is why compliance with the UCC is critical, notwithstanding variations in state property law governing the mortgage. According to section 3–301 of Article III, one currently in possession of a properly endorsed instrument is generally entitled to enforce it. This legal requirement helps explain why the information contained in the robo-signed documents is crucial. Robo-signing is also a serious issue when the lender cannot submit competent evidence of how much the borrower owes. Affidavits are only valid if signed by a person with knowledge of the facts. The affidavit is usually necessary to show that the lender possessed the note and to establish how much money was owed to the lender.

If the note was diverted somewhere along the securitization chain – or never transferred to the foreclosing lender at all – the plaintiff trustee or its servicer would not be able to proceed. If it was permitted to continue foreclosing, situations could occur where two different parties (the plaintiff and the actual holder) both attempted to foreclose on the same home. Obviously, only one party can legitimately hold a particular note at one time.

---

[50] U.C.C. § 3–301 (AM. LAW INT. & UNIF. LAW COMM'N 2002).

The Mortgage Electronic Registration System (MERS), further complicated the situation. MERS was launched in 2004, with input from the Mortgage Bankers Association, after the GSEs recommended an electronic system to register mortgages. Ordinarily, when a mortgage is transferred (assigned) between parties, the transaction must be recorded in the appropriate county, which entails a recording fee. The note, on the other hand, is subject to Article III of the UCC and its possession and endorsement requirements. The mortgage and note can become separated when transferred, creating much confusion. Given the multiple transfer obligations required in securitizations, recording each assignment can become expensive. Thus, MERS was created to efficiently maintain a private online registry of mortgage transfers so that all members could keep track of each movement.

In theory, the idea is not a bad one, but in practice, it turned out to be vastly inferior to the public registration and recording system because each lender keyed its own data into the MERS system. Some data were considerably less accurate and complete than others – many transfers were not entered at all. A voluntary, individually operated system like this is subject to the "garbage in, garbage out" principle for each member lender. Plus, what happens when the mortgage goes one way and the note another? Under common law the "mortgage follows the note," but not all courts follow this rule. We will explore the implications of these rules in depth in Chapter 6. For now, it is only necessary to understand that MERS did nothing to resolve these contradictions. Instead, it accentuated them: securitization process inadequacies combined with mortgage registration problems to produce complete chaos.

Robo-signing became acutely important because of securitization and the passage of mortgage notes from one entity to another in the securitization chain. Robo-signed affidavits had the potential to undermine the entire assembly line foreclosure system almost universally used by lenders in the United States. Testifying before the House Financial Services Committee in 2010, Linda Fisher noted:

> These affidavits can violate state … statutes, as well as the due process rights of homeowners … [C]ourt rules requiring an evidentiary basis for all filed submissions may be violated. For instance, an affidavit may falsely state that a homeowner has been served with process, that the foreclosure plaintiff is the holder of the mortgage obligation, that an assignment of a mortgage and note timely took place, or that inflated amounts are owed to the lender. When the plaintiff is not the party entitled to foreclose because the wrong party was named or because the plaintiff trust did not hold the obligation at the time of filing, it does not have standing and is not entitled to judgment. Yet every day foreclosures proceed to judgment because a court relied on a plaintiff's inaccurate attestations. A colleague calls these widespread practices "servicer civil disobedience."[51]

---

[51] *Hearing on Robo-Signing, Chain of Title, Loss Mitigation & Other Issues: Before the Subcomm. on Housing & Comm. Opp. of the H. Fin. Serv. Comm.* (Nov. 18, 2010) (Testimony of Linda E. Fisher).

DOCUMENT CREATION AND "ART DEPARTMENTS"

Gaps in the documentation needed to establish the necessary chain of title in a mortgage loan were another common problem plaguing foreclosure during (and after) the crisis. These gaps were often filled in "creatively," in so-called art departments of documentation, companies working with servicers on foreclosures. Lender Processing Services (LPS) and its affiliates, including DocX, were major players in the servicing industry during a substantial part of the foreclosure crisis. (LPS is now known as Black Knight Financial Services; it is related to Fidelity Information Services.) Through its Mortgage Servicing Platform, LPS produced a very high percentage of the affidavits and other documentation used across the entire country to support foreclosures.[52] A former executive of LPS, Lorraine Brown, pled guilty to federal charges of conspiracy to commit wire fraud and was sentenced to five years in prison.[53] In 2011, several federal agencies entered into a consent decree with LPS, DocX and LPS Default Solutions – both subsidiaries – relating to allegations of robo-signing and actual forgery, but it appears to us that little has changed as a result.[54]

It is important to realize that firms like LPS and DocX were not on the fringes of the industry. They were in the mainstream and their activities affected real people. On December 13, 2011, Belinda Murphy was served with a complaint to foreclose on her Indiana home.[55] She claimed to have sent $3,000 in mortgage payments to her mortgage loan servicer, Guaranty Bank of Texas, not knowing that the bank had been closed by federal regulators. Guaranty Bank of Texas agreed to return the money to her, but instead held the funds for over a year, causing Ms. Murphy's home to go into foreclosure. Nonetheless, she believed she had the matter under control because she was working directly with her new servicer, Bank of America, to obtain a loan modification. She did not know that the foreclosure was proceeding in state court. She had been caught in the "dual track," a practice that resulted in thousands of unnecessary foreclosures across the nation before the Consumer Financial Protection Bureau stepped in to outlaw it in 2014.[56]

---

[52] *See,* David Dayen, Chain of Title (2016) for an absorbing explanation of the chain of paper issues.

[53] Press release, U.S. Dept. of Justice, Former Executive at Florida-Based Lender Processing Services Inc. Sentenced to Five Years in Prison for Role in Mortgage-Related Document Fraud Scheme (June 25, 2013), https://www.justice.gov/opa/pr/former-executive-florida-based-lender-processing-services-inc-sentenced-five-years-prison.

[54] Lorraine Brown was the CEO of DocX. *See,* David Dayen, *supra* note 52.

[55] Bank of America v. Dona Streetman, 64-D02–1212-MF-013023.

[56] Dual tracking was a controversial procedure used by mortgage servicers wherein an employee would be working with a homeowner to apply for a loan modification while, at the same time and usually without the knowledge of the homeowner, the servicer was proceeding with the foreclosure. For a more in-depth analysis of the issue, *see,* Sharon Schmickle & Sarah Rose

A default foreclosure judgment was entered against Ms. Murphy on February 20, 2013, followed by a writ of assistance to evict her from her home on October 24, 2013.[57] Upon learning this, she filed a complaint with the Indiana attorney general, claiming to have been unaware of the foreclosure action until "she came home after taking care of [her] bed ridden mother" to find an eviction notice on her door.[58] Ed Hutchison, an investigator for the Indiana attorney general received the complaint. He initially did not believe he could do much to assist her, but since it was close to Thanksgiving, he reached out to Bank of America's attorneys to see if anything could be done to prevent the eviction, at least until after the holiday.

Thus, began a multiyear investigation into how Ginnie Mae handled the assets of failed banks and the effect on thousands of homeowners, many of them in Indiana.[59] What Mr. Hutchinson uncovered was shocking. The governmental response to his findings was even more so. The first step in the investigation was to examine Ms. Murphy's loan documentation. She had obtained the loan from Guarantee Residential Lending. The mortgagee was Mortgage Electronic Registration System, Inc. (MERS) "as nominee for Guaranty Residential Lending," recorded on June 1, 2004.[60] On April 13, 2010, the mortgage was allegedly transferred by way of a corporate assignment from Guaranty Residential Lending to Guaranty Bank of Wisconsin.[61] The assignment was signed by Rhonda Wetson, allegedly a Bank of America employee at the time. This was the first sign of trouble. In 2010, Guaranty Residential Lending did not exist. It had been assumed by Guaranty Bank of Austin Texas in 2006.[62] In fact, in 2010, Guaranty Bank of Austin Texas also did not exist. Guaranty Bank of Texas had failed years earlier. It was closed by the Office of Thrift Supervision and the Federal Deposit Insurance Corporation (FDIC) appointed receiver.[63]

Miller, *'Dual tracking' Trap: Owners Lose Homes while Trying to Modify Mortgages*, Minneapolis Post (Mar. 21, 2013), http://www.minnpost.com/politics-policy/2013/03/dual-tracking-trap-owners-lose-homes-while-trying-to-modify-mortgages. The Consumer Financial Protection Bureau banned dual tracking in 2014 when it enacted its new mortgage servicing rules, specifically 12 §CFR 1024.41.

[57] Bank of America v. Dona Streetman, 64-D02–1212-MF-013023.
[58] Complaint to Indiana attorney general (on file with author).
[59] Since opening the investigation, numerous other homeowners have filed complaints that all relate to the same Taylor Bean Whitaker, Ginnie Mae transfer that Ms. Murphy's case first uncovered. The Indiana attorney general reached out to the author, who has been assisting with this matter since early 2015.
[60] Mortgage recorded June 1, 2004, document 2004–017764; Title Report, Nationwide Title Clearing, 2014.
[61] *Id.*
[62] Title II: Lender Summary, U.S. Dept. of Housing and Urb. Dev., https://entp.hud.gov/sfnw/public/lendinfo.cfm?RequestTimeout=500&lendlist=79215&lendstat=%27A%27&orderkey=lender_branch_id&report=BOTH&varorder=ASC&lender_type=t2&CFID=9492236&CFTOKEN=8b5317d58533da2c-5DC15E76–0B45-BD43-C83085B28A5D95D4.
[63] Press Release, Federal Deposit and Insurance Company, BBVA Compass, Birmingham, Alabama, Assumes All of the Deposits of the Deposits of Guaranty Bank, Austin, Texas (Aug. 21, 2009), https://www.fdic.gov/news/news/press/2009/pr09150.html.

According to an FDIC attorney, if the 2010 assignment of the mortgage from Guaranty Residential Lending to Guaranty Bank of Wisconsin had taken place as represented, it would have constituted the transfer of an FDIC asset without permission of that agency. The FDIC claimed to have no record of this loan having been transferred.[64] In fact, its records indicated that Bank of America was billing the FDIC for servicing the loan, suggesting that the FDIC still owned the loan. Even more confusing was the presence of Guaranty Bank of Wisconsin in this chain of title. Nothing in the file indicated that the bank had ever been involved in this loan. Mr. Hutchinson pressed on. He had been told that all the assets of Guaranty Bank of Austin, the bank that may have once owned the loan, had been sold to BBVA Compass Bank in 2009.[65] Real questions began to emerge regarding this mortgage's chain of title. How could the mortgage have been transferred by Guaranty Residential Lending in 2010 when all the records indicate that Guaranty Residential Lending did not exist in 2010?[66] Even if the mortgage had been transferred, the record should have shown a transfer from Guaranty Residential Lending to Guaranty Bank of Texas and then to BBVA Compass Bank or, perhaps, Ginnie Mae. Instead, the documents submitted in the foreclosure indicate a transfer from Guaranty Residential Lending to Guaranty Bank of Wisconsin and then, in an assignment dated October 25, 2010, from Guaranty Bank of Wisconsin to BAC Home Loan Servicing, formally known as Countrywide Home Loan Servicing.[67]

The October 25, 2010, mortgage assignment was signed by Debbie Kiss, allegedly an employee of Guaranty Bank of Wisconsin. The problem, however, is that Guaranty Bank of Wisconsin was never the mortgagee of this loan, nor did Ms. Kiss ever work for Guaranty Bank of Wisconsin.[68] A search for mortgage documents filed throughout the country at about the same time as the assignment in question revealed that Ms. Kiss had identified herself as having multiple jobs for a variety of lenders, including "Assistant Secretary" of Bank of America Home Loans,[69] an officer of MERS[70] and "Secretary of Veterans Affairs."[71] This evidence suggests that

[64] Indiana Attorney General *supra* note 58.

[65] *Id.* In January of 2015, Ginnie Mae told Mr. Hutchinson that they still had the note because BBVA "didn't want it."

[66] *Id.* It should be noted that Guaranty Bank of Wisconsin was also contacted. They have no record of ever owning or originating the Murphy loan. (11/22/2013).

[67] *Id.* Title report; because the foreclosure was subsequently dismissed before the file has been destroyed. The Indiana attorney general retained its copies.

[68] *Id.* Paul Guardalabene, email dated Nov. 22, 2013, confirming that "Guaranty Bank FSB (my employer) was definitely not part of the chain of title for the Streetman loan. We did not originate it and, furthermore, the individual who signed the Assignment of Mortgage in October 2010, Debbie Kiss, was not an employee of our bank."

[69] Document 1019851, filed with the St. Joseph County, Indiana Recorder, July 7, 2010.

[70] Document 2010121026, dated Nov. 5, 2010, filed with the Lake County, California Clerk of Court, Dec. 1, 2010.

[71] Document 201000157930, signed May 25, 2010. Filed in the Dallas, Texas County Records, June 23, 2010.

Ms. Kiss was most likely an employee of MERS in 2010. MERS operated by having its employees designated as officers for each of its member banks. In that way, a single person could appear as an assistant secretary for one bank and officer of another. The lending institutions sign corporate designations, designating certain MERS employees to act on their behalf. In that way, one woman can be an "employee" of multiple lending institutions. This would appear to explain the discrepancy. However, a spokesperson for MERS admitted to Mr. Hutchinson that no one at their firm could have been authorized to assign a mortgage in 2010 from Guaranteed Residential Lending or Guaranty Bank of Texas because they were both closed institutions in 2010.[72]

Puzzled, Mr. Hutchinson returned to the FDIC to determine if it had sold the loan to Bank of America. According to its records, the answer was "No."[73] In fact, the FDIC agreed the loan in question probably was included in the loans sold to BBVA Compass Bank along with all the other assets formerly owned by Guaranty Bank of Austin, Texas.[74] However, in 2015, it retracted this position and claimed it probably still owned the note.[75] Unable to obtain an accurate chain of title for the mortgage, Mr. Hutchinson began looking instead for the note. In the 2011 foreclosure case, Bank of America filed a lost note affidavit. The UCC permits a lost note affidavit when a negotiable instrument, in this case the note secured by the mortgage, is lost.[76] Not everyone can enforce a lost instrument. The person seeking to enforce the mortgage note (known as the "PETE") must prove that it was the PETE when "loss of possession occurred"[77] or that it "acquired ownership of the instrument form a person who was entitled to enforce the instrument when loss of possession occurred."[78] Therein lies the problem. To be eligible to file a lost note affidavit, Bank of America must have had actual possession of the note before it was lost, or prove that Guaranty Bank of Wisconsin possessed it when it was lost. The investigation had already determined that Guaranty Bank of Wisconsin, the entity that Bank of America allegedly obtained the loan from, had never owned or had possession of the loan. Bank of America could not have obtained possession from Guaranty Bank of Wisconsin. In fact, in conversations with the FDIC, it denied the note was lost. But, where was it?

The representations to the court had been false, and the apparent chain of title was flawed.[79] Bank of America was not entitled to enforce the Murphy note. In addition, according to MERS, the assignments used to transfer the mortgage were

---

[72] Indiana A.G. notes, *supra note 58.*
[73] Id.
[74] Id.
[75] Id.
[76] U.C.C. § 3–309(Am. Law Int. & Unif. Law Comm'n, 2002).
[77] U.C.C. § 3–309(1)(A)(Am. Law Int. & Unif. Law Comm'n, 2002).
[78] Id.
[79] Bank of America had filed a lost note affidavit in the foreclosure action.

invalid and did not comply with MERS rules. According to the MERS signing officer primer, "any reference to MERS as a nominee must also include the language 'its successors and assigns' behind the name of the Lender that MERS was originally a nominee for. This is important because at the time MERS is acting (e.g., assigning the mortgage) MERS may no longer be nominee for the original Lender."[80] So, the investigator concluded that the Bank of America "assignments of mortgages used after the death or bankruptcy of the original lenders, regardless of whether they were lawful, were not allowed under MERS rules."[81] When the inaccuracies in the filing documents and the apparent fraudulent assignments were pointed out, Bank of America set aside its foreclosure judgment and dismissed the case. But the story does not end there.

The investigator began to dig deeper. The loan in question was insured by the Government National Mortgage Association, better known as Ginnie Mae. To understand the next part of this tale, it is important to understand what Ginnie Mae is and does. Ginnie Mae is wholly owned by the federal government. It does not buy and sell loans. Instead, it insures them or, in its own words it "guarantee[s] investors the timely payment of principal and interest on [mortgage-backed securities] backed by federally insured or guaranteed loans-mainly loans insured by the Federal Housing Administration (FHA) or guaranteed by the Department of Veterans Affairs (VA)."[82] When a loan originator goes out of business the loan "become[s] the absolute property" of Ginnie Mae.[83]

While this investigation was progressing, several other homeowners filed complaints related to Ginnie Mae-insured mortgages. Most of them involved another failed lender, Taylor, Bean and Whitaker. It now appeared that the answer to the puzzle lay in the practices of Ginnie Mae, which had also guaranteed the Taylor, Bean and Whitaker loans. When this firm declared bankruptcy in July 2009,[84] Ginnie Mae took its place as originator of the loans.[85] Loans originated by Taylor, Bean and Whitaker were especially problematic in the mortgage crisis, as was the collapse of the bank that originated them. The loans it originated were predatory and the paperwork fraught with problems. When Ginnie Mae acquired these loans, it acquired a flawed portfolio. Necessary paperwork was missing. An audit of Ginnie Mae loan files in 2010 and 2011 found significant deficiencies in documentation of the loan files and cited the "[n]eed to improve Compliance Control to Ensure the Safety, Completeness and Validity of Collateral Loan Files."[86] Ginnie Mae assured Congress that its

---

[80] Indiana A.G. notes, *supra* note 58.

[81] *Id.*

[82] Ginnie Mae, http://www.ginniemae.gov/pages/default.aspx.

[83] 12 U.S.C.§ 1721(g).

[84] Reuters, *After Suspension, Lender Seeks Bankruptcy Protection*, N.Y. Times, Aug. 25, 2009, https://www.nytimes.com/2009/08/25/business/25lender.html

[85] 12 U.S.C. § 1721(g).

[86] Audit Report of Ginnie Mae's FY 2011 Financial Statements No. 2012-FO-001, Dep't Housing and Urban Dev. 6 (Nov. 7, 2011), https://www.ginniemae.gov/about_us/what_we_

Master Subservicer (Bank of America) had hired a contractor that would "cure all unclear or indefinable documents" and "recreate" all documents not found.[87] How one "recreates" loan documents missing from a file is curious. Ginnie Mae promised this recreation process would be completed by February 20, 2012.

This date is significant. It was in February of 2012 that the National Mortgage Settlement was reached.[88] The US Justice Department and forty-nine state attorneys general had begun investigating the five biggest servicing banks in the country (Ally, Bank of America, Citi, JP Morgan Chase and Wells Fargo) and their practices related to robo-signing, settling in February 2012 for relief to states and homeowners worth over $50 billion and requiring certain reforms to servicing standards.[89] Soon afterwards, the five largest servicers, including Bank of America, signed a consent agreement with the Justice Department and the attorneys general of forty-nine states and the District of Columbia.[90] The agreement gives Bank of America immunity against a lawsuit for any documents that may have been fraudulently created before the agreement, documents Ginnie Mae apparently paid Bank of America to create. It also appears that Ginnie Mae, knowing another branch of government was negotiating a settlement that would result in immunity for the recreated documents, wanted to ensure that Bank of America completed the job of recreating those documents in time to be included in the immunity of the settlement agreement. The attorneys general were never informed of this arrangement.

Even more disturbing, Bank of America was at the time utilizing the services of DocX, described earlier as an affiliate of Lender Processing Services that advertised its ability to recreate missing loan paperwork.[91] Its rate sheet advertised that, for a mere $12.95, it would "cure [a] defective mortgage" and for $95 it could "recreate [an] entire collateral file."[92] On November 20, 2012, a year after Ginnie Mae assured regulators it would have Bank of America fix its loan files, the chief executive of DocX pleaded guilty to a "scheme to fabricate mortgage-related documents at the height of the financial crisis."[93] It is not certain that DocX fraudulently recreated the documents in Ms. Murphy's file, but the circumstantial evidence is compelling.

---

do/Financial_Statements/annual_financials11.pdf; AUDIT REPORT OF GINNIE MAE'S FY 2010 FINANCIAL STATEMENTS NO. 2011-FO-001, DEP'T HOUSING AND URBAN DEV. 5–6 (Nov. 5, 2010) https://www.ginniemae.gov/about_us/what_we_do/Financial_Statements/annual_financials10 .pdf.

[87] FY 2011, App. B, *supra* note 86.

[88] JOINT STATE-FED. NAT'L. MORTGAGE SERVICING SETTLEMENTS, http://www.nationalmortga gesettlement.com/about.

[89] *Id.*

[90] U.S. v. Bank of America, Case, 1:12-cv-00361-RMC,
https://d9klfgibkcquc.cloudfront.net/Consent_Judgment_BoA-4-11-12.pdf.

[91] 60 MINUTES, *supra* note 49.

[92] DocX term sheet, http://www.lsnj.org/NewsAnnouncements/Foreclosure/materials/EXHIBITB LenderProcessingServices.pdf.

[93] Press Release, U.S. Dep't of Justice, Former Executive at Florida-Based Lender Processing Services Inc. Admits Role in Mortgage-Related Document Fraud Scheme, (Nov. 20, 2012),

What is most distressing is that neither Ginnie Mae, which paid for some of this fraud, nor the Justice Department prosecuting the fraud, notified the attorneys general involved in the global mortgage settlement relating to robo-signed documents, nor did they notify affected homeowners. Ginnie Mae refused to respond to a subpoena sent by the Indiana attorney general's office. Bank of America and MERS also refused, citing instructions from Ginnie Mae. It appeared the government was still protecting Wall Street, disregarding Main Street.

Additional examples exemplify government agencies' aversion to pursuing this systemic misconduct. While litigating a New Jersey foreclosure matter, we obtained an affidavit from Adrian Lofton, a former employee of LPS's predecessor company Fidelity National Default Solutions. Mr. Lofton stated that, despite policy to the contrary, many employees had access to borrower information in the system and were able to change it at will. Once the security of a supposedly safe system is compromised, its information is no longer reliable. Yet Mr. Lofton was terminated after reporting the system breach and the company apparently did not follow up. Nor did the court in our case pay attention to his affidavit. Around the same time, we received a call from two assistant attorneys general in Florida, June Clarkson and Theresa Edwards. They were among the very few people in the country conducting a serious investigation into the potential frauds of LPS and related players. Their story is recounted in David Dayen's absorbing book *Chain of Title*. Yet the deeper they dug into the mess, the more their office resisted, eventually firing both of them.[94]

We also received a call from John Kelleher, chief deputy attorney general in Nevada, who was conducting a similar inquiry. Later, it was terminated abruptly when he was pulled off the investigation.[95] No one, it seemed, wanted to unearth the extent of the irregularities and fraud occurring in the national foreclosure process. And like the banks, the foreclosure system apparently is too big to fail. Very few financial industry executives were ever prosecuted, let alone convicted, for mortgage-related fraud.[96] By contrast, hundreds were successfully prosecuted during

http://www.justice.gov/opa/pr/former-executive-florida-based-lender-processing-services-inc-admits-role-mortgage-related.

[94] *See,* Stefan Kamph, *June Clarkson and Theresa Edwards Were Fired after Revealing Widespread Foreclosure Fraud,* BROWARD PALM BEACH NEWS (June 21, 2012, 4:00 AM), http://www.browardpalmbeach.com/news/june-clarkson-and-theresa-edwards-were-fired-after-revealing-widespread-foreclosure-fraud-6348374.

[95] Scot Paltrow, *Special Report: Watchdogs that Didn't Bark,* REUTERS (Dec. 22, 2011, 7:12 AM), http://www.reuters.com/article/us-usa-foreclosure-idUSTRE7BL0M020111222.

[96] *See,* Chris Isidore, *35 Bankers Were Sent to Prison for Financial Crisis Crimes,* CNN MONEY (Apr. 28, 2016, 6:53 AM), http://money.cnn.com/2016/04/28/news/companies/bankers-prison/index.html; Jesse Eisinger, *Why Only One Top Banker Went to Jail for the Financial Crisis,* N.Y. TIMES (Apr. 30, 2014), https://www.nytimes.com/2014/05/04/magazine/only-one-top-banker-jail-financial-crisis.html; Jed S. Rakoff, *The Financial Crisis: Why Have No High-Level Executives Been Prosecuted?* N.Y. REV. BOOKS (Jan. 9, 2014), http://www.nybooks.com/articles/2014/01/09/financial-crisis-why-no-executive-prosecutions.

the savings and loan debacle of the 1980s.[97] Many have questioned and criticized the federal government's failure to prosecute during the later era.[98]

RESPONSES TO ROBO-SIGNING AND OTHER
REACTIONS TO THE CRISIS

The entire foreclosure system was called into question by the robo-signing revelations. Some courts and judges responded by requiring lenders to produce the proper documentation before granting a default foreclosure. The result was to slow the foreclosure process in many states. Once again, New Jersey provides a representative example. On December 20, 2010, the chancery court overseeing the Office of Foreclosure issued an order to show cause to six large national bank servicers and high-volume foreclosure filers, requiring them to demonstrate that their foreclosure practices were not tainted by robo-signing and other irregular practices. In response, the servicers largely halted foreclosures until the early fall of 2011. By then, the New Jersey Supreme Court was considering a challenge to the standard servicer practice of including the name of the servicer, but not the "lender," in notices of intent to foreclose. The notices are required by statute before filing a foreclosure complaint. In its February 2012 decision in *US Bank v. Guillaume* the Court held that notices of intent must include both the name and address of the servicer, and of the lender, i.e., the ostensible holder of the mortgage note. Although servicers were not prohibited from foreclosure activity during this period, it did not resume to any significant extent until later in 2012.[99] It should be noted that the New Jersey reforms were future-oriented and no investigation concerning past robo-signing ever took place, though servicers did agree to improve their practices. We attempted to intervene on behalf of our client population of lower-income homeowners but were rebuffed.

Forty-nine attorneys general, including those of Indiana and New Jersey, began a nationwide investigation of robo-signing. In 2011, they reached the National Mortgage Settlement, which ultimately delivered much less than promised.[100] Around the same time, several federal banking regulators began an "independent foreclosure review" to attempt to ascertain the extent to which robo-signing had tainted foreclosures across the country, causing consumers financial injury. Private consultants

---

[97] *See,* Joshua Holland, *Hundreds of Wall Street Execs Went to Prison during the Last Fraud-Fueled Bank Crisis,* Moyers & Co. (Sept. 17, 2013), http://billmoyers.com/2013/09/17/hundreds-of-wall-street-execs-went-to-prison-during-the-last-fraud-fueled-bank-crisis.

[98] *See,* e.g., Jesse Eisinger, The Chickenshit Club: Why the Justice Dept. Fails to Prosecute Executives (2017).

[99] *See,* Fisher, *supra* note 51, at 1284–285.

[100] Press Release, U.S. Dep't of Justice, Federal Government and State Attorneys General Reach $25 Billion Agreement with Five Largest Mortgage Services to Address Mortgage Loan Servicing and Foreclosure Abuses, (Feb. 9, 2012), https://www.justice.gov/opa/pr/federal-government-and-state-attorneys-general-reach-25-billion-agreement-five-largest.

were hired to conduct an audit, which was halted after officials decided that the exorbitant costs did not produce sufficient benefits to continue. But in 2013, a settlement with the participating mortgage servicers was reached and small payments – some as low as $300 – were made to more than 4.2 million affected borrowers.[101]

By this time, the primary locus of foreclosure activity had shifted from the "sand states," e.g., Nevada, Arizona and California, to Eastern states, including Florida, New Jersey and New York. While foreclosures rose and fell across the country, it remained high in the Rust Belt states. Indiana and Ohio consistently appeared in the top ten states with the highest number of foreclosures. While foreclosures and delinquencies have declined in many areas, many pockets of distress remain. According to the Mortgage Bankers Association's fourth quarter report in 2017, New Jersey had the highest number of active foreclosures, followed by New York.[102] The highest foreclosure rate was in the Mid-Atlantic region (New York, New Jersey and Pennsylvania).[103] New Jersey retained the dubious distinction of having the highest foreclosure rate in the nation in early 2018 as well.[104]

Many of the issues that caused the crisis have not been addressed. Worse yet, some of the few successful actions are being dismantled. In future chapters we move our focus from the financial crisis to its aftermath. Despite several premature pronouncements that the foreclosure crisis is over, it lingers in specific regions and isolated communities. In the rest of the book we will explain how that lingering crisis is affecting people like our clients.

---

[101] Independent Foreclosure Review, https://independentforeclosurereview.com.

[102] Nat'l Delinquency Survey, Q4, 2017, Mortgage Bankers Assoc., CHART 2 (2018)

[103] *Id.* at, 5–8 (2018).

[104] Brian O'Connell, *Do You Live in One of the 10 States with the Highest Foreclosure Rates in the US?* Experian (May 10, 2018), https://www.experian.com/blogs/ask-experian/do-you-live-in-one-of-the-10-states-with-the-highest-foreclosure-rates-in-the-us. "New Jersey takes the cake as the state with the highest rate of foreclosures, with one in 605 properties in some stage of foreclosure in 2018, according to RealtyTrac. That's 1.61% of housing units with a foreclosure filing in the Garden State. Bank repossessions hit an 11-year high in 2017, against a national average of an 11-year low repossession level at an 11-year low, on average across the U.S."

2

The Breakdown of Mortgage
Servicing and Loss Mitigation

Faced with a wave of unanticipated delinquencies coming out of the housing crisis, servicers built systems quickly and inflexibly, often held together with rubber bands, bandages, spit, glue, and a bit of duct tape. Their personnel were often ill-equipped to handle the new demands, making mistakes in dealing with distressed borrowers.

Laurie Goodman, The Urban Institute

SERVICING AND SECURITIZATION

This chapter discusses the role mortgage servicing played after the foreclosure crisis appeared to be over. First, though, we set the stage by identifying the genesis of current problems within the history of the crisis itself, notably issues with mortgage servicers, the companies that collect payments for trustees of mortgage-backed securitized trusts and other loan holders. Servicers not only collect borrowers' payments, passing them on to investors, but also manage defaults, with foreclosure law firms serving as subagents. Handling defaults is part of the function the industry calls "loss mitigation." That term encompasses measures taken to work out or renegotiate terms with borrowers to avoid foreclosure. The typical options include repayment plans, mortgage modifications, short sales, forbearance plans and deeds in lieu of foreclosure.[1]

Complex contracts called "pooling and servicing" agreements govern the relationship between the entities. During the crisis, servicers were most often affiliated

---

[1] Repayment plans allow the homeowner to become current by paying the existing mortgage payment and an additional sum. Mortgage modifications are agreements that change the original terms of the loans. Short sales are sales of a property in foreclosure for less than the homeowner owed in which the lender accepts the sale price in full payment of the mortgage balance. Forbearance plans are agreements that allow debtors to stop making payments for a defined period of time. Deeds in lieu of foreclosure is a form of loss mitigation that allows the homeowner to deed the property back to the lender in full payment of the mortgage lien.

with the banks that originated mortgages; now they are increasingly affiliated with nonbank lenders.[2] After the crisis began, new private label securitizations dwindled to almost nothing (though they are just starting to revive now). The vast majority of new mortgage-backed trusts have been guaranteed by one of the government-sponsored enterprises (GSEs): Fannie Mae, Freddie Mac and Ginnie Mae (for FHA and VA loans). According to Recursion Co, a mortgage analytics firm, by early 2018 more than half of new Freddie Mac securities and 83 percent of FHA loans were being serviced by nonbanks.[3] This shift has raised some concerns. While these servicers may be subject to regulation via GSE rules, their size may also exempt them from some of the Consumer Financial Protection Bureau's regulations.[4]

For borrowers, servicing banks are the sole liaison with lenders and the entities to which all communications and issues must be addressed. A consumer can neither hire nor fire them. Thus, when servicers failed to hire sufficient numbers of trained employees to manage the cascade of defaults and foreclosures that ensued after the crisis began, borrowers were left out in the cold, or lost in an endless telephone loop. Congresswoman Maxine Waters went public with this problem after spending two hours in vain on live TV attempting to contact a servicing agent on behalf of a constituent.[5] We spent forty-five similar minutes, finally hanging up after being transferred to five different agents, the last of whom then transferred the call back to the first. Nobody knew anything about the client's situation.

Lack of borrower contact with their lenders was – and is – far from the only issue. Even when borrowers reach the right employee to address their concerns, the representatives generally are neither sufficiently trained nor competent enough to provide correct or consistent answers to even the most basic questions. Unsurprisingly, these poorly paid workers with high turnover have been dubbed the "Burger King Kids." Their disorganized offices often lose borrowers' applications for loss mitigation. Housing counselors knew that faxes on behalf of borrowers had to be sent first thing in the morning because they pile up over the course of the day and are thrown out at the end, requiring borrowers to start over again the next morning. The treatment of mailed applications was similar. The third quarter 2016 report of the Special Inspector General of TARP (Troubled Asset Relief Program, the federal bank bailout) indicates that at one bank, "[T]he floor of the room in which the bank dumped the voluminous unopened HAMP (Home Affordable Modification

---

[2] Richard Koss, *The Mortgage Market Is Moving into the Shadows*, BLOOMBERG VIEW (Feb. 23, 2018, 6:00 AM), https://www.bloomberg.com/view/articles/2018-02-23/mortgage-loans-the-market-is-moving-into-the-shadows.

[3] *Id.*

[4] 12 C.F.R. §.1026.41(4)(ii) (2014).

[5] Brian Ross & Avni Patel, *On Hold: Even Congresswoman Gets Runaround on Bank Help Lines*, ABC NEWS (Jan. 22, 2009), http://abcnews.go.com/Blotter/story?id=6702731&page=1.

Program) applications actually buckled under the packages' sheer weight."[6] Thus, borrowers frequently spend years trying to get their mortgages modified, thanks also to the especially large number of errors made by servicers in interpreting and applying highly technical federal regulations and guidance, as well as accounting errors.[7] For most of the crisis, while borrowers were working with their servicers towards modification, lenders often were pursuing foreclosures, surprising borrowers when their homes were sold just as they thought they had worked out a solution with their lenders. Although this practice known as "dual-tracking" was prevalent for years, it is now prohibited by federal regulations.[8]

As we mentioned earlier, modifications are not the only relief borrowers may receive in loss mitigation. A "short sale" can also occur when a borrower finds a buyer offering less than the unpaid principal balance of the mortgage, which the lender accepts. Before the crisis, a short sale usually satisfied the debt. This practice changed during the crisis when lenders slipped clauses into short-sale agreements allowing them to pursue a deficiency judgment even after accepting the short sale amount. Even when the deficiency is waived, lenders often fail to inform borrowers that they may be responsible to pay federal income tax on that amount. Alternatively, a lender may propose a deed in lieu of foreclosure, which is exactly what the name suggests: The borrower deeds the property to the bank in return for the lender's promise not to foreclose on the mortgage. Again, the borrower's responsibility for the difference between the amount of the underwater mortgage and the actual market value of the home remains at issue, a topic we will revisit in Chapter 7. Yet in some areas servicers have been recalcitrant about permitting short sale or deed in lieu transactions, and even more intractable when it comes to serious mortgage modifications.

There are various reasons for these unfortunate circumstances, including that high-quality customer service has been a low priority for many years. In fact, loss mitigation departments were generally small before the financial crisis, requiring servicers to scale up at an unaccustomed pace that they were unable to maintain. In addition to keeping costs at a minimum, those drafting and negotiating pooling and servicing agreements in the early 2000s never contemplated that millions of complex

---

[6] OFF. OF THE SPECIAL INSPECTOR GENERAL OF THE TROUBLED ASSET PROGRAM, THIRD QUARTER REP. 21 (Oct. 26, 2016), https://www.sigtarp.gov/Quarterly%20Reports/October_26_2016_Report_To_Congress.pdf.

[7] *The New York Times* reported that, according to a series of audit reports from the program's regulatory watchdog, the Office of the Special Inspector General for the Troubled Asset Relief Program, "[T[he business has long been littered with errors, confusion and outright abuses." In addition, "[b]anks and servicers routinely flouted the rules by rejecting eligible homeowners, processing applications at a snail's pace and tossing people out even when they made modified payments on time," Stacy Cowley, *Foreclosure Prevention Returns to the Unknown*, N.Y. TIMES, Jan. 26, 2017. *See also* SIGTARP, *supra* note 6, Consumer Complaint Database, CONSUMER FIN. PROTECTION BUREAU (Apr. 21, 2018, 9:14 PM), https://www.consumerfinance.gov/data-research/consumer-complaints.

[8] 12 C.F.R.§ (c)(3)(i)(D).

defaults would have to be processed. The agreements were drafted to allow for the management of the pools, not individual loans that may default – let alone millions of such loans.[9] Earlier in the crisis, servicing contracts actually financially incentivized foreclosure over working with borrowers to maintain homeownership. Servicers can make money by charging late fees and various other administrative fees, some of which are illegitimate.[10] The longer a servicer interacts with a loan, the larger the potential for accruing fees.

Once they choose to foreclose, servicers tend to use the cheapest providers, often the law firms pejoratively referred to as "foreclosure mills." Mistakes in foreclosure proceedings are all too common. For example, in one of our cases the wrong lender filed a foreclosure action against a client whose loan was actually held by a completely different entity. Another client lost her home after she represented herself *pro se* (without the aid of an attorney) in a foreclosure. The plaintiff lender inadvertently filed two different foreclosure complaints against her on the same mortgage default. She contested one, but was never made aware of the second action, so it went through to judgment and sale uncontested.[11] Foreclosure firms that tried to follow the law by requiring their clients to provide the correct paperwork found themselves losing business as the industry apparently favors those attorneys who skirt the rules.

FRAUD AND SERVICING

Servicer fraud has exacerbated the legal issues. The number of forgeries and robo-signed foreclosure documents astonished many when these practices were uncovered in 2010. As we explained in Chapter 1, Lender Processing Services (LPS) and its affiliates produced most of the foreclosure documentation in the country during the foreclosure crisis. The 2011 consent decree between LPS, its subsidiaries DocX and LPS Default Solutions, and several federal agencies required the affected entities to do remediation, including "remediat[ing] affected documents."[12] This decree was amended in 2017 to include a civil penalty of $65,000,000 and the removal of the remediation obligation.[13] We have been unable

[9] Adam J. Levitin & Tara Twomey, *Mortgage Servicing*, 28 YALE J. REG. 11, 31–7 (2011); Larry Cordell, Karen Dynan, Andreas Lehnert, Nellie Liang & Eileen Mauskopf, *The Incentives of Mortgage Servicers: Myths and Realities* (Fed. Reserve Bd., Fin. & Econ. Discussion Series, Working Paper No. 2008–46, 2008)

[10] Levitin, *supra* note 9, at 42–3; *see also* Daniel Wagner, *Abusive Mortgage Servicers Profit from Government Help*, ABC NEWS, http://abcnews.go.com/Business/story?id=8263629&page=1.

[11] The appellate courts were uninterested in rectifying the injustice and the indigent client was forced to move across the country to live with family.

[12] Written Agreement between Lender Processing Serv. Inc. et al., and the Board of Governors of the Fed. Res., Docket No. 11–052-B-SC-1, 11–052-B-SC-2 & 11–052-B-SC-3 (Apr. 13, 2011), https://www.occ.gov/news-issuances/news-releases/2011/nr-occ-2011-47f.pdf.

[13] Written agreement between Service Link Holding, LLC as a Successor to Lender Processing Serv. et al. and the Board of Governors of the Fed. Reserve, Docket Nos. 11–052-B-SC-1, 11–052-B-SC-2,

to find evidence that a systematic review and remediation ever took place, but servicers reviewing these files often made the situation worse. Fraudulent documents are still circulating and causing headaches for both borrowers and lenders.

The Indiana attorney general investigated several cases involving such forged documents.[14] You will recall that DocX was the entity hired by Ginnie Mae to do document "recreation" for any loans missing proper documentation by February 20, 2012. This date is significant. It was in February of 2012 that the National Mortgage Settlement reached its agreement with attorneys general and federal regulators.[15] Soon afterwards, the five largest servicers, including Bank of America, signed a consent agreement with the Justice Department and the attorneys general of forty-nine states and the District of Columbia.[16] The agreement gives these banks immunity from lawsuits for any documents that may have been fraudulently created before the date of the agreement; documents Ginnie Mae apparently paid Bank of America to create. Neither the attorneys general, nor any affected homeowners, were informed that their loan files contained fraudulent documents. While the creation of fraudulent and forged documents has abated since the beginning of the crisis, documents created during the crisis are still making their way through foreclosure proceedings.

Much more troubling situations can occur when servicers go out of business. Only five of the most active servicers in 2007 were still in business in 2017. An official in the Indiana attorney general's office told us a horrifying story about one such servicer who rented a storage locker for its files. When it went out of business, it stopped paying the storage fees, and the locker went up for auction. Someone purchased the contents of the locker in the auction and discovered the mortgage notes. Having possession of these mortgages, it began foreclosure proceedings. The problem was that many of these people now being foreclosed upon had long since paid off their mortgages. How do homeowners gather documents to prove they made thirty years of mortgage payments? In telling this story, the official also predicted more such surprises awaiting discovery across the industry. This unfortunate circumstance has prompted us to request that the lender return the original note to the homeowner whenever a house is foreclosed. Theoretically at least, if the homeowner possesses the original note, no one can attempt to collect on the note a second time.

Although outright forgeries may have ceased since the crisis, affidavits are still being filled out and signed by employees lacking personal knowledge of the practices they are attesting to. This practice compromises the validity and stalls the

---

11–052-B-SC-3, 17–002-CMP-SC (Jan. 23, 2017), https://occ.gov/static/enforcement-actions/ ea2017–004.pdf.

[14] Bank of America v. Dona Streetman, 64-D02–1212-MF-013023.

[15] Nat'l Mortgage Servicing Settlements, Joint State-Fed. Nat'l. Mortgage Servicing Settlements, http://www.nationalmortgagesettlement.com/about.

[16] Consent Judgment, U.S. v. Bank of America (Apr. 4, 2012), https://d9klfgibkcquc.cloudfront .net/Consent_Judgment_BoA-4–11-12.pdf.

completion of foreclosures, but it may never stop. Few judges are willing to sanction servicers or their principals for this conduct and the industry continues to resist any requirement that they prove their right to foreclosure.

SERVICER INCOMPETENCE AND DYSFUNCTIONAL BUREAUCRACY

These are not the only hurdles borrowers face when dealing with servicers who lack knowledge of basic legal issues and procedures. Some tell homeowners that their home is "scheduled for sale" when no foreclosure judgment has been entered. Although lenders have had loan modification programs for at least ten years, many struggle to handle the paperwork involved. As recently as May 2018 we have engaged in foreclosure mediations with servicers that had no knowledge of what loss mitigation offers were available or how to instruct homeowners to access them. Some unfortunate families have endured this incompetence for years. Ray McCarthy was the four-term mayor of the working-class community of Bloomfield, New Jersey, who by day was a real estate appraiser. High school football was his passion. He and his family had lived in town for over thirty years. Ray's wife Janet helped with the business. Predictably, their appraisal work declined quickly after the housing crash. But business had been decent in 2006 when Ray and Janet decided to refinance their home with Wells Fargo to include extra cash to help their son purchase his own home.

Not long thereafter, in December 2007, the recession began. The McCarthy's son lost his home to a short sale. The real estate market plummeted, and the appraisal business dried up, making the McCarthys unable to keep up with their sizeable monthly payments. They defaulted and sought their first mortgage modification in hopes of affordable payments. But they had no idea they would have a foreclosure filed against them, go through five modification attempts and only achieve a permanent modification in bankruptcy court, a long six years later. As one clinic student wrote in a complaint to the CFPB about the servicer's recalcitrance during the modification process: "The consequence of ASC's [America's Servicing Company] inadequacy has left the McCarthys on a perpetual application, denial and reapplication merry-go-round." This, despite plentiful evidence that the McCarthys met the net present value standards for a permanent modification and had the income to make payments. Granting a modification was less costly to the lender than proceeding with a foreclosure.

Following is a history of the McCarthy's loss mitigation attempts: In March 2008, they obtained a trial Special Forbearance Plan. They put $25,000 down to qualify. After months of payments, Ray and Janet were denied a permanent modification because it was "not in the best interest of the investors." No further explanation was given. Next, in December of that year, they obtained a second trial modification plan after putting $11,000 down. The McCarthys made their trial payments, and in considering them for a permanent modification, ASC asked for additional documentation, which they promptly sent over and over again. Nonetheless, the modification was denied in October 2010 for "lack of information." A few months later, Ray and Janet applied for a third time. ASC told Ray that after his fifth trial payment, the modification would be made permanent. But the package with materials for the permanent modification never arrived. The McCarthys were unable to get ASC to respond and never received an official denial.

They began a fourth attempt at modification in October 2011, submitting all requested documents and information. After running into difficulties, Ray contacted us to help him navigate the extremely confounding process. But to our surprise and frustration, things only worsened after our legal representation began. In February 2012, an ASC representative made one attempt to call us, but the call inadvertently dropped. We called back and left a message but received no response. We kept attempting to contact the representative, but several days later ASC sent a letter denying the modification and claiming that the McCarthys were not only "unreachable," but also had failed to send all required documents. We once again faxed a letter in response, but never received a reply.

In October 2012, we sent a Request for Escalation to HAMP, protesting the reasons for denying the fourth application. This time, ASC said that it was denied because of "insufficient income," stating that the McCarthys made only a bit more than $1,000 per month, which was untrue. Inexplicably, ASC had used outdated and inaccurate figures from 2010 in its determination, even though Ray had subsequently documented his current income of many times that amount. Nonetheless, HAMP rejected the escalation. In the spring of 2013, we filed a complaint with the Consumer Financial Protection Bureau. It began: "Raymond and Janet McCarthy file this complaint to expose the dysfunctional nature of the mortgage modification process at America's Servicing Company and the Department of the Treasury's HAMP escalation process." The upshot of this complaint was yet another application, this time as part of the New Jersey Foreclosure Mediation Program. Eventually, after many sessions and failures of ASC to provide a knowledgeable employee, we referred the McCarthys to a bankruptcy lawyer. It was in federal bankruptcy court near the end of 2013 that a final mortgage modification contract was reached, more than six years after this exhausting saga began. We learned quite viscerally that the system was still broken, though it could operate more efficiently if servicers would only view loss mitigation as essential, and part of their customer service obligations.

Recurring issues with loss mitigation are only the tip of the servicing iceberg. Misapplied payments and other accounting mistakes remain frighteningly common. Mr. and Mrs. Owens experienced these problems for years before, during and now after the crisis. The couple refinanced their mortgage in 2004. In 2008, Mr. Owens was deployed to Iraq and Mrs. Owens temporarily relocated to the military base to be close to the families of other deplored forces. A few months later the couple's monthly mortgage payments inexplicably increased from $539.42 to $1,870.49. When asked, the customer service representative told them it was an "Indiana tax issue." It was not. Their taxes had not increased. Instead, the city had assessed a civil penalty for some unresolved code enforcement issues. The couple insists they had no notice of the property code violations, but nonetheless the fine was assessed. The bank misunderstood the $5,000 fine as a $10,000 increase in property taxes. (Indiana property taxes are assessed in two installments per year.) As a result, the lender increased the required escrow payments by $1,300 per month.

This was only the first of the long list of errors made by Ocwen, the servicer in this case. The Owenses had begun to make double payments on their loan. Instead of applying these to the principal due, Ocwen put the payments in a suspense account. A suspense account is exactly what it sounds like, an account where the money is placed "in suspense," instead of applying it to the loan and reducing the principal due. This once-common practice violates numerous regulations and basic contract law, but it was all too common during the crisis. At one point, over $10,000 in payments had accrued in the Owenses' suspense account, and then it disappeared. During depositions, Ocwen claimed the money was in suspense because the customer had requested that the payments be unapplied to their loan. The request does not appear anywhere in the telephone logs, and the homeowners deny it. The lender has never properly accounted for this money.

The loan ultimately went into foreclosure, after which their lender, Patti Realty (a subsidiary of GMAC), went into bankruptcy. Everything stopped for over a year. Ocwen purchased GMAC's loans out of the bankruptcy. To add insult to injury, the bankruptcy judge determined that the homeowners could proceed with loan modifications and offsets to their balances but were not entitled to any damages for actions that occurred before the bankruptcy. The couple made multiple attempts to obtain a loan modification. Statements they received did not match from one month to another. The principal balance rose and fell, varying by as much as $30,000 a month. The interest rate jumped from 2.1 percent to 5 percent with no explanation. We attended two court-ordered mediations, but the parties were unable to agree on the balance due. Ocwen filed and lost two motions for summary judgment (a legal procedure in which you ask the court for judgment without trial).

In 2017, the case finally went to trial. By then, the Consumer Financial Protection Bureau had filed a lawsuit against the servicer alleging, among other things, that Ocwen "improperly calculated loan balances, misapplied borrower payments, failed to correctly process escrow and insurance payments, and failed to properly investigate and make corrections in response to consumer complaints."[17] Soon afterward, Indiana revoked Ocwen's license to originate mortgage loans within the state.[18] The allegations in this action mirrored all the problems our clients were experiencing

[17] Consumer Financial Protection Bureau v. Ocwen Financial Corp, et al., Case. No. 9:17-CV-80495, https://files.consumerfinance.gov/f/documents/20170420_cfpb_Ocwen-Complaint.pdf.

[18] In the Matter of: Ocwen Loan Servicing, LLC, Notice of Charges and Emergency Order to Revoke Licenses Under IC 24-4.4-2 and IC 24-2.5-3, Apr. 21, 2017, http://www.dfi.wa.gov/sites/default/files/consumer-services/enforcement-actions/C-13-1153-14-CO01.pdf.

with their mortgage. More important, it suggests that mortgage servicing problems are far from resolved. Immediately before the trial, the servicer changed yet again. Interestingly, we had to inform the lender's own lawyer that he had a new client since the lender had apparently not done so. Such lapses are all too common in the industry. Servicers routinely fail to communicate with their lawyers, who are forced to use the same 1–800 lines to reach their clients that our clients use, with much the same result.

At the trial, the new loan servicer was unable to explain the inconsistent records. Unfortunately, by this time the Owenses had split up and moved to different states. The judge ruled that they had defaulted on their payments, something they never really denied. They had stopped making payments because they had doubled for no apparent reason, in their mind justifying the default. The judge disagreed. In the 2018 foreclosure judgment, the judge commented on Ocwen's "abysmal record keeping" and admitted being "completely flummoxed as to what actual interest accrued over time and at what interest rate."[19] He awarded the bank an *in rem* judgment (one that can only be collected by selling the property) in the amount of the balance that had existed in 2008, and none of the additional money it claimed was owed. The saga was finally over – or was it? A few months later, the servicer changed again. The new servicer is now trying to collect over $100,000. Not only does the order disqualify the lender from collecting any money from the couple; they are seeking an amount twice that ordered by the judge. The litigation begins again.

The Owenses' story illustrates the servicer incompetence we saw during the crisis. Even when all forms and supporting documentation were given to the lender in time, the lender would fail to timely evaluate it. When a lender fails to evaluate an application within sixty days, it is considered stale. Even if nothing has changed, a borrower is required to submit an entirely new packet. Whistle-blowers have reported being instructed to tell homeowners that the loan modification was under review when it was not, and encouraged to delay modification in favor of foreclosure.[20] Forms were rejected for silly, minor issues. Servicers routinely requested paperwork that did not exist or could not be reasonably obtained.

The HAMP loan modification program was intended to assist borrowers either currently in default or in imminent danger of default. Servicers regularly encouraged homeowners to stop making their mortgage payments in order to become eligible to apply for it. Most of our clients were so advised. At least one study has suggested that the possibility of a loan modification induces people to strategically

---

[19] Order, 71C01–1009-MF-000542, Jan. 25, 2018.
[20] John W. Schoen, *Bank of America Former Employees: "We Were Told to Lie,"* NBC NEWS (June 17, 2013, 3:29 PM), https://www.nbcnews.com/businessmain/bank-america-former-employees-we-were-told-lie-6C10351458.

default.[21] As a result, FHFA has been preoccupied by the notion that thousands of people strategically defaulted on their mortgages instead of acknowledging they had been advised to default. The problem with this study and similar ones that rely solely on large datasets is that they have no information about what is occurring on the ground. While we do not dispute that many people defaulted when they could have made a few more payments, these were usually not strategic defaults by sophisticated borrowers. Instead, they were defaults induced when servicers instructed homeowners what to do to save their homes. All too often, the process to obtain a loan modification dragged a homeowner who never intended to default into foreclosure. Review after review has found that the largest servicers failed to properly handle loan modifications.[22]

SERVICING TRANSFERS

The servicing transfers the Owenses experienced (four in the life of their loan) are far from unusual. As mentioned previously, there has been a massive exodus of big banks from the servicing industry. According to a 2016 Government Accounting Office report, nonbank mortgage loan servicers increased from 6.8 percent in 2012 to slightly over 24 percent in 2015.[23] This market shift has continued, raising concerns, including liquidity issues last seen during the crisis.[24] These liquidity issues create pressure for a servicer to forego loss mitigation and foreclose quickly in order to recoup needed capital.[25] Servicing rights are bought and sold frequently, creating numerous other issues for homeowners. Servicing transfers tend to complicate borrowers' attempts to negotiate with their lenders for a loan modification. In this new reality, it is relatively common for borrowers to work out a modification with their one servicer only to have the new servicer refuse to honor it. The story of Linda and Dave Smith offers a striking example. A housing counselor first referred the Smiths to the Notre Dame Clinical Law Center in 2009. At the time, Mrs. Smith was disabled, and Mr. Smith was still working. They were both in their early sixties. Shortly after contacting us, Mr. Smith, a diabetic, became too ill to continue

---

[21] Xianghong Li & Xin Lei Shelly Zhao, *Strategic Defaults Induced by Loan Modifications* (2015), https://papers.ssrn.com/sol3/papers.cfm?abstract_id=2586072.

[22] U.S. Dep't of Treas., Rep., Hamp Application Activity by Servicer, https://www.treasury .gov/initiatives/financial-stability/reports/Pages/HAMP-Servicer.aspx (quarterly reports from the third quarter of 2015 through the fourth quarter of 2017 indicate the need for servicer improvement).

[23] U.S. Gov't Accountability Off., GAO-16-278 Rep. to Congressional Requesters: Nonbank Mortgage Servicers 9 (2016).

[24] *Nonbank Share of Top 500 Mortgage Servicers up Sharply in q416, Plenty of Upheaval Ahead*, inside mortgage finance (Feb. 2, 2017), https://www.insidemortgagefinance.com/issues/ imfpubs_imf/2017_5/latest_data/Nonbank-Share-of-Top-50-Mortgage-Servicers-Up-Sharply– 1000039985-1.html; You Suk Kim, Steven M. Laufer, Karen Pence, Richard Stanton & Nancy Wallace, *Liquidity Crisis in the Mortgage Market* (Brookings Papers of Economic Activity Conference Draft, Mar. 8–9, 2018).

[25] Kim, *supra* note 24, at 33–4.

working. Deutsche Bank had filed to foreclose on their home in March 2009, and the housing counselor was helping the couple apply for a HAMP modification. The servicer, First Franklin, abruptly halted the foreclosure process and stopped responding to the counselor. We intervened and were ultimately able to negotiate a repayment plan wherein the couple would pay $500 per month – principal only – with no accruing interest. Despite agreeing to the terms and accepting the monthly payments, the lender refused to put the agreement into writing. A series of letters were exchanged confirming the arrangement. About once a year we checked in with the servicer to be sure they were properly crediting the payments. They were.

In 2011 Bank of America became the new servicer, and things quickly fell apart. Bank of America filed a notice of intent to foreclose. We contacted the foreclosing attorney, giving her copies of the agreement documents. She never filed the foreclosure complaint. We complained to the Indiana attorney general and the Consumer Financial Protection Bureau about the bank's failure to honor the loan modification. Bank of America finally complied with the previous servicer's contractual changes, but in 2014, servicing transferred again, this time to Select Portfolio Servicing (SPS). Again, the lender refused to honor the payment deal, claiming it had no record of it. SPS sent numerous letters threatening foreclosure. The stress of possibly losing her home put Mrs. Smith in the hospital many times. We sent SPS a notice of error, a legal process that requires acknowledgement and resolution within a specified time period.[26] That was in 2014. SPS spent several years "investigating." The Smiths could have filed a lawsuit, but the prospect was too stressful for them. Instead, they kept making their payments. SPS never replied to the notice of error. Instead, in early 2017, it sent the clients an unsolicited offer for a loan modification with a very, very low payment. It was actually a very good offer. When we contacted the clients to see if they wanted to accept, a family member answered the telephone instead. The Smiths were both very ill and unable to live in the home. The good news: We had kept them in the home for eight additional years. The bad news: The constant stress of their ordeal caused their health to deteriorate. Our clients soon passed away and the family chose not to pursue any further legal action.

Mrs. Miller is yet another client whose account became incomprehensible after a servicing transfer. She had fallen behind in payments when her husband passed away. Servicing was transferred from Bank of America to Ditech. The bank notified her in 2016 that her escrow account was short several hundred dollars. Her son paid the amount requested, but the bank inadvertently applied the amount to her next payment. Her next two statements directed her to make payments of approximately thirty dollars less than previous statements, which she did. She did not realize – nor was it explained – that the lender had accidently applied the money meant to bring the escrow current as if it was a regular monthly payment. After paying the reduced amount for two months, the homeowner received a statement indicating that the

---

[26] 12 C.F.R. §1024.35(e)(3).

homeowner's mortgage payment was zero dollars for that month. She checked with the servicer and was assured she owed no payment for the month. She did not send a payment.

In 2017, the servicer realized its error. It backed out the payments and applied them to escrow. It did not explain its action to the owner – it simply sent a notice that she was nearly three months delinquent and threatened foreclosure, even though it had been the cause if the delinquency. While the servicer finally acknowledged what it had done in response to a formal request for information, it still refused to accept any responsibility for the delinquency. It refused to provide a loan modification or a repayment plan. Ironically, the servicer's reason for refusing to give Mrs. Miller a loan modification is that she can afford to make payments. While she can, she cannot afford to make up the deficiency caused by the lender. Loan servicers see no duty to their customers, the homeowners. Homeowners cannot hire or fire their loan servicer. With none of the traditional market forces keeping them in check, the servicers have no incentives to serve the interests of the homeowners.

SERVICER EXCUSES AND DEFENSES

Lenders and their servicers also fail to recognize a need to explain their actions. When pressed, they often justify the low numbers of modifications with reference to something called the net present value (NPV) formula. The NPV test permits modification only if modifying the loan is less expensive to the lender than foreclosing. This particular formula was developed as part of the federal government's Home Affordable Modification Program (or HAMP, discussed further in Chapter 4).[27] Its rubrics have shaped the framework now used by almost all lenders, even in their proprietary, in-house modification programs. The rationale is that a lender should not have to modify a mortgage if it will lose money modifying the loan rather than foreclosing. It can be difficult to definitively refute a lender's claim that a borrower's situation fails the NPV test, as the actual NPV algorithm is not publicly available. However, using the actual formula, a site called checkmynpv.com (which HUD encouraged borrowers to use) allows borrowers to determine whether they might be eligible for a HAMP modification.[28] Servicers in regions with high-value homes

[27] The HAMP program formally stopped accepting applications on December 31, 2016, though the program will not expire entirely until the mortgages currently in the pipeline have been processed. Interestingly some servicers are still referring to their loan modifications as "HAMP mods" even though such mods really do not exist. In reality, these are loan modifications that use the previous HAMP guidelines.

[28] The frequently asked questions for checkmynpv.com explains:

CheckMyNPV.com is required to use the same formula for evaluating NPV as that used by HAMP mortgage servicers. However, differences in input data and other industry-related data referenced by the NPV formula may result in different outputs. CheckMyNPV.com

often deny modifications because of the NPV even when there is every indication that homeowners are eligible for modifications and would pass the NPV test.

Early in the HAMP program, borrowers frequently were denied relief through claims that their pooling and servicing agreement did not permit modification. In reality, most pooling and servicing agreements do. Others neither authorize nor prohibit loan modifications, but are silent.[29] We have seen a few pooling and servicing agreements that permit modifications only until the number reaches a certain percent of the remaining loans in the pool. Some of the worst subprime trusts can reach this threshold. But these claims often seem to have been merely an excuse for a denial. In fact, it is not clear that the servicers ever really look at the pooling and servicing agreements. One of our clients, for instance, was denied a loan modification allegedly because of investor restrictions. When we asked to see the provision of the pooling and servicing agreement containing this information, we were sent a document that clearly stated there were no restrictions on loan modifications. The modification was granted once we pointed out this inconsistency. The servicer had either never looked, or had deliberately misrepresented the situations.

All stakeholders are concerned about the redefault rates on modified mortgages. Obviously, nobody benefits when a modified mortgage fails. Early loan modifications often raised monthly payments and failed, as a result.[30] HAMP modifications have performed better than private label modifications, which tend to decrease payments less. HAMP Tier II modifications performed better than Tier I.[31] This may be because interest rates in HAMP Tier I modifications increase over time. In 2017, more than 450,000 families experienced their third rate increase.[32] Family incomes did not increase in the ensuing years. It therefore stands to reason that many of the latter have little chance of surviving.

---

calculates the proposed loan modification terms based on the input values you provide. The inputs you enter may be different than ones used by your servicer based on documentation you previously provided. You should work with your servicer on significant differences in input values. Also, servicers have access to non-GSE investors' guidelines or restrictions on performing modifications on mortgages owned by them; CheckMyNPV.com does not. For this reason, it is important to understand thatCheckMyNPV.com provides only an estimate of a mortgage servicer's NPV evaluation.

Checkmynvp.com Frequently Asked Questions, MAKING HOME AFFORDABLE, https://www.checkmynpv.com/bnpv-ui/pages/start.xhtml. (This webpage is scheduled to be retired on May 1, 2018. A copy is on file with the authors.)

[29] John Patrick Hunt, *What Do Subprime Securitization Agreements Say About Mortgage Modification?*, 31 YALE J. REG. 11, 17–8 (2013).

[30] *See*, Alan White, *Deleveraging the American Homeowner: The Failure of 2008 Voluntary Mortgage Contract Modifications*, 21 (2009), http://ssrn.com/abstract=1325534.

[31] MAKING HOME AFFORDABLE: PROGRAM PERFORMANCE REP. THROUGH THE FOURTH QUARTER OF 2017, DEPT. OF TREASURY 8–9 (Mar. 16, 2018), https://www.treasury.gov/initiatives/financial-stability/reports/Documents/4Q17%20MHA%20Report%20Final.pdf.

[32] *Id.* at 6.

PRINCIPAL REDUCTION AND CONSEQUENCES
OF FAILURE TO TAKE IT

Not all loans can be modified into an affordable loan. This is especially true in urban areas where many foreclosures were put on hold for years while lenders caught up with their foreclosure inventory. While foreclosures were stalled, loan balances continued to increase; at the same time, housing values in these distressed areas plummeted (though they have been rising lately in gentrifying areas). Lenders' reluctance to reduce principal has made many modifications offers unaffordable. When lenders did reduce principal, it was rare that such reductions were large enough to have a real impact.[33] When all the interest and fees are capitalized, i.e., added to the amount due, the principal naturally increases, and the resulting payment must be large in order to amortize the full amount of the loan in a reasonable amount of time. However, it is important to remember that the industry defines "principal reduction" in a manner that, in our opinion, is not entirely accurate. The industry capitalizes all principal, fees and interest before considering the loan modification. If the lender waived the interest and dubious fees that accrued while it was stalling the mortgage foreclosure or loan modification process and refusing any payments, the resulting principal balance would not be unreasonably large. Loan modification thus would be feasible. What the industry considers unjustified principal reduction, we consider fundamental fairness.

Until recently, the percentage of underwater mortgages (those with principal balances higher than the market value of the property) was quite high, providing justification for cutting those balances to reflect the actual worth of the collateral. After all, lenders will not recover more than the market value in a resale after foreclosure; in fact, they generally recover much less. Lenders have given many reasons for their reluctance to write down principal. Of these, research suggests that much of the aversion is related to accounting, including an unwillingness to "mark to market," or price mortgage collateral at its fair market value, which could impact stock value.[34] Other reasons include the view that write-downs will incentivize borrowers to default and seek a modification with lower payments. Research has shown, however, that the percentage of intentionally defaulting borrowers is quite low and that borrowers will go to great lengths to maintain their commitments.[35] On the other hand, plentiful evidence exists of lenders' intentional refusals to modify

---

[33] The fourth quarter 2017 HAMP performance report shows that, after 2012, more than half the loan modifications included principal reductions. These reductions were much more common in areas where the housing bubble had been extreme, and not in neighborhoods were our clients lived. *See*, supra note 31.

[34] Sanjiv R. Das & Ray Meadows, *Strategic Loan Modification: An Options-Based Response to Strategic Default*, 3 J. BANKING FIN. 636, 637 (2013).

[35] Brent T. White, *Underwater and Not Walking Away: Shame, Fear and the Social Management of the Housing Crisis*, 45 WAKE FOREST L. REV. 971, 972 (2010).

mortgages when doing so would serve the interests of all parties – lenders, investors and borrowers.

Consumer advocates are puzzled. Servicers' refusal to modify mortgages in cases where the borrowers are willing and able to consistently pay seems irrational. In fact, we have several recent instances where the lender refused a loan modification but then unilaterally released the mortgage. We can only conclude that servicing is a highly dysfunctional business, frequently unable to act even in the interest of the securitized trusts and investors that servicers represent. Another client story provides an illustration. This story begins during the second round of foreclosures – those occurring after recession-related unemployment or underemployment set in. Although these events occurred a number of years ago, they remain relevant, given that servicer conduct generally remains the same. Here, the servicer fought every reasonable option to avoid foreclosure tooth and nail, despite the financial advantage that would have accrued to the defrauded borrowers, the investors and taxpayers (given that the mortgage was guaranteed by Ginnie Mae), had a reasonable modification (as opposed to one with substantially higher payments) been fashioned. Principal reduction was warranted but it was not considered. Unfortunately, this course of conduct often extends into litigation, if a foreclosure proceeds in that manner. Servicers' counsel often combat every issue in court, filing repeated motions to cut off discovery and grant summary judgment, and endlessly resisting requests for relevant documents, despite the exorbitant legal fees that ensue.

Juan Guaraco,[36] a Peruvian immigrant in his fifties (and US citizen), who had worked at the same bread bakery job in New Jersey for over twenty years, was having trouble making his mortgage payments in 2010. He had even missed a payment or two on the mortgage on the old wood-frame house in an inner-ring suburb of Newark, where he lived with his wife, children and one grandchild. He was getting fewer hours and less overtime at work, as was his wife Cristina, and making the monthly payments over the last six years had never been easy. Nor was raising kids in America, where new expenses seem to crop up daily. Because the Guaracos speak little English, they thought there wasn't much they could do about their situation.

Mr. Guaraco was therefore curious and relieved when he heard about a Spanish-speaking business, Time Consulting, which all but guaranteed its customers mortgage modifications. He had a good feeling about its proprietor, Adan Cueva, when they met face-to-face –Cueva seemed trustworthy and sincere, shaking hands and looking Juan right in the eye. Mr. Cueva promised the Guaracos lower mortgage payments if they paid him $3,500 in monthly payments of $500 after a down payment of $1,000. They began doing so. Shortly thereafter, Time Consulting did indeed obtain a mortgage modification, but it had both a higher interest rate and higher monthly payments! After Juan complained, Cueva said he would work on

---

[36] The clients' names have been changed. Although they are legally in the United States, they are concerned about possible repercussions if their names are revealed.

getting a better deal. Many months elapsed. Sometimes Cueva would instruct Juan not to make monthly payments, telling him – inaccurately – that nonpayment was necessary to qualify for a modification. This is something we commonly hear from clients. Servicers told them to stop making payments if they wanted a loan modification.

In 2011, Cueva instructed the Guaracos to send their monthly mortgage payments directly to Time Consulting so that he could forward them to the servicing bank. By now you may have guessed that Mr. Cueva kept all those payments – $20,000 worth by 2013. The Guaracos only became suspicious in 2012 when Cueva told them he achieved a mortgage modification with a much lower payment and gave them a letter stating the terms. The letter looked forged. The Guaracos also had attempted to pay the servicer directly one month, but their payment was returned with a letter indicating that foreclosure proceedings had begun. This clinched it – Mr. Cueva was not on the up-and-up.

Mr. Guaraco sought legal advice from us late in 2012. Around the same time, the clinic received additional calls about Time Consulting and began representing another of its victims as well. We started investigating and in April 2013 were unsurprised to hear that Adan Cueva, as well as his father and brother, had just been arrested and charged with theft and fraud regarding the operation of Time Consulting. The brothers pleaded guilty in the summer and received short prison sentences, plus a restitution order for over $800,000. We filed a consumer fraud lawsuit on behalf of the Guaracos against Time Consulting, Adan Cueva and other defendants; all defaulted. The next year, we obtained a judgment against them for $60,000, but are still attempting to collect on it. Ironically, Adan Cueva fell into foreclosure himself and the Guaracos are in line to collect from any surplus funds, though it is unlikely any will exist after the house is sold.

We have focused up to this point on Time Consulting, which set the foreclosure juggernaut in motion. Now we will shift to the servicer (actually, there were several, as servicing rights on the Guaracos' mortgage were sold and resold), and the foreclosure action against our clients. The Seton Hall Civil Litigation Clinic began representing the Guaracos as foreclosure defendants in late summer of 2013, filing defenses and defeating a motion to strike. Discovery in the case took almost two years (with much attendant drama!). In the meantime, we filed for simultaneous mediation, in another attempt to obtain a workable mortgage modification. Once again, the Guaracos laboriously filled out an application for a modification, attaching recent pay stubs, consenting to release their tax returns, itemizing monthly income and expenses in detail and submitting a hardship letter that described their need for lower payments. They appeared eligible for a modification, based on the NPV test.

Over a year later the Guaracos finally received a trial modification they could (barely) afford, but only after enduring five mediation sessions made even more difficult by servicer negligence, e.g., servicer representatives missing some of the meetings, losing documents and requesting multiple resubmissions of pay stubs. Under the federal government's FHA HAMP modification program, borrowers had to make three timely trial payments before being eligible to receive a permanent modification, the terms of which might differ slightly from the trial plan. We had had to educate opposing counsel and the servicer – using government-issued interpretive guidance – about how to calculate the Guaracos' eligibility as we lumbered through the mediation process. Eventually, though, the Guaracos made a substantial down payment and four trial payments before the servicer provided a permanent modification offer. Surprisingly and unfortunately, the final offer's terms included significantly *higher* monthly payments than those under the trial plan (not to mention the original mortgage). The lender was utterly unwilling to reduce the principal amount of the mortgage at all, much less by the $20,000 that Adan Cueva had stolen from the Guaracos. Cueva's crimes had caused the Guaracos to fall into default to begin with, but the servicer refused to take that into account, even though the foreclosure judge had repeatedly requested it to make efforts to rectify the injustice of the situation.

At the end of 2014 the Guaracos reluctantly turned down the permanent modification offer because it was unaffordable. The servicer then filed a summary judgment motion, which we lost in November 2015. Yet the Guaracos still owned their home and continued to reside there because the lender had never finalized the foreclosure, despite paying taxes, hazard and flood insurance (after Hurricane Sandy, the home ended up on FEMA's expanded flood zone map) since default. Meanwhile, the Guaracos – who could afford to make monthly payments and were entirely willing to do so – were unable to pay for the home because servicers do not accept payment from borrowers in foreclosure. The family saved every mortgage payment from the time we began representing them until the trial modification plan (for which they used escrowed funds as a down payment); afterwards, there was no point in continuing to escrow.

The Guaracos temporarily lived in their home without paying the mortgage. Like so many families in foreclosure, they stopped putting money and sweat equity into home improvements, since their place in the neighborhood was uncertain. Any community is better off when homes remain occupied, not tempting to vandals and squatters, but the lack of investment in maintenance and improvements made economic sense for the Guaracos, whose long-term prospects of keeping the home were uncertain. Still, the deterioration of the property will eventually adversely affect the entire neighborhood by depressing surrounding home values.

It makes little financial sense to refuse sustainable modifications to middle-class working people like the Guaracos who can afford to make reasonable monthly payments to stay in their homes, benefiting themselves, their communities and the investors relying on the stream of income that securitized mortgages generate. Property values in the Guaracos' neighborhood are low and the house remains underwater, such that a sale of the home after foreclosure will not net the lender anything but a substantial loss. These are the homes that most often become zombies, something we explore in the next chapter.

As a postscript, servicing rights on this loan were transferred to a new servicer several years ago (and transferred again more recently). The new servicer reached out to the Guaracos and allowed them to apply once again for a modification. After the initial application was denied, they were considered for a grant under a New Jersey state program that could have reduced their principal balance. The new servicer may have learned that it pays to keep homeowners who can afford to pay in their homes.

FORECLOSURE MEDIATION

Policymakers have heard numerous complaints about the flaws in the loss mitigation system from both constituents and consumer advocates. More than half of all states have enacted some kind of mediation program, whether statewide or local.[37] Foreclosure mediation programs have been very effective in assisting homeowners seeking loan modifications.[38] One of the earliest and most successful was Philadelphia's Residential Mortgage Diversion Program. Its success can be attributed partially to its mandatory nature – homeowners had to "opt out" of participation – and partially to the passion of its creator and implementer, Judge Annette M. Rizzo.[39] While most programs have been successful, servicer compliance has been consistently difficult to secure.[40] Effective programs enable borrowers to connect with a servicer employee with the knowledge and authority to act.[41] They also include protocols for the timely exchange of documents – such as payment histories and

---

[37] *Foreclosure Mediation Programs by State*, NAT'L CONSUMER L. CTR. (Apr. 19, 2018, 1:07 PM), https://www.nclc.org/issues/foreclosure-mediation-programs-by-state.html, *see also* Alan White, *Foreclosure Diversion and Mediation in the States*, 33 GA. ST. U. L. REV. 411, 416 (2017).

[38] White, *supra* note 37, at 422–24.

[39] *Id.* at 422–24, *see also* PHILA. RESIDENTIAL MORTGAGE FORECLOSURE DIVERSION PROGRAM, REP. OF FINDINGS, UPDATE, 2014, THE REINVESTMENT FUND (2012), https://www.reinvestment .com/wp-content/uploads/2015/12/Diversion_Court_Findings-Update_Report_2014.pdf.

[40] *See*, i.e., White, *supra* note 37, at 421 (reporting that one-half of all Nevada mediations failed due to servicer noncompliance); when Maryland was creating their program, Judith Fox and Tom Cox were asked to assist in the training. We both stressed that the program design was missing a key element, a way to require compliance from the servicers. They did not believe us because they had consistent compliance from employers and employees in their unemployment mediation program. It was barely two months into the program that Maryland, too, had to change the program to strengthen compliance requirements.

[41] "An effective foreclosure mediation program addresses one of the most troublesome features of foreclosures involving securitized mortgages, namely the inability of homeowners to reach a live person with whom they can communicate about options other than foreclosure." NAT'L CONSUMER L. CTR, FORECLOSURES AND MORTGAGE SERVICING §8.8.1, https://library.nclc.org/ forcl/080801.

origination and assignment documents – and providing adequate notice.[42] Mediation has frequently enabled borrowers to work with housing counselors, these relationships leading to more favorable outcomes.[43] Because mediation programs tend to be considerably more effective than leaving borrowers to fight foreclosure *pro se*, they can help to preserve homeownership for lower-income people, including minorities, whose ownership rates were hit particularly hard by the crisis.[44]

As a rule, foreclosure mediation has been a positive development in that it forces servicers to engage with homeowners, their alleged clients. The mediation experience can be either positive or negative and depends very much on local factors. In Indiana, for example, some counties provide for third-party facilitators (we deliberately do not call them mediators in Indiana so as not to invoke the mediator rules and processes), and others do not. The outcomes are quite good for homeowners in facilitated programs and only fair in un-facilitated counties. The program the Guaracos participated in had many inadequacies but was better than trying to negotiate with a lender on their own. Still, our experience with the voluntary New Jersey foreclosure mediation program illustrates some of the problems facing homeowners. Although the mediators we encountered have been quite professional, servicers frequently have not taken the process seriously. Not only have they repeatedly failed to provide – even by phone – a knowledgeable employee empowered to enter into an agreement, they sometimes have refused to honor mediated settlement agreements. That was our experience representing several nonprofits as *amicus curiae* in a New Jersey Supreme Court case in which that occurred. TamiLynn Willoughby had represented herself in foreclosure court for years in an attempt to save her small old house in a working-class community near the New Jersey shore. Eventually she was able to reach an agreement with her servicer in mediation, but the servicer refused to comply with the terms, instead offering her a permanent modification with far worse terms.

---

[42] "Federal oversight of servicers' practices in reviewing homeowners for eligibility for loan modification has failed. This failure leaves states in the position of having to take over the task. Since early 2008, mandatory foreclosure diversion and mediation programs have been implemented in at least nineteen states. While procedures vary from program to program, they typically include mechanisms to counteract the most common deficiencies in servicers' loss mitigation reviews." Geoff Walsh, *Rebuilding America: How States Can Save Millions of Homes through Foreclosure Mediation*, NAT'L CONSUMER L. CENTER 6 (Feb. 2012).

[43] "An important feature of most foreclosure conference and diversion programs is that they connect homeowners in foreclosure with housing counselors. Another study released in 2011 documented the impact of a borrower's working with housing counselors on the likelihood that the borrower will lose the home to foreclosure. The study found that homeowners who received counseling were 1.7 times more likely to avoid a foreclosure sale than those who did not. The counseled homeowners had a forty-five percent higher probability of avoiding redefault than borrowers who obtained loan modifications without counselor assistance." *Id.*

[44] *Id.* "Policymakers at the state level should see foreclosure conference and mediation programs as important tools for the preservation of minority homeownership ... Today, African American and Latino families are facing a doubly high foreclosure rate, even when income differences are taken into account." *Id.* at 9.

To illustrate exactly what happened, we have reproduced the relevant text of the text mediated settlement agreement (emphasis added in bold; strike-throughs appear in the original):

Foreclosure Mediation Settlement Memorandum (Page 1)

Docket No: F19159–06

GMAC	v.	Willoughby
Plaintiff's Name		First Defendant's Name

The terms of this settlement memorandum were arrived at through mediation conducted on May 25, 2010 in settlement of the foreclosure action initiated by GMAC [herein lender] against Willoughby [herein borrower].

The parties agree that the foreclosure action is resolved upon the following terms, conditions and covenants:

1. Borrower is being offered a **trial to permanent modification plan contingent on signed modification documents and an initial down payment.** Borrower must make a down payment of $6,000.00 ... on or before 11am Monday June 7, 2010.
2. At that point lender will adjourn sale for 6 weeks ... There are no grace periods on any payment.
3. The loan will be amortized at 5 percent for 480 months making the new payment amount estimated at 1,678.48 PITI.
4. New payments start on July 6, 2010 in certified funds and are to continue on or before the 1st of each month thereafter. There are no grace periods.
5. **The parties agree that when executed this mediation settlement memorandum shall be final, binding and enforceable upon all parties** ~~and resolves the lender's claim that the borrower's default under the terms of the note and mortgage permit the initiating of the foreclosure action.~~ This memorandum shall be admissible in any action or legal proceeding to enforce its terms.
6. ~~The pending foreclosure action will be dismissed without prejudice, subject, however, to the right of the lender, in the event that the borrower fails to fulfill the terms of this settlement memorandum, to move on or before one year from the date hereof to reinstate the complaint at the point previous processing ceased.~~
7. ~~...~~
8. **The parties acknowledge that: (1) they have reviewed this memorandum and understand and agree with the terms and provisions contained herein and enter into it freely.**

/s/ [Attorney], Esq. 5/25/10

Lender's Representative Signature Date

/s/ Tami Lynn Willoughby 5/25/10

Borrower's Signature Date

Foreclosure Mediation Settlement Memorandum (Page 2)

The terms of this settlement memorandum were arrived at through mediation conducted on May 25, 2010 in settlement of the foreclosure action initiated by GMAC [herein lender] against Willoughby [herein borrower].

The parties agree that the foreclosure action is resolved upon the following terms, conditions and covenants:

1. The new estimated unpaid principal balance is $215,365.30 after lender recapitalizes 32,764.28 in negative escrows and corporate advances.
2. 71,736.39 in arrears will be put into a non interest bearing balloon that is payable upon maturity, refinance, or sale.
3. **If all trial payments are made lender will make modification permanent**.
4. If any payment is missed, lender will continue with foreclosure.
5. **The parties agree that when executed this mediation settlement memorandum shall be final, binding and enforceable upon all parties** and resolves the lender's claim that the borrower's default under the terms of the note and mortgage permit the initiating of the foreclosure action. This memorandum shall be admissible in any action or legal proceeding to enforce its terms.
6. The pending foreclosure action will be dismissed without prejudice, subject, however, to the right of the lender, in the event that the borrower fails to fulfill the terms of this settlement memorandum, to move on or before one year from the date hereof to reinstate the complaint at the point previous processing ceased. ....

/s/ [Attorney], Esq. 5/25/10
Lender's Representative Signature
/s/ Tami Lynn Willoughby 5/25/10
Borrower's Signature Date
Ms. Willoughby and GMAC signed both pages of the agreement on May 25, 2010. Nonetheless, the Chancery Court found that no permanent mortgage modification existed because Willoughby supposedly had failed to sign the agreement. The Appellate Division affirmed the glaring factual error, stating: "Willoughby never accepted GMAC's [the lender/plaintiff's] offer of a permanent loan modification ... [because] [s]he never signed the documents tendered by GMAC to implement its offer."

Ms. Willoughby had not only signed the original but also signed subsequent modification documents from GMAC and made all required payments on time, including the $6,000down payment on June 7, 2010. (Both parties signed an acknowledgement of this transaction.) On June 25, 2010, Ms. Willoughby signed the "trial plan documents," styled as a "forbearance agreement," which required her to make trial payments for twelve months. Although GMAC may not have counter-signed this agreement, Ms. Willoughby made all trial payments on time and continued to make monthly payments for an additional sixteen months after the trial plan period concluded, with all payments totaling $58,790.69. She only stopped submitting checks after GMAC began rejecting them.

GMAC confirmed Willoughby's compliance with trial period requirements three times. Nonetheless, the terms of the permanent loan modification proposal differed substantially from those agreed upon in mediation. The offer of June 7, 2011 shortened the loan term by about fourteen years, tacking on a large balloon payment at the end. Subsequent offers on December 5, 2011 and May 23, 2012 also raised the interest rate by .5 percent, substantially increasing monthly payments. Ms. Willoughby rejected these offers, since she had already accepted and executed the mediated agreement. Hurricane Sandy then swept through the area on October 29, 2012, necessitating an insurance claim for damage to the home, with $132,000 going to GMAC. A sheriff's sale was held on November 4, 2013, six years after entry of judgment, despite continuing litigation.[45]

During this period, Ms. Willoughby had to leave New Jersey at times to stay with her mother in another state. This "dual-tracking," through which the lender pro-ceeded with foreclosure while working on loss mitigation efforts with the borrower, was the norm during the crisis. It is now prohibited by regulations promulgated under the Dodd-Frank Wall Street Reform and Consumer Protection Act.[46]

As we argued in our initial brief supporting the Petition for Certification [citations omitted]:

> Created in 2008 to assist the Chancery Courts and Office of Foreclosure to resolve foreclosure cases, the Mediation Program has successfully mediated 17,548 cases, from its inception through June of 2015 ... An effective mediation program is needed now more than ever, as New Jersey continues to lead the nation in foreclosure. According to RealtyTrac, "New Jersey foreclosure activity in the first half of 2015 increased 24 percent from a year ago, boosting the state's foreclosure rate to second highest nationwide." The Chancery Courts and the Office of Foreclosure have struggled for years to handle the constant and growing influx of foreclosure cases, and there is no end in sight. A fully functioning foreclosure alternative, such as the Mediation Program, can help courts manage their foreclos-ure dockets, while also benefitting borrowers, lenders, communities, and the

---

[45] These points come from our brief on the merits after certification was granted.
[46] Pub. L. 111–203 (2017).

housing market in this State ... The Program can only work effectively, however, if parties abide by commitments entered into during mediation sessions. In the matter at hand, this was not the case, as Plaintiff GMAC repeatedly and unilaterally altered the material terms of the settlement agreement.

Inexplicably, the lower courts overlooked the existence of the fully executed mediation agreement (as well as performance by the homeowner) and found none existed. Had the lower courts accurately apprehended the facts, they might have reached a different result, but the broader, unfortunate consequence of their erroneous decisions is subversion of the Mediation Program ... Permitting fore-closing lenders to disregard voluntary settlements incentivizes servicing banks' dysfunction, stalling, and gaming of the system. Servicers demonstrate disrespect towards the mediation process in multiple ways, ranging from losing documents and requiring repeated resubmissions ... to assigning insufficiently trained employ-ees to evaluate borrowers' eligibilities, declining to make trial modifications per-manent when borrowers comply with all conditions, and–as occurred here–failing to honor settlement agreements. Similar practices occur across the country, as exemplified by the Consumer Financial Protection Bureau's database of mortgage complaints; the New Jersey experience is no different. Foreclosure defense attor-neys and housing counselors in New Jersey have been sharing these experiences for many years.

The oral argument in March 2017 reinforced to the court not only that the mediation program is worth retaining, but also that the court system needs to have an active role in enforcing its strictures to make sure servicers do not weaken the program. On July 31, the court ruled unanimously:

We now reverse and conclude that Willoughby and GMAC entered into an enforceable settlement agreement through the Foreclosure Mediation Program.

The language of the 2010 mediation agreement ... spoke of a "permanent modification" that was final and binding. The specificity of the terms ... did not suggest that the agreement was a temporary placeholder awaiting a final resolution. The 2010 mediation agreement was worded as a final settlement, not a prelude to further negotiations. Willoughby has endured years of litigation, ending with the loss of her home. She was entitled to the benefit of the agreement for which she had bargained.[47]

As of this writing, Ms. Willoughby has won the battle but lost the war. Her home had mistakenly been sold to a third party, so only a damages remedy is available to her. For some time, she was forced to live out of her car, but is now staying temporarily with various friends and relatives, doing odd jobs while the damages case continues. As Ms. Willoughby herself puts it:

I have rented and stayed outside under the stars and near the ocean. I have stayed in nice rooms and bug-infested rooms and tents and I have couch-surfed and even sat

---

[47] GMAC Mortgage, LLC v. Willoughby (A-97-15) (076006) (July 31, 2017).

inside a hotel lobby till the sun rose and I have eaten in soup kitchens and visited pantries to assist in my survival since becoming homeless ... It is unbelievable how much of one's life you can fit into one duffle bag and one backpack.[48]

The Seton Hall Center for Social Justice now represents her directly and just successfully defended against a motion to dismiss.

The Supreme Court meanwhile convened a New Jersey Residential Foreclosure Committee to improve foreclosure processes and rules. We issued a report recommending legislation and rules amendments that will, among other things, make the mediation program permanent and give it sharper teeth.[49] Like many states, New Jersey does not provide unique protections to litigants trying to enforce a settlement agreement entered into in mediation. Six states require lenders to negotiate in good faith.[50] Some of these provide equitable enforcement remedies.[51] Certain other states also impose sanctions, that

> exist to compel parties to come to the negotiation table prepared to work out viable alternatives to foreclosure. For example, borrowers and lenders that fail to appear at the mediation session, fail to cooperate and participate in it, or fail to exchange required documents before deadline are subject to sanctions.
>
> Additionally, failure to have someone with authority to make decisions about the loan present at the mediation session, or connected via teleconference, exposes a party to sanctions. Both parties can be sanctioned for failing to take the negotiation seriously, but some sanctions only target loan servicer behavior for example proceeding with foreclosure even though it is not in investors' best interest.[52]

Truly effective programs require a provision for pro bono lawyers for borrowers, as well as sufficient training for all personnel involved.[53] They also require a committed judiciary willing to enforce the mediations.[54] Federal bankruptcy courts joined the mix a bit later than the states. The program in the Southern District of New York is unique in that it does not employ full-time professional mediators, yet still has

---

[48] Letter from Tamilynn Willoughby to Linda Fisher, Feb. 7, 2019 (on file with Linda Fisher).

[49] New Jersey Judiciary, *Report of the Special Committee on Residential Foreclosures*, Aug. 2018 (on file with Linda Fisher).

[50] White, *supra* note 37, at 442.

[51] Foreclosure Mediation Programs, *supra* note 37.

[52] Lydia Nussbaum, ADR's *Place in Foreclosure: Remedying the Flaws of a Securitized Housing Market*, 34 Cardozo L. Rev. 1889, 1944–45 (2013). *See also* Foreclosures and Mortgage Servicing, *supra* note 41, at §8.8.7: "[T]he program must impose consequences on mortgage holders who do not cooperate in good faith to ensure full consideration of a loan modification and other options. At a minimum, mortgage holders who do not cooperate in good faith to provide data for modification decisions or who fail to have authorized representatives available for negotiations should not be permitted to proceed with foreclosures."

[53] Foreclosures and Mortgage Servicing, *supra*, note 41 §8.8.8: "The availability of experienced counsel for borrowers has been a major factor in the success of the mediation programs in New York, Connecticut, and Philadelphia."

[54] White, *supra* note 37, at 437–38.

resolved a high percentage of cases.[55] Its success can be at least partially attributed to virtually all of the debtor participants having counsel. Unfortunately, many of the programs created during the crisis are either subject to sunset provisions or have been eliminated by their creators as no longer necessary. Homeowners have been left to fend for themselves.

CONTINUING MORTGAGE SERVICING ISSUES, CONFLICTS OF INTEREST AND BANKING CULTURE

Servicing problems – often exacerbated by servicing transfers – persist, not only in states like New Jersey, where high-volume foreclosures remain, but anywhere foreclosures continue to be mishandled. Hence, the comedy of errors plays on and Laurie Goodman's quotation at the beginning of this chapter still resonates. The first quarter 2017 report by SIGTARP (Special Inspector General of the Troubled Asset Recovery Program) recounts numerous lingering servicer misbehavior, such as wrongfully terminating borrowers from HAMP, misapplying payments, failing to notify borrowers of rate raises and failing to reduce principal on mortgages despite having been paid by the Treasury Department.[56]

Servicing dysfunction seems immutable. In fact, we appear to be returning to some of the worst moments of the early crisis as large banks leave the servicing market to be replaced by smaller nonbank entities. These new servicers appear to have neither the capacity nor the training for this job, a problem signaled by many new instances of the lost paperwork we remember from early in the crisis. As long as borrowers need to seek relief from their lenders, and as long as loan servicing continues to be done on the cheap, these problems will not disappear. Moreover, as the inequality gap widens between low-to-moderate income (LMI), often African-American or Latino areas and wealthier white ones, the dual housing market persists, and residents of poorer neighborhoods are thus more likely to have continued contact with their servicer. Servicing issues thus remain both critical and topical. Effective loss mitigation practices could help prevent – or at least moderate – the next housing crisis.

These issues have, in fact, prolonged the foreclosure crisis: Servicers fail to accommodate borrowers who can afford to make mortgage payments, but who cannot afford to keep paying back the abusive loans they took out before the recession. We continue to see multiple errors ranging from improperly calculated escrow accounts to misapplied payments. Our clients are unable to pay the incorrectly calculated mortgage payments, so they end up in foreclosure and, even after the error is corrected, cannot

---

[55] *See*, David Gill, *Bankruptcy Court's Mortgage Mediation Program a Success*, BLOOMBERG BANKRUPTCY L. REP. (Feb. 24, 2017), https://www.bna.com/bankruptcy-courts-mortgage-n57982084348.

[56] OFF. OF THE SPECIAL INSPECTOR GENERAL OF THE TROUBLED ASSET PROGRAM, FIRST QUARTER REP.74–83 (Jan. 27, 2017), https://www.sigtarp.gov/Quarterly%20Reports/January_27_2017_Report_To_Congress.pdf.

catch up largely because of the mounting fees. The only option – hiring a lawyer and funding a lawsuit – is simply not available to most homeowners.

Conflicts of interest can help explain some of the dysfunction still seen in in the industry. Until very recently, servicers were paid more to foreclose on than to modify mortgages, even though proper servicing can be less costly than foreclosure or holding REO (real-estate-owned) inventory repurchased after foreclosure. Some lenders have avoided modifying when their affiliates hold second mortgages on the same property, since holders of seconds may lose value or leverage after a modification of a first mortgage. Even more irrationally, we have seen examples of one bank – Wells Fargo – hire one law firm to foreclose on the first mortgage on a property, and another to foreclose on their second mortgage on the same property. Two attorneys, ostensibly representing the same client, appeared in court, one to argue for foreclosure and one to argue against. Both will add attorney's fees to the loan balances of the homeowners. Servicers seem to operate entirely independently of the trusts or the lenders, which are, allegedly, the principals in this relationship.

As a recent report from the Urban Institute noted, servicer compensation systems remain misaligned:

> Under the current compensation structure, which has been in place since the 1980s, servicers are paid a flat 25 basis point fee for conventional mortgages. According to Housing Finance Policy Center codirector Laurie Goodman, "this regime pays servicers too much for servicing performing mortgages and too little for servicing nonperforming ones." Data from the Mortgage Bankers Association show that the average cost to service a performing mortgage was only $181 per loan in 2015 but was $2,386 for a nonperforming loan—roughly 13 times more.[57]

Banking culture may help explain why servicers seem unresponsive to the institutions' rational self-interest. Certain norms and practices in financial institution culture work to promote dysfunction or worse. Prevailing attitudes include a highly adversarial mindset that recoils from compliance with federal programs and regulations. Enormous sums are spent on lobbying and fighting borrower lawsuits. Moreover, role behavior leads individuals to act in ways that comport with banking norms and values, sometimes contrary to their own values and moral code. A 2014 study found that bankers were more likely to promote the interests of their employers than that of their customers when reminded beforehand of their employment role. Employees in other professions were not more likely to do so.[58] Incidents like the recent Wells Fargo push to sign up customers – often without their knowledge – for

---

[57] Karan Kaul, *To Ease Access to Mortgages, We Must Reform Mortgage Servicing Now*, URB. INST. (Aug. 29, 2016), https://www.urban.org/urban-wire/ease-access-mortgages-we-must-reform-mortgage-servicing-now. Volatility in pricing also adds to uncertainty in servicing. *Id.*

[58] *See*, Kerri Smith, *Banking Culture Primes People to Cheat: Individual Bankers Behave Honestly – Except When They Think About Their Jobs*, NATURE (Nov. 19, 2014), https://www.nature.com/news/banking-culture-primes-people-to-cheat-1.16380.

fake accounts, reflect this culture, as does Wells Fargo's targeting of minority borrowers for inferior mortgages before the Great Recession. Wells Fargo is far from the only bank engaging in these practices.

Another problem known as "short-termism" plagues financial institutions and corporations. Executives tend to be more concerned with the short-term profits than longer-term institutional health, driven, no doubt by the relentless demand to increase shareholder value. Thus, servicers frequently agree to mortgage modifications that are unaffordable for borrowers and even increase monthly payments, in part because they can benefit financially over the short run by getting their loans out of default. Lenders appear confident that banks will be bailed out again in the event of another financial catastrophe and therefore make decisions secure in the knowledge that borrowers and investors are likely to bear the costs. The rules enacted to prevent this kind of behavior are under attack by the Trump administration and the financial services industry. Protected against externalities, banks lack incentives to change their behavior, creating moral hazard. Reforms that alter financial incentives would go a long way toward rectifying the situation, but institutional culture must also change in ways that give more weight to the interests of borrowers, who are, after all, the banks' customers.

3

Zombie Mortgages and Abandoned Properties

You cannot shoot the financial meltdown in the head—you can do that with zombies.

Max Goss, author of *Zombie Survival Guide*

As the foreclosure crisis was plaguing America, so, apparently, were zombies. *The Walking Dead*, set in a post-apocalyptic world, was cable's most popular television show.[1] During the height of the financial crisis, best-selling books (e.g., *Pride and Prejudice and Zombies*), video games (e.g., *Alive-4-Ever*) and movies (e.g., *Zombieland*) began featuring the undead. When numerous abandoned homes and half-finished foreclosures also started to appear across America, reporters and policy makers dubbed them "zombie mortgages,"[2] and in February 2015, RealtyTrac reported that one-quarter of all foreclosures in America fell into this category.[3] Florida and New Jersey led the nation in zombie foreclosures, but Indiana and Ohio were not far behind. In fact, the problem was so widespread at the height of the crisis that one Cleveland municipal judge created a web page specifically to explain both what a zombie mortgage was, and how a homeowner could determine if he or she were its victim.[4] The phenomenon shows few signs of letting up in poor cities in the New York metropolitan area – and particularly Long Island – as profiled recently in the NPR program *Marketplace*.[5]

When calculating its statistics, RealtyTrac defined a zombie foreclosure very narrowly as a property "actively in the foreclosure process" that had been "vacated by the homeowner prior to [repossession by] the bank."[6] To our clients it is so much more. We have seen the development of three varieties of the so-called zombie mortgage. We will distinguish them as the "stalled foreclosure," the "abandoned foreclosure" and the full-fledged, back-from-the-dead "zombie mortgage."

STALLED FORECLOSURES

Ned Carey's story illustrates the first type of zombie mortgage. In 2009, Mr. Carey's mother became ill. He was a match to donate a kidney to her, so he did. His altruism

---

[1]   Allen St. John, *The Most Watched Hour Ever: Why 'The Walking Dead' Season Finale Will Break a Ratings Record*, FORBES (Mar. 20, 2014), http://www.forbes.com/sites/allenstjohn/2014/03/30/the-most-watched-hour-ever-why-the-walking-dead-season-finale-will-break-a-ratings-record.

[2]   *See*, Andrea Clark, *Amidst the Walking Dead: Judicial and NonJudicial Approaches for Eradicating Zombie Mortgages*, 65 EMORY L.J. (2016); David P. Weber, *Zombie Mortgages, Real Estate, and the Fallout of Survivors*, 46 N.M.L. REV. 37 (2014); Michelle Conlin, *Special Report: The Latest Foreclosure Horror: The Zombie Title*, REUTERS (Jan. 10, 2013, 7:04 AM), http://www.reuters.com.article/2013/01/10/us-usa-foreclosures-zombies-IDusbre90909g920130110 CFPB, Monitor, *CFPB Considering Action on Zombie Foreclosures*, BALLARD SPAHR, L.L.P (Mar. 18, 2014), https://www.consumerfinancemonitor.com/2014/03/18/cfpb-considering-action-on-zombie-foreclosures.

[3]   *One in Four US Foreclosures Are "Zombies" Vacated by Homeowner, Not Yet Repossessed by Foreclosing Lender*, REALTYTRAC (Feb. 5, 2010), https://wpnewsroom.realtytrac.com/news/zombie-foreclosures-q1-2015/

[4]   Raymond L. Pianka, *Zombie Mortgages and Zombie Titles*, CLEV. MUN. CT. HOUS. DIV., http://clevelandhousingcourt.org/zombies.html.

[5]   Marielle Segarra, *10 Years after the Housing Crisis, Thousands of Zombie Homes Are Still Stuck in Foreclosure Limbo*, MARKETPLACE WEEKEND (June 13, 2018) (quoting Linda Fisher).

[6]   REALTYTRAC, *supra* note 3.

put him out of work for several months, and he fell behind on his mortgage. Unfortunately, when he reached out for help, it was to a fraudulent mortgage foreclose rescue company, which charged him several thousands of dollars. Mr. Carey turned to us when the bank filed for foreclosure in 2010. Nothing happened at all for the next two years. The bank did not move forward on the case and refused all his attempts to make payments. He tried to negotiate a loan modification but was unsuccessful. He tried to sell the house but received no offers. In 2013, the bank finally filed a motion requesting a foreclosure judgment from the court, but it did not have the proper documentation, and the motion was denied. For the next two years, the court repeatedly instructed the lender to provide the correct documentation to allow it to proceed with the foreclosure, and for the next two years the lender failed to provide it. Frustratingly, the court would not dismiss the foreclosure action outright.

Mr. Carey was eventually offered a modification capitalizing all the interest that had been building up for years – along with multiple fees. Acceptance of the modification would have required him to pay a mortgage now twice as large as the home was worth. He rejected the offer. The property ultimately sold at a sheriff's sale for much less than he owed the lender, and the foreclosure – stalled for nearly six years – caused him extreme stress.

This case illustrates the potential harm of a stalled mortgage, especially if a lender refuses payment. Even if the mortgagor saves up every mortgage payment due, he or she may not have enough to bring a loan current because of additional interest and fees that begin to accrue. For instance, once a property falls into foreclosure, the servicer begins charging a monthly inspection fee of between $12 and $25 to make sure the property is not abandoned. There is rarely a need for such inspections, and many doubt they actually take place. When there has been regular and sustained communication with the lender, as there was here, inspections are especially unnecessary. At the same time, homeowners – Mr. Carey included – often fail to make improvements or do maintenance on the property during the pendency of the foreclosure because they fear they would be throwing money away. As a result, the value of the property decreases, while the balance due increases due to the unpaid fees and mounting interest. This lethal combination explains why these properties often become abandoned, adding to growing urban blight.

ABANDONED FORECLOSURES

The second type of zombie loan we observed during the crisis can best be categorized as an abandoned foreclosure. Mr. and Mrs. Jordan Reynolds, the unhappy homeowners in this situation, chose Countrywide Mortgage, a lender that originated some of the worst subprime loans in the run-up to the foreclosure crisis. When their loan payment suddenly increased by more than $100, the Reynolds contacted the loan servicer for an explanation. Unable to afford this increased monthly payment, they were offered a loan modification with a new payment of $617.22 per month. When the paperwork arrived, however, the payment reflected was $846.79. The couple called the loan servicer in a panic but were assured it was a simply a typographical error. They were instructed to cross out the $846.79, fill in $617.22 and sign and return the document. They followed these instructions and happily made their first payment.

The next month they received a statement requesting a payment of over $900. They immediately called Countrywide and were told not to worry. The loan modification had not been "booked" yet. This was a common occurrence during the crisis. Homeowners could wait months, even years, for the company to input their new loan information into the computer. During the interim they would receive late notices, statements with ever-increasing loan payments and sometimes even foreclosure notices. Countrywide instructed the Reynoldses to pay the agreed-upon amount, which they did. This pattern continued until Bank of America acquired Countrywide's loan portfolio.

Bank of America informed the Reynoldses that the loan modification was invalid because they had crossed out the payment amount, even though the servicer had instructed them to do so. The modification was voided, and the couple suddenly found themselves six months delinquent. Reluctantly, they agreed to sign a new modification, increasing their payment by $100 per month. They made the three trial payments required before a loan modification becomes permanent only to be informed that the servicer could not find any of those payments. They were considered delinquent again and the loan modification was canceled. This was too much for the couple. They stopped making further payments and called a lawyer. The bank filed for foreclosure. Although they did attempt to negotiate yet another trial modification, the Reynoldses could not afford the increasing payments on offer. More importantly, the stress and continued uncertainty had simply become too burdensome. They no longer wanted to litigate. They wanted to move on with their lives. We negotiated an agreed "in-rem" judgment of foreclosure.

An "in-rem" judgment authorizes the bank to take possession of the property and sell it. The lender retains the proceeds of the loan and does not have the right to pursue any additional funds from the homeowner if the house sells for less than is owed. The Reynoldses thought it finally meant an end to the saga. In exchange for having no personal judgment against them, they turned the property over to the lenders and moved into an apartment. It was not a perfect resolution but one they were happy with at the time. They settled into their apartment, believing the situation was resolved. They were wrong.

The bank obtained its foreclosure judgment and then did nothing. Soon, the couple was contacted by the city's code enforcement office, which informed them of maintenance issues with the property. The couple was surprised because they thought the bank had taken possession of the property and, as a result, should be responsible for the maintenance. It is noteworthy that they only learned of the maintenance issues because they had remained in the same small town, enabling the city to locate them. During the crisis, many similarly situated homeowners did not realize they remained responsible for the upkeep on their foreclosed property because the title of that property had not been transferred to a third party through the foreclosure sale. Many were never located by their former municipalities. They only learned of judgments against them later, when trying to buy a car or rent an apartment. At this point, it is often too late to correct the problem. While people are required to know the law, it is easy to understand how a homeowner who has moved from the property as part of an agreement with the lender would believe that she or he is no longer responsible for the property. This is especially true when, as with the Reynoldses, the lender had taken possession of the property, locking them out.

The litigation began again. This time, the couple was attempting to force the bank to set the property for foreclosure sale – not an easy process. In Indiana, for instance, the party requesting the sale must post a hefty bond. The statute allowing the sale is written in a way that may well preclude a former homeowner from requesting it. The issue was made somewhat easier for the Reynolds because the court order in the foreclosure said that the bank "shall" sell the property. In law, that is a nonnegotiable court order, and the bank did set the sale. Then, with no notice to the homeowner[s], the lender canceled it. (Many foreclosure orders specifically allow the bank to cancel the sale if they so desire.) The judge agreed with the homeowner in this case and finally forced the bank to put the property up for sheriff sale.

For the Reynoldses, the entire foreclosure process took nearly four years of litigation. Interestingly, the mortgage industry would cite a four-year foreclosure as an example of why judicial intervention is harming the country by keeping homes that could be resold off the market. Much of the delay in the low-income neighborhoods we serve is caused by lenders, not courts. This is the kind of foreclosure that Michelle Conlin of Reuters first dubbed a "zombie mortgage," and it was frighteningly common at the height of the crisis.[7]

"Just *how* common?" we wondered, so we conducted a small empirical study of bank walkaways (stalled/abandoned foreclosures) in Newark in 2011 and 2012. Newark – New Jersey's largest city – has been one of the hardest hit cities in a state frequently reporting the highest foreclosure and default rate in the country. The study involved a random sample of 100 foreclosures from a single neighborhood, all filed from 2007 to 2009, during the height of the crisis.[8] This research complemented similar studies undertaken in Cleveland, Chicago and Florida and

[7] *See*, Conlin, *supra* note 2.
[8] Linda E. Fisher, *Shadowing the Shadow Inventory: A Newark, New Jersey Case Study of Stalled Foreclosures and Their Consequences*, 4 U.C. IRVINE L. REV. 1265 (2014), *see also* Linda E. Fisher, *Bank Walkaways and Undead Foreclosures Continue to Haunt the Economy*, COLUMBIA L. SCHOOL BLUE SKY BLOG (July 10, 2015), http://clsbluesky.law.columbia.edu/2015/07/10/bank-walkaways-and-undead-foreclosures-continue-to-haunt-the-economy.

nationally by the General Accounting Office (GAO), all of which determined that banks were stalling or abandoning foreclosures.[9] The GAO surveyed six servicers as well as Fannie Mae and Freddie Mac during 2008 and 2010. The study found that people tend to abandon their property if the foreclosure has been initiated and the bank fails to follow through, but not if the foreclosure is never initiated, despite a default by the borrower.[10] This finding has a logical explanation: People abandon their properties because they believe them to have been lost in foreclosure.

Our Newark study was the first to trace the disposition of each property in the sample through both public and private sources, allowing us to draw highly accurate conclusions similar to those of the previous studies: Without legal excuse or ongoing workout efforts, banks frequently ceased prosecuting foreclosures. The findings conclude that uncontested foreclosures were stalled or abandoned at all stages of the process, from failures to serve process on homeowners to failures to move for judgment. Forty-four cases never even reached judgment, a prerequisite to a public foreclosure sale. Fifteen post-judgment cases never reached sale; seven sales were stayed, vacated or took one to two years to reach sale. Twelve cases settled at some point during the foreclosure process, and eight cases were dismissed voluntarily. Altogether, the very conservative finding was that 37.8 percent of the sample cases remained in limbo, qualifying as stalled foreclosures or bank walkaways/abandoned foreclosures.[11]

As a partial update, RealtyTrac, a real estate information company and online market for distressed properties, issued a Zombie Foreclosure Report in the first quarter of 2015. It found that at the end of January 2015, homeowners had vacated 142,462 homes still in the foreclosure process. This figure represented 25 percent of all active foreclosures in the United States. Zombie foreclosures – using this definition – had increased 109 percent in New Jersey since the previous year, and the state had the second-highest numerical total of any state, with 17,983, representing 23 percent of all properties in foreclosure. By contrast, New York zombie

---

[9]   U.S. Gov't Accountability Off., GAO-11–93, Mortgage Foreclosures: Additional Mortgage Servicer Actions Could Help Reduce the Frequency and Impact of Abandoned Foreclosures (2011); *Unresolved Foreclosures: Pattern of Zombie Properties in Cook County*, Woodstock Inst. (Jan. 2014), http://www.woodstockinst.org/sites/default/files/attachments/140123_unresolved_foreclosures_final_0.pdf; Alison Fitgerald & Jared Bennett, *'Zombie' Homes Haunt Florida Neighborhoods: Aborted Foreclosures Leave Thousands of Properties in Legal Limbo*, The Center for Public Integrity (Sept. 15, 2014, 5:00 AM, updated Jan. 7, 2015, 4:48 PM), https://www.publicintegrity.org/2014/09/15/15519/zombie-homes-haunt-florida-neighborhoods; Kermit J. Lind, *Perspectives on Abandoned Houses in a Time of Dystopia*, 29 Probate Prop. 1 (2015);

[10] *See*, GAO-11–93, *supra* note 9; *see also* Katie Buitrago, *Deciphering Blight: Vacant Building Data Collection in Chicago Six County Region*, Woodstock Inst. 3 (June 2013), http://www.woodstockinstorg/sites/default/files/attachments/dechipheringblight_buitrago_june2013.pdf (finding abandonment more likely when foreclosure is initiated, but not pursued).

[11] We informally checked the limbo cases again a year later; very few had made any progress in the interim.

foreclosures had increased 54 percent from the previous year to 16,777, the third-highest numerical total, representing 19 percent of all residential properties in foreclosure.[12] The RealtyTrac definition focuses on vacant properties in the foreclosure process, but the totals still indicate the continuing severity of the problem of incomplete foreclosures, regardless of cause. While this study was quite small in scale, the results can be extrapolated to the City of Newark, and, to some extent, similar lower-income urban neighborhoods in states with judicial foreclosure regimes.

In 2015, we looked back at all the foreclosures filed in two counties in northern Indiana during 2010. We discovered that a significant number appeared to have been abandoned by the lender. In some, the foreclosure was initiated and later dismissed. The court dismissed about 2 percent of the cases because the lender failed to pursue the litigation. Another 2 percent were still pending five years after filing, not because of court delays but because the lender had never requested a judgment. A third group of cases showed facts resembling those faced by the Reynoldses. The foreclosure judgment had been entered, and the sheriff's sale was either never set or set and then canceled by the lender. These represented roughly 5 percent of the filings.[13] The most disturbing group, which we will discuss in more detail, were cases in which the lender had obtained a judgment and then asked the court to set that judgment aside. This represented 10 percent of the filings. Overall, the lenders had abandoned at least 133 of the foreclosures filed in two counties in 2010. This represents just two of Indiana's ninety-two counties, and far from the most populated two. While that number appears small, when combined with the stalled and abandoned mortgages in those same counties that year, they equaled nearly 20 percent of all the foreclosure filings. Interestingly, this is consistent with Reality-Trac's findings that, at the time, more than 20 percent of the foreclosures in the country had become zombies.

It is easy to see how Indiana would have amassed tens of thousands of abandoned foreclosures during the life of financial crisis.[14] And the numbers were much greater in states like Florida, New York and New Jersey.[15] The lenders that securitized mortgages during the housing boom followed standard practices of targeting

---

[12] *See*, REALTYTRAC, *supra* note 3. According to RealtyTrac, its methodology is to "gather ... data for vacant foreclosures by matching foreclosures in the RealtyTrac database with data collected from the United States Postal Service for addresses that the agency has deemed vacant or where the owner has requested a change of address."

[13] The data were collected from doxpop, an online docket service and Odyssey, Indiana's state court online docket, during the months of March and April 2015.

[14] Matt R. Kinghorn, *Indiana's Ongoing Foreclosure Crisis*, 86 IND. BUS. REV. (2011), http://www.ibrc.indiana.edu/ibr/2011/summer/article1.html. (Indiana's foreclosure filing began to rise sharply in 2006 and remained substantially higher than the national average until the rest of the county caught up in 2009).

[15] REALTYTRAC, *supra* note 3.

communities of color for the worst subprime loans.[16] They also followed national servicing and foreclosure practices adapted to each state's laws, so it is entirely logical to assume that bank walkaways occurred at comparable levels in much of the country. Did these abandoned foreclosures eventually become abandoned properties? Not all municipalities kept lists, and not all homeowners moved out, but research has shown that an increase in foreclosure activity corresponds with an increase in abandoned properties.

Dealing with an abandoned mortgage can make a homeowner feel like Alice falling down the rabbit hole. The world is turned upside down, and progress seems impossible. Mr. and Mrs. Miller had that disorienting experience in 2015, when trying to pay their mortgage. The couple had taken out the mortgage with Key Bank in 2002. It was immediately transferred to Bank of America, though the 2002 assignment was not recorded until 2012. In 2013, the couple fell behind on their payments. They were in contact with Bank of America for a short period, and then the communication stopped. Whenever they contacted Bank of America, they were told they had no loan. The couple wanted to pay the mortgage but had no idea whom to pay. A title report on the property indicated one lien, a mortgage with Bank of America, but Bank of America denied having a mortgage. We filed a "Quiet Title Action," a judicial procedure where one party – in this case the homeowner – asks the court to clear all liens from the property. We got an immediate response from Bank of America, asking why we had named them in our suit because "they had no record of ever having this mortgage." We had not expected that response. The case was quickly settled with the bank releasing the lien (which they still claimed they did not have) on the property. Yet, the Millers were still concerned. They knew they borrowed money and that another party had probably bought the underlying mortgage loan, but who could it have been? Borrowers have no definite way of knowing who might own their loans at any given time. Someday, another bank could appear, and while they cannot claim to have a mortgage lien, they could ask for repayment of the underlying loan. In this crazy world of lost and fabricated paperwork, such a scenario is all too likely.

ZOMBIE MORTGAGES

An abandoned foreclosure presents a homeowner with a nasty problem, but a real zombie mortgage is even worse. The real zombie mortgage occurs when a lender

---

[16] Matthew J. Rossman, *Counting Casualties in Communities Hit Hardest by the Foreclosure Crisis*, 16 UTAH L. REV. 245, 258 (2016); Patrick Bayer, Fernando Ferreira & Stephen L. Ross, *What Drives Racial and Ethnic Differences in High Cost Mortgages? The Role of High Risk Lenders*, (Econ. Research Initiatives at Duke, Working Paper No. 206, 2016), https://ssrn.com/abstract=2730894; Debbie Gruenstein Bocian, Wei Lei & Keith S. Ernst, *Foreclosures by Race and Ethnicity: The Demographics of a Crisis*, CTR FOR RESPONSIBLE LENDING 6 (June 18, 2010); MONIQUE W. MORRIS, DISCRIMINATION AND MORTGAGE LENDING IN AMERICA: A SUMMARY OF THE DISPARATE IMPACT OF SUBPRIME MORTGAGE LENDING ON AFRICAN AMERICANS, NAACP (Mar. 2009);

forecloses on a property and then – months or even years later – goes back to the judicial body and sets aside the judgment, claiming to have reinstated the note.[17] Notice of this action, if sent at all, is sent to the property address, an address the homeowner has long abandoned, believing the property to be lost to foreclosure. Evidence of these zombie mortgages can be found throughout the judicial records. In our examination of 2011 mortgage filings in two Indiana counties, we found that 318 (10 percent) of the foreclosure judgments were later vacated by the bank. When combined with stalled and abandoned foreclosures, at least 25 percent of all the foreclosures filed in these counties in 2010 entered this netherworld.[18]

It is hard to find victims of true zombie loans because most have moved on and have no idea that their foreclosure judgment has been set aside. When they do come forward, the lender always requires a confidentiality agreement in exchange for a settlement, preventing the homeowners from telling their story. Occasionally a case does come into court, however, and the story can be told. The following examples illustrate some of the harm that zombie mortgages can cause.

John Doe was in the National Guard and deployed overseas until 2008.[19] When he returned, he was stationed in a city distant from his home. He attempted to commute for nearly a year, but the strain on his family was too much. Mr. Doe contacted CitiMortgage to try to give the home back to the lender, either by short sale or by a deed in lieu of foreclosure.[20] They told him Citi could not assist him because he was an active duty soldier, although he was not. Even if he had been on active duty, federal law has placed restrictions on interest rates and foreclosures for active duty military, not on assistance with a foreclosure. Nonetheless, the family received no assistance. They moved from the property in 2010.

In 2013, Mr. Doe retired from the military and sent the documentation to the bank. The bank still refused to assist him. In 2015, the Does were surprised to receive notice that the bank had filed a motion to set aside their foreclosure judgment. They had never received notice that a foreclosure had been filed, let alone that a

---

[17] For an extensive discussion of these, *see*, Judith Fox, *The Foreclosure Echo: How Abandoned Foreclosures Are Re-Entering the Market through Debt Buyers*, 26 LOY. CONSUMER L. REV. 25, 43–62 (2013).

[18] The number is likely larger. The 200 dismissals are out of a possible 725 total dismissals. Some of these are the result of settlements reached in the Indiana foreclosure mediation program. Unfortunately, there are not accurate statistics, nor are the settlements reflected on the court docket sheets. I chose to use the one-year cutoff because it is unlikely that a loan modification or payoff would have occurred after that much time. Therefore, it is likely that more than 200 are actually abandoned foreclosures.

[19] Transcript of Record at Vol I, 6, CitiMortgage v. John Doe and Jane Doe, 02D01–1401-MF-000054, Vol. I, Page 6 (Feb. 18, 2015). The court file does indicate the party's names, but the court that supplied this transcript requested that we identify them as Jane and John Doe, so we have honored that. We did not represent this couple.

[20] A short sale allows the homeowner to sell the home for less than is owed, with no personal judgment for the difference. A deed in lieu is simply a direct transfer from the borrower to the lender, releasing any further payment obligations.

judgment had been reached. They also were unaware that a sheriff's sale had been scheduled and canceled by the bank in 2014.[21] Mr. and Mrs. Doe called the bank and were told that the lender was setting aside the mortgage because Mr. Doe was an active member of the military. Back on that merry-go-round, the Does decided to attend the court hearing to finally resolve the matter.

At the hearing, the judge inquired as to why CitiMortgage would want to set aside a judgment now. The bank's attorney told the court that the lender wanted to "charge off"[22] the loan, so it needed to set aside the judgment. CitiMortgage admitted it had not been maintaining the property, nor had the Does, who had vacated the property in 2010. Mr. Doe began getting notices from neighborhood code enforcement in 2011 and had contacted the bank. He testified that the bank had changed the locks on the home and winterized it. He consequently had had no access to the property. The exchange between the judge and the lender's counsel was typical of lenders' positions in this circumstance:

JUDGE:	"So would it be safe to say, Mr. McKay, that the reason that CitiMortgage wanted to turn around now and dismiss this lawsuit is so that they wouldn't be responsible for the property anymore?"
LENDER'S ATTORNEY:	"I don't know if that's a fair characterization or not."
JUDGE:	"Do you know why they waited three years to file their foreclosure after they had possession of it in 2011?
LENDER'S ATTORNEY:	"Well, I don't think they had possession. They were able to secure it under the terms of the mortgage, but that doesn't—"
JUDGE:	"Well, if they changed the locks, and they had the key to the lock, then ostensibly the borrowers don't have possession. If your mortgage company came in and winterized it and changed the locks, out of the two parties that are involved in this, which would one would have possession?"
LENDER'S ATTORNEY:	"Fair enough, your Honor."[23]

In the end, when it was very clear that the court was not going to allow the judgment to be set aside, CitiMortgage withdrew the request and set a sheriff's sale. The property was finally sold in July 2015, five years after the Does had first reached

---

[21] In Indiana and New Jersey these are sheriff's sales, but they could also be called Trustee sales or a variety of other variations of these names. They are the final step where the property is sold to a buyer to satisfy the lien. During the crisis, the buyer was very often the bank itself.

[22] "Charge off" is an accounting term. A bad debt is charged off when the lender determines it is no longer collectable. It moves the debt off the assets column of the lender's balance sheet. It does not mean anything in practical terms to the debtor. The debt is still owed.

[23] *See*, transcript, *supra* note 19.

out for help. By the time the case was resolved, the property had decreased in value from $118,000 to less than half that amount. CitiMortgage sold the property to CKS Properties in 2015 for $25,000.[24]

An even more extreme manifestation of the zombie loan is the case of CitiMortgage versus Jeffrey Winston. Mr. Winston's home was foreclosed upon and set for sheriff's sale in 2014. CitiMortgage purchased the property and obtained a deed for it in December 2014. In April 2015, CitiMortgage filed to set aside the sheriff's sale. If granted, this request would have taken the property out of the bank's name and put it back in the name of the previous homeowner. CitiMortgage represented to the court that "no other party" would be affected by setting aside the sheriff's sale. Mr. Winston appeared at the hearing and explained to the court that the home had not been habitable and was demolished by the city's building code enforcement office. CitiMortgage was the owner of the property at the time of the demolition, the cost of which was $8,000. CitiMortgage represented to the court that it had paid the cost of the demolition, so Mr. Winston would not be harmed by putting the property (now an empty lot) back in his name.[25]

The court was skeptical. The judge asked CitiMortgage to come back with proof of the demolition payment. At a subsequent hearing, CitiMortgage admitted that the $8,000 cost had not been paid and that, if the sheriff's deed were set aside, the debt would become Mr. Winston's obligation. Citi pushed ahead nonetheless, insisting it had the right because, unless they did so, "the property cannot be conveyed back to HUD." The court rightly determined that servicer's ability to convey a debt back to HUD does not constitute a legal reason to unwind a sheriff's sale, especially if in doing so the court would be taking a debt legally owed by CitiMortgage and dumping it on the previous homeowner. The court refused to set aside the deed. Had Mr. Winston not accidentally discovered there was a hearing and appeared, he might well have found himself owing an $8,000 debt to the city.[26]

Mr. Doe and Mr. Winston were fortunate. They both discovered their bank's efforts to create zombie loans. Most homeowners in this situation are less lucky. Lenders rarely tell homeowner that his or her foreclosure has been abandoned, despite the federal guidance requiring such notice.[27] In 2012 the Board of Governors of the Federal Reserve System responded to this practice by issuing guidance to lenders regarding when and how they should discontinue a foreclosure. Specifically, the guidance encourages lenders to notify homeowners and communities at the

---

[24] Docket sheet, 02-D01–1401-MF-000054, https://public.courts.in.gov/mycase/#/vw/CaseSummary/eyJ2Ijp7IkNhc2VUb2tlbiI6IlpEEWXpNalF3ToRFM01UUXdPakoyTiRVME16VXhZVoo9Im19.

[25] Citimortgage v. Wilson, 02 D01–1209-MF-001197, order dated Sept. 17, 2015.

[26] *Id.*

[27] *See,* Kate Berry, *Banks Halting Foreclosure to Avoid Upkeep,* Am. Banker (Apr. 23, 2013), http://www.americanbanker.com/issues/178_78/banks-halting-foreclosures-to-avoid-upkeep-1058558-1.html?zkPrintable=true.

time they abandon a foreclosure in order to avoid incidents of abandoned properties.[28] Compliance with that directive is spotty at best. The Consumer Financial
Protection Bureau found it "'extremely common' for servicers to charge off
low-balance loans and not notify borrowers or municipalities if they did not complete the foreclosure."[29] Lenders typically decide not to proceed with foreclosure for
economic reasons.[30] As one Federal Reserve economist put it, "It may cost more to
cure the back taxes and bring the property up to code than they could ever get from
selling the property itself."[31] In addition, there are significant costs in owning the
property. A lender's ability to repackage the loan and sell it back into the market
provides another incentive to abandon a nonperforming mortgage loan.[32]

Currently, there is no law or regulation preventing a lender from initiating and
then abandoning a foreclosure. Many homeowners thus leave their residences
mistakenly believing that title to the home has passed to the bank. In fact, regulations that existed during and immediately after the crisis may have caused more
confusion for homeowners. Lenders are required by the Truth in Lending Act to
send monthly statements to any borrower who has a delinquent mortgage debt.[33]
Lori Maggiano, an official with the CFPB, suggested that lenders' desire to avoid
this requirement may be pushing "servicers to release the borrower from liability for
the debt," without expressing the clear effects on the corresponding lien.[34] Does this
mean that the homeowner's debt is simply charged off, or is it truly forgiven?[35] The
Office of the Comptroller of the Currency instructs mortgage lenders to give no
indication "to the borrower that the accounts have been charged off."[36] Anyone who

---

[28] BD. OF GOVERNORS OF THE FED. RES., SR 12–11/CA 12–10, *Guidance on a Lender's Decision to Discontinue Foreclosure Proceedings* (July 11, 2012).

[29] Kate Berry, *CFPB Takes Aim at 'Zombie' Foreclosures*, NAT'L MORTGAGE NEWS (Sept. 29, 2014), http://www.nationalmortgagenews.com/news/servicing/cfpb-takes-aim-at-zombie-fore closures-1041319-1.html. In the year prior to this announcement the author was approached by the CFPB on this issue and asked to discuss and share data. I shared all my findings with the agency.

[30] The examination procedures issued by the Federal Home Finance Agency Office of Inspector General requires a bank to make "[a] comparison of the option of continuing the foreclosure or abandoning the foreclosure, considering the cost and potential recovery in a net present value analysis." EXAMINATION PROCEDURES FOR REVIEWING A BANKING ORGANIZATION'S ABAN-DONED FORECLOSURE PROCESS, FED. HOME FINANCE OFF. OF INSPECTOR GENERAL, http://www.federalreserve.gov/bankinforeg/srletters/sr1211.pdf.

[31] Berry, *supra* note 29 (citing Thomas Fitzpatrick economist, Federal Reserve Bank of Cleveland).

[32] *See*, Fox, *supra* note 17; Berry, *supra* note 29.

[33] *Id.*

[34] Berry, *supra* note 29.

[35] "Charged off" is an accounting term to refer to the act of moving the debt from accounts receivable to losses. It does not, however, mean the debt is no longer owed.

[36] OFF. OF CURRENCY ADMIN. OF NAT'L BANKS, *Allowance for Loan and Lease Losses, Internal Control Questionnaires and Verification Procedures*, (Dec. 2007), https://www.occ.treas.gov/publications/publications-by-type/comptrollers-handbook/internal-control-question-verif-pro cedures/pub-ch-internal-controls-questionnaire.pdf.

has ever attempted to get information about their zombie loan has experienced the frustration of trying to determine what is owed to whom. No one will tell you the status of your account. The lender will not accept payment, nor will it tell you what entity, if any, currently owns the debt.

The legal requirements intended to provide consumers with information about their accounts also can have unintended consequences. Take, for example, the confusion of Jeffery Vallancy, who had not heard from his lender in years, then suddenly received a statement in the mail. Chase had foreclosed on the Vallancy home via a default judgment in August 2012. The judgment was for slightly more than $106,000. The property was set for sheriff's sale at the time, but the bank canceled it without notifying Mr. Vallancy. In November 2015, he received a statement showing a balance of over $114,000, of which $35,182.21 was now due. The bill also reflected charges for taxes and property preservation fees, post judgment. A lawyer reading this statement would immediately see the problem, but most consumers would not.

Let us explain. The statement was issued in November 2015. The home had been foreclosed and a legal judgment rendered in August 2012. When a judgment is entered in a court of law, the document that sets out the homeowner's obligation to pay (in this case the mortgage note) is said to merge into the judgment. The ongoing obligation to pay according to the promissory note ends, and the duty to pay the judgment takes over. From the point of the judgment forward, the borrower no longer has a loan contract. Therefore, any amounts that would have come due after August 2012 as a result of the contractual relationship, such as property preservation fees, corporate advances and inspection fees, do not apply because, legally, the loan contract no longer exists. The amounts due are set out by the judgment alone. Depending on state law, the judgment may continue to grow due to added accrued interest, but that is distinct from additional fees. Servicers do not seem to understand this legal distinction, and our clients are continuing to receive bills after foreclosure for charges that are not owed or are the legal responsibility of the lender.

To say the least, Mr. Vallancy was confused by the statement he received and came to us for advice. Complicating matters further for him, a 1099-C tax form from the lender indicated that it had forgiven $52,922.19 in debt. Lenders send out a 1099-C form when they are reporting to the Internal Revenue Service that they have forgiven a debt obligation. When a debt is forgiven, the IRS considers this income, and taxes may be due on it. Mr. Vallancy was presented with two separate documents, both generated by his lender. One said he owed $114,937.69 and another that said the bank had forgiven a debt of $52,922.19. Making the situation murkier still, he had a third document from the court – the judgment – that said he owed the bank $106,000. Who wouldn't be confused?

We began going through the records, trying to sort out exactly how Chase had calculated the numbers and what, in the end, it all meant for poor Mr. Vallancy. After much effort, the answer was a resounding, "We have no idea!" We finally were able to discover that in September 2015, Chase had reset a previously canceled sheriff's sale, now three years after the foreclosure judgment. The bank had purchased the home at the sheriff's sale for $41,674.50. This left a balance of approximately $64,000 due on the judgment. The bank forgave just under $53,000 of that amount. The difference, a little over $11,000, is unaccounted for. Likely, that amount was covered by either a guarantee or primary mortgage insurance.[37] But we are only guessing – the lender has no obligation to explain where the numbers come from. It does not have to explain why it bid one amount on the property as opposed to another. It does not have to explain why it canceled one sale, only to set another three years later. It could sell the court judgment of $106,000 to a debt buyer under no obligation to inform anyone that a substantial portion of that judgment was forgiven or paid.

As it turns out, Mr. Vallancy had a stalled foreclosure and not an abandoned foreclosure or a zombie loan. Some of the foreclosures we originally classified as abandoned appear to have been simply stalled. As the official foreclosure crisis ended, we have noticed that entities, often hedge fund investors who apparently purchased these loans on the secondary market, are returning to the courts and have begun to set sales. The delay in doing so has had real consequences for Mr. Vallancy and for homeowners like him. It also has real consequences for his former neighbors. Mr. Vallancy's property sat empty for three years and maintenance on it was deferred. While the negative effects of abandoned properties may be obvious to someone driving through a neighborhood, the negative effects on the homeowner are not. Just when these families began to recover from the financial crisis, the stress and uncertainty of the foreclosure returns.

The purpose of the sheriff's sale is to sell the property to obtain funds to satisfy the judgment. As the property sits empty, it loses value. Property values increased ever so slightly during the time of Mr. Vallancy's stalled foreclosure, but not for abandoned properties. Abandoned properties always lose value. By delaying the sale, the lender decreased the amount of money the sale could generate, increasing the amount the homeowner would owe in deficiency. In Mr. Vallancy's case, that deficiency was more than $60,000. There are longstanding rules in contracts that preclude a party from obtaining damages they could have mitigated.[38] Since the crisis, we have only been able to convince one judge that the lender, not the homeowner, should bear the loss when it is the lender that fails to put the home up for sale, causing the home to lose value during the long delay between judgment and sale. This delay, we argued, was a failure by the lender to mitigate his damages. In our case, the judge refused to allow the lender to collect the deficiency judgment it would otherwise have been entitled to. This should be the result in all such cases, but it is not.

---

[37] Primary mortgage insurance is insurance that the borrower pays for but that compensates the lender for losses above and beyond 80 percent of the home's value.

[38] Restatement (Second) of Contracts, §305(1)75(1981).

In our studies, we found many examples of judgments that increased due solely to the lenders' delays. One of the stranger cases involved the property of a deceased borrower. The lender filed for foreclosure in October 2010 and obtained a foreclosure judgment of $22,644.22 two months later. At all times in this action, the homeowner was deceased. The lender set and canceled two sheriff's sales. The record shows that the property was sold to a third party in June of 2011 for slightly more than $20,000. A week later, the lender moved to set aside the judgment and reinstate the note. Shortly afterwards, the lender filed for a second judgment, this time for $31,445.52. The property was again set for sheriff sale, this time in September 2011, but there is no record of the result.[39] We know of no other area of civil law where a party can ask the court to set aside its judgment so that it can ask for a higher amount in a few days or weeks. In the end, the lender was found to be entitled to an additional $9,000 bonus for their act of delay.

CONSEQUENCES OF A ZOMBIE LOAN

All the iterations of a zombie loan we have mentioned – the stalled foreclosure, the abandoned foreclosure and the zombie foreclosure – have significant consequences for a homeowner, not all of which are negative. If the homeowner remains in the home, there can be long periods of time with no mortgage or rental payments. Our clients in this position have used this opportunity to make payments on other goods or services that may have lapsed during the crisis. At the same time, even these clients complain of the stress of being unable to do anything about the underlying problem, the delinquent mortgage. As mentioned, the servicer, the entity the homeowner has always dealt with, may be unaware of who now controls a charged-off loan. If the foreclosure is simply stalled, the lender will refuse all payments unless borrowers can bring the loan current. Everything remains in limbo.

While free rent may seem like a positive outcome, the related negative financial implications are greater. If the mortgage loan has actually been charged off by the creditor or a judgment of foreclosure has been entered, that incident will be reflected on the borrower's credit report. That notation, known as a "tradeline," will remain on the credit report for seven years. If the loan is just in zombie state, with no judgment having occurred, it remains on the homeowner's credit report as an active mortgage foreclosure. Every month a new entry appears on the credit report, stating that he or she has failed to make a payment. Theoretically, the foreclosure could appear for the remaining term of the loan plus seven years. Realistically, one's credit score never recovers. A homeowner in this position faces numerous obstacles, ranging from being forced into purchasing more expensive subprime credit products to having trouble obtaining a job.

---

[39] Park Tree Investments III v. Devisees the Unknown Heirs-At-Law, 71 C01–1010-MF-00600.

Significant research has shown that people in foreclosure, whether they have vacated the home or not, fail to maintain the property to previous standards.[40] This is logical behavior. If the owner has moved out in the belief that she no longer owns the home, performing maintenance would be irrational. If she remains in the home, she may be reluctant to invest in an asset she could lose at any moment. In both scenarios, the condition of the property deteriorates. If it declines to the point of violating local safety regulations, fines and fees for not maintaining a property begin to mount. In some jurisdictions, these are civil matters, but in others they are criminal charges. For homeowners who did not even realize they still owned the property, receiving a criminal summons can be a shocking experience.

We mentioned some of the negative aspects of tax foreclosure in the previous chapter. Ironically, tax foreclosure is one of the best-case scenarios for homeowners with a zombie mortgage. Tax foreclosure occurs when the homeowner fails to pay property taxes. The length of delinquency before a tax sale occurs varies by state. A tax sale might at least get the property out of the homeowner's name. During and immediately after the crisis there were so many properties in arrears on taxes and so few buyers at the tax sales that many properties did not sell at all. In some cases, the lender continued to pay the taxes during the pendency of the delay. Such payment can signify that the lender intends to eventually proceed with the foreclosure, but it can also be the result of bad record keeping. A bank holding many mortgages receives one consolidated bill for the taxes due. One department of the bank pays the entire amount while another is charged with sorting out which taxes correspond to which properties. Thus, lenders may keep paying taxes on properties they have decided to abandon. None of this provides much reassurance for the homeowner left in limbo. In another situation, our clients and the lender both paid the taxes, leading to the complicated question of who was owed a refund.

In Indiana, as in many other states, once the requisite number of tax payments has been missed, the governing municipality is required to sell the property to pay the taxes due. The homeowner then has a designated period of time to redeem the property by paying all the back taxes and a fine before the statutory redemption period expires. Buyers at these tax foreclosure sales are often investors who really do not want the property. Instead, they are buying the tax certificate at the sale in the hope that the homeowner will redeem the certificate, thereby giving them a profit in the amount of the fines and fees. In recent years, we have seen these investors returning to the tax foreclosure market. They are not returning, however, to

---

[40] *See,* John Harding, Eric Rosenblatt & Vincent W. Yao, *The Contagion Effect of Foreclosed Properties,* 66 J. Urb. Econ. 164 (2009), Danielle Wallace, E. C. Hedberg & Charles M. Katz, *The Impact of Foreclosures on Neighborhood Disorder before and during the Housing Crisis: Testing the Spiral of Decay,* 3 Soc. Sci. Q. 625 (2012).

purchase abandoned properties whose value exceeds the tax due. There is no economic reason to pay, for instance, $20,000 in back taxes for a property only worth $5,000. The original owners are also unlikely to redeem such a property. As a result, the worst of the abandoned properties remain so.

The tax foreclosure process works in the opposite way as well. We have recently come across evidence of one method fraudulent actors use to take advantage of homeowners. A property is sold at a tax sale. An investor purchases the tax certificate, but not the pseudo-investor starring in our tale. Rather, this fraudulent actor claims to have purchased the home and demands that the homeowner move or pay rent. Unwitting homeowners comply by either abandoning the home – creating another problem for the community – or paying rent on a home they own, and thereby becoming unable to catch up on the taxes. The fraudulent actor takes advantage of the year-long redemption period to work his scam. Then, when the investor gains legal title, the scammer moves on to his next victim.

The number of properties left unsold even after a tax sale has mounted around the country, and the lost revenue has had devastating effects on cities. Significant research shows that these foreclosures cause a variety of societal harms, a topic we will take up in Chapter 6. An increase in foreclosures corresponds with an increase in abandoned properties. Whether the cause is the foreclosure or the abandonment or both, neighboring property values decrease.[41] Investment in the neighborhood decreases. This results in a decline in the value of the neighboring properties and neighborhoods in general. As most property taxes are tied to the value of the property being taxed, tax revenue decreases. As tax revenue decreases, so does the available money for infrastructure improvements and other governmental services. It is easy to see how zombie loans and the associated abandoned properties create a fatal spiral downward.

At the height of the Indiana foreclosure crisis, many properties placed for tax sale did not sell. Indiana reacted by creating a second, commissioners' sale, through which the properties can be purchased for as little as twenty-five dollars, regardless of the property tax owed. This sounds like a great deal, especially to an unsophisticated buyer. However, to obtain clear title to the property, buyers still need to go through an often laborious and sometimes expensive process. For low-value abandoned properties, the costs to the buyer do not always make this a wise investment. Interestingly, and atypically for us, clearing title has become a common request in our low-income legal clinics, something not seen before. All these complications often result in the homeowner unwillingly retaining the home.

---

[41] *See*, Daniel Hartley, *The Effect of Foreclosures on Nearby Housing Prices: Supply or Dis-Amenity?*, 49 REGIONAL SCI. URB. ECON. 108, 113 (2014); Atif Mian, Amir Sufi & Francesco Trebbi, *Foreclosures, House Prices, and the Real Economy*, 70 J. FIN. 2587, 2590, (Dec. 2015).

STRATEGIC DEFAULT AND OTHER THEORIES
BEHIND ABANDONED PROPERTIES

There is no longer any doubt that foreclosures were stalled, abandoned and even set aside during the crisis. Lenders blame homeowners and homeowners blame lenders. One recent study attempted to determine the cause of zombie loans (which the study calls "limbo loans"). The researchers looked at a set of loans in Florida, well known for having the highest number of these problem foreclosures during the height of the crisis.[42] Their study explored three possible hypotheses for the foreclosure delay. The first they termed the "bottleneck hypothesis." This theory suggests the delay may have been caused by efforts to require the originating banks to repurchase securitized loans that were not of the quality originally warranted. The sheer volume of these loans, it was posited, may have caused a bottleneck and even limited the resolve of servicers to deal with the remaining loans in that "their fees are a function of the volume of loans" left in the trust.[43]

The second possible reason they dubbed the "bank capital constraint hypothesis." This theory holds that banks may have been unwilling to foreclose because doing so would have required them to report the loss on their balance sheets, affecting their ability to meet the capital requirements of the banking regulators.[44] Finally, the researchers tested their third theory, the "operational risk hypothesis." This theory suggests that in the rush to originate and securitize as many loans as possible in the run up to the foreclosure crisis, lenders grew careless with the paperwork. They relied heavily on the Mortgage Electronic Registration System (MERS). MERS was created by the lending industry to keep track of the paperwork involved in all the transfers necessary to create the securitized trusts, though it has since been determined that it was not up to the job.[45] The study concluded that the foreclosure delays can be attributed to the use of MERS. "[A] 10 percent increase in the presence of MERS in county-level foreclosures increases the length of time a loan spends in limbo by around 10 months."[46]

This study is interesting because it debunks most of the common narratives about zombie loans. The lending industry often cites the length of time needed to foreclose, or the "bottleneck hypothesis," for zombie loans. The study found the opposite: "The probability of a limbo classification, either foreclosure or

---

[42] Linda Allen, Stavros Peristiani & Yi Tang, *Bank Delays in the Resolution of Delinquent Mortgages: The Problem of Limbo Loans*, 37 J. REAL ESTATE RESEARCH 65 (2015).

[43] *Id.* at 4.

[44] *Id.*

[45] *See,* Alan White, *Losing the Paper-Mortgage Assignments, Note Transfers and Consumer Protection*, 24 LOY. CONSUMER L. REV. 468, 486 (2012).

[46] Allen, *supra* note 42, at 69.

non-foreclosure limbo, decreases as the length of the foreclosure proceeding increases."[47] Likewise, the study found a negative relationship between bank capitalization and zombie loans. Undercapitalized banks were actually more likely to complete the foreclosure than well-capitalized banks.[48] In layman's terms, small neighborhood banks have not caused the zombie loan problems, big banks have. In the end, though, it was the presence of MERS and lack of proper paperwork to foreclose that not only predicted the likelihood that a loan would become a zombie, but also how long it would remain one.[49]

Homeowners and communities have dubbed these loans "zombies," but to the governmental entities that insure them—Fannie Mae, Freddie Mac and HUD— they are simply "nonperforming assets." A nonperforming asset is one that is no longer making money. Regardless of the reason, the loan payments have stopped coming in. Congress began to pressure these GSEs to do something about all these loans on their books. HUD was the first to act. It created the Distressed Asset Stabilization Program to resell the loans to investors. There has been some suggestion, mostly coming from foreclosure attorneys, that some lenders have worked to set aside previously obtained foreclosure judgments so the properties could be included in these sales. In other words, the foreclosure was stalled specifically so the asset could be resold. We inquired at both HUD and FHFA as to whether the lenders had been instructed to do so, but neither replied to our inquiries.

While our research documents that a significant percentage of the abandoned properties can be attributed to stalled or abandoned foreclosures and zombie loans, some were simply properties abandoned by their owners. This reality helped create an enduring myth: that abandoned properties are the result of an epidemic of strategic defaulters. The definition of a strategic defaulter that has gained the most acceptance is the one adopted by Experian, a credit reporting agency. Experian conducted a study in which it defines a strategic defaulter as someone who pays his nonmortgage debt while at the same time failing to pay his mortgage loan.[50] The study estimates that hundreds of thousands of borrowers defaulted on their mortgages not because they could not afford the payments but because the homeowner owed more on the mortgage than the home was worth. The research has also shown that most strategic defaulters were prime borrowers who had money and intended to remain in their homes. In the end, most did.[51] These are not the clients we represent.

Most of the studies on strategic default focus on two things: credit behavior (whether you pay nonmortgage and other debt) and whether you have equity in

---

[47] *Id.* at 90.
[48] *Id.* at 89.
[49] *Id.*
[50] Oliver Wyman, *Understanding Strategic Default in Mortgages Part 1*, EXPERIAN-OLIVER WYMAN MARKET INTELLIGENCE REP. 8(2009), http://www.marketintelligencereports.com.
[51] *Id.* at 13.

the home. More recent studies have begun to question this methodology because it does not take income fluctuation into account.[52] Another recent study by Jonathan Morduch and Rachel Schneider, reported in *The Financial Diaries*, focuses on the central role of income fluctuation in many Americans' inability to progress financially. Any accumulated savings are swallowed up by emergencies and unforeseen expenses, an increasingly common phenomenon in our age of job insecurity.[53] We find this argument more persuasive and more consistent with our experience. Our clients often paid their car loans and credit cards before their mortgage, not because they were strategically defaulting on the mortgage but because they simply could not pay for everything. Transportation was essential to employment, without which there would be no income at all. Many were using their credit cards to pay for living expenses and paying the minimum due allowed them to eat. Most did not have the sophistication even to imagine a strategic default. They were simply trying to survive in a crisis.

Unfortunately, because the federal government has adopted Experian's definition of a strategic defaulter, these same people are the most likely targets for post-foreclosure collection. This is probably the single most disturbing finding about zombie loans. The government seeks to punish borrowers whom they imagine to be strategic defaulters while at the same time taking no action against lenders who have strategically abandoned properties on a regular basis. A recent study confirmed that many strategic defaulters were actually real estate investors and home flippers with prime loans, rather than families residing in the homes, yet very little attention has been paid to this fact.[54] A review of the study explains:

> The mortgages these prime borrowers were able to secure were much bigger than those taken out by poor borrowers. Worse, speculators have less incentive to hold onto their extra homes than those who only own one home. So when the housing market started tumbling and the economy soon followed, they were much more willing to default and foreclose.[55]

Defaulting by necessity is seen as an immoral act and strategic defaulting as a wise business decision when neither is the case. In fact, according to a popular narrative, "The financial problem of poor and middle-class people were treated as moral

---

[52] Saura Mocetti & Eliana Viviano, *Looking behind Mortgage Delinquencies*, 75 J. of Bus. & Fin. 53, 55 (2017).

[53] Jonathan Morduch & Rachel Schneider, The Financial Diaries: How Am. Families Cope in the World of Uncertainty (2017).

[54] *See*, Stefania Albanese, Giacomo DiGiorgi & Jaromir Nosal, *Credit Growth and the Financial Crisis: A New Narrative*, NBER Working Paper 23740 (Aug. 2017). ("The rise in mortgage defaults during the crisis was concentrated in the middle of the credit score distribution, and mostly attributable to real estate investors.")

[55] Gwynn Guilford, *House Flippers Triggered the U.S. Housing Market Crash, Not Poor Subprime Borrowers*, Quartz (Aug. 29, 2017), https://qz.com/1064061/house-flippers-triggered-the-us-housing-market-crash-not-poor-subprime-borrowers-a-new-study-shows.

failings, while rich people's debt is either ignored or spun as a sign of intrepid entrepreneurism."[56] Yet again, we see a false and misleading narrative shaping public perceptions and informing policy decisions.

Some of our clients, it is true, did attempt to abandon their homes, not because they sought a strategic advantage but because they had no other choice. Usually, these were elderly clients unable to live in the home any longer who had not been able to sell. Other people who abandoned were younger clients who were forced to move in search of jobs. Unable to sell their homes and unable to pay their mortgages, they walked away from both. What they learned, however, is a long-standing principle in the law: You cannot simply walk away from a piece of real property.[57] Sometimes the owner is permitted to abandon the benefit, but not the burden, of the property. Interestingly, zombie mortgages have shown that courts are willing to allow mortgage lenders – but not homeowners – to walk away from all the burden of ownership, while retaining all the benefits. We think they have it backwards.

Several of our clients entered agreements with the lenders to accept a deed to their properties instead of judicial judgments. In legal terms, this is called a deed "in lieu of foreclosure." Unfortunately, even in these cases, some homeowners found they could not abandon their properties because the lender had not recorded the deed with the requisite authorities and, as a result, the borrower appears to be the owner, subject to all the burdens, while the lender can file the deed at any point, claiming all the benefits of ownership. This kind of zombie loan is much harder to trace because there is no court record. Consumer advocates in states not requiring court involvement in the foreclosure identified these as their most common iteration of zombie loans.

One justification for not allowing homeowners to simply abandon their homes is that it shifts the burden of ownership to another party, such as a neighbor or city government, without their consent. Ironically, in the case of a zombie loan, there are often homeowners or community organizations willing to accept the responsibility of the property, but they are prevented from doing so because of the lender's outstanding mortgage. The lender is receiving the benefit of the mortgage but has discharged all the responsibility to others. By far the best and most efficient way to clean up the zombie loans that have plagued the country since the beginning of this crisis is to consider the mortgages on those properties abandoned. Homeowners and communities can then more easily move in to deal with the related, abandoned properties.

---

[56] Michelle Goldberg, *Don't Shame Candidates for Debt*, N.Y. TIMES, Aug. 19, 2018.

[57] Pocono Springs Civic Ass'n v. Mackenzie, 667 A.2d 233, 235–36 (PA. Super Ct. 1995), *see* Eduardo M. Penalver, *The Illusory Right to Abandon*, 109 MICH. L. REV. 191, 211 (2010); Lior Jacob Strahilevitz, *The Right to Abandon*, 158 U. PA. L. REV. 355, 399 (2010).

Another source of abandoned properties has been Real Estate Owned Property (REO), property owned by a bank because of foreclosure. For many years during the crisis, the banks were simply overwhelmed by this shadow inventory. Hedge funds hoping to make money flipping or renting properties purchased large numbers of foreclosed properties. Many of these properties were in no shape for either. As a result, institutional buyers have been trying to sell off or abandon these properties, returning them to the abandoned property statistics.[58]

The foreclosure crisis has officially ended, though in some areas there are still historically high foreclosure filings. Vast swathes of urban America are still littered with abandoned properties. Many of them have been torn down, never to be rebuilt. The physical properties are not the only remaining shadows of the crisis. Many of the loans associated with these properties remain abandoned as well.

---

[58] Matthew Goldstein, *Investors Who Bought Foreclosed Homes in Bulk Look to Sell them*, N.Y. TIMES, June 27, 2014.

4

The Benefits and Harms of Interventions

A government that robs Peter to pay Paul can always depend on the support of Paul.

George Bernard Shaw

Thus far, we have focused our story on the mortgage industry participants as we outlined the causes and some of the resulting fallout of the financial crisis. The government played – and continues to play – an important role in the story because of actions it took, and actions it failed to take, before, during and after the crisis. While a growing number of scholars credit the Federal Reserve's policy of quantitative easing for helping to rein in the effects of the financial crisis,[1] the government's response has been viewed more critically. Its first interventions were intended to stabilize the mortgage markets and insure that additional financial institutions did not fail. Foreclosure issues came second. The depth and breadth of that crisis would develop over time. We have already explained how abandoned properties – largely the result of foreclosures – continue to harm communities across America. The following chapter walks through government actions before and after the crisis and discusses how they helped, how they hurt and what they left behind.

THE FEDERAL HOUSING FINANCE AGENCY (FHFA)

One of the federal government's earliest interventions in the crisis was the Housing and Economic Recovery Act (HERA). The act was primarily designed to stabilize the housing markets but not affected homeowners.[2] HERA created the Federal Housing

---

[1] *See,* Edison Yu, *Did Qualitative Easing Work?* FED. BANK OF PHILA. RES. DEPT. (2016), https://www.philadelphiafed.org/-/media/research-and-data/publications/economic-insights/2016/q1/eiq116_did-quantitative_easing_work.pdf?la=en; Alexander Rodnyansky & Olivier Darmouni, *The Effects of Quantitative Easing on Bank Lending Behavior,* 30 THE REV. OF FIN. STUDIES 3858 (Nov. 2017)(which argues that quantitative easing did have a positive effect, but only when targeted to a specific sector).

[2] Housing and Economic Recovery Act of 2008, Pub. L. 110–289, 122 Stat., 2654 (2008).

Finance Agency (FHFA), which was designated to oversee Fannie Mae and Freddie Mac.[3] As previously mentioned, Fannie Mae and Freddie Mac are hybrid organizations, chartered by the federal government but with private shareholders. As such, they are referred to as GSEs, or government sponsored entities. At the beginning of the crisis, Fannie Mae and Freddie Mac owned or guaranteed nearly half of all mortgage loans in the United States and they were in financial trouble.[4]

Soon after being created, FHFA placed Fannie Mae and Freddie Mac into a conservatorship. Its stated purpose was to "enable them to continue to provide liquidity and stability to the mortgage market."[5] The conservatorship was supposed to be temporary, remaining in place only as long as Fannie and Freddie remained unstable.[6] However, that was in 2008. Ten years later, Fannie and Freddie have returned to profitability, yet they remain in a conservatorship. This arrangement has allowed all the profits from the two entities to be returned to the Treasury Department and not the shareholders. Fannie and Freddie shareholders have filed numerous lawsuits challenging the conservatorship.[7] The shareholders' lawsuits have not been successful, though some of these cases are still pending. While a favorable outcome does not seem likely for these shareholders, nothing can be ruled out. Much that occurred in this crisis has bucked conventional wisdom.

From very early in the crisis, FHFA took an almost imperialistic position regarding its oversight role. It has successfully argued that its actions as conservator are completely immune from all local laws and ordinances as well as from judicial review. This position has been especially harmful with respect to abandoned properties. When FHFA became conservator, Fannie Mae and Freddie Mac owned a significant number of foreclosed homes. In 2010 they were estimated to have been taking possession of as many as one home every ninety seconds. By June, they owned 163,828 homes, more than in the entire city of Seattle.[8] In the meantime, cities spent millions of dollars securing and repairing abandoned properties during a time when their own revenue was declining – a direct result of the financial downturn.[9]

---

3 Nicole Summers, *Fannie Mae and Freddie Mac's Subversion of State Consumer Protection Law under the Guise of HERA: Post-Foreclosure Litigation in Massachusetts*, 20 U. PA. J. L. Soc. CHANGE 273, 274 (2017).

4 Charles Duhigg, *Loan-Agency Woes Swell from Trickle to Torrent*, N.Y. TIMES, July 11, 2008; *see also* David Reiss, *An Overview of the Fannie and Freddie Conservatorship Litigation*, 10 N.Y.U J. L. BUS. 479 (2014).

5 *History of Fannie Mae and Freddie Mac Conservatorships*, FED. HOUSING FIN. AGENCY, https://www.fhfa.gov/Conservatorship/Pages/History-of-Fannie-Mae-Freddie-Conservatorships.aspx.

6 Reiss *supra* note 4, at 483.

7 *Id.* at 493–98 (explaining the earliest suits filed).

8 Binyamin Applebaum, *Cost of Seizing Fannie and Freddie Surges for Taxpayers*, N.Y. TIMES (June 19, 2010), https://www.nytimes.com/2010/06/20/business/20foreclose.html.

9 *Zip Code Inequality: Discrimination by Banks in the Maintenance of Homes in Neighborhoods of Color*, NAT'L. FAIR HOUSING ALLIANCE 9 (Aug. 27, 2014), http://www.nareb.com/publications/zip-code-inequality-discrimination-by-banks-in-the-maintenance-of-homes-in-neighborhoods-of-color; *see also* Kathleen C. Engler, *Local Governments and Risky Home Loans*, 69 SMU

They were thus desperate for revenue and many sought to acquire additional funding by enacting abandoned property ordinances. By 2011, 439 jurisdictions had established some sort of vacant property ordinance.[10] These ordinances usually involved the registration of abandoned properties as well as certain basic forms of upkeep.

Fannie Mae and Freddie Mac refused to pay the fees required to register their properties and failed to maintain them. The legislation installing FHFA as the conservator of these two GSEs gave the entity broad powers, "including those arising from the failure of any person to pay real property, personal property, probate or recording tax or any recording or filing fees when due."[11] Essentially, the legislation gave FHFA a free pass regarding all property it owned. While FHFA theoretically had the power to force Fannie Mae and Freddie Mac to register and maintain the properties they owed, no one could force FHFA to exercise that authority.

The City of Chicago provides a good example of struggles between municipalities and FHFA as it relates to abandoned property ordinances. Chicago's ordinance required owners of abandoned properties to pay a $500 registration fee within the latter of either thirty days of abandonment or mortgage default.[12] The logic behind the ordinance was that the registration fee could then be used by the city to help maintain these properties, many of them REO (real estate owned) as a result of foreclosure.[13] Because Fannie Mae or Freddie Mac owned the vast majority of mortgages, they also owned the bulk of these properties. As a result of the conservatorship, these properties became the responsibility of the FHFA.[14]

In 2013, FHFA sued the City of Chicago alleging, among other things, that federal law preempted the ordinance and that FHFA was immune from fines and any judicial oversight of its actions as a conservator.[15] FHFA argued in response that it had policies in place to ensure that properties were being maintained.[16] The facts on

---

L. REV. 609, 629 (2016); Karl W. Smith, *The Effect of the Global Economic Crisis on State and Local Tax Revenues*, 3 UNC S. GOV'T (2009); Carrie Wells, *Fannie Mae Accused of Neglecting Foreclosures in Minority Neighborhoods*, THE BALTIMORE SUN (May 13, 2015, 6:06 PM), http://www.baltimoresun.com/bs-bz-fannie-mae-housing-complaint-20150513-story.html.

[10] U.S. GOV'T ACCOUNTABILITY OFF., GAO-12-34, VACANT PROPERTIES: NUMBER INCREASES COMMUNITIES' COSTS AND CHALLENGES 61 (Nov. 2011).

[11] 12 U.S.C. § 4617(j)(4).

[12] Mary Ellen Podmolik, *Federal Agency Sues Chicago Over Vacant-Property Rules: FHFA Says City Lacks Authority to Assess Fines on Properties with Freddie, Fannie Mortgages*, CHI. TRIB. (Dec. 12, 2011), http://articles.chicagotribune.com/2011-12-12/business/ct-biz-1213-housing-suit-20111213_1_mortgage-servicers-vacant-property-ordinance-vacant-buildings.

[13] An REO property is one that has been foreclosed and is now owned by a third party, usually the lender but sometimes a third-party investor. If a third party buys a foreclosed property for personal use, it loses this designation.

[14] Geoff Smith & Sarah Duda, *Left Behind: Troubled Foreclosures Properties and Servicer Accountability in Chicago*, WOODSTOCK INST. (Jan. 2011), http://www.woodstockinst.org/sites/default/files/attachments/leftbehind_jan2011_smithduda_o.pdf.

[15] Fed. Housing Fin. Agency v. City of Chi., 962 F. Supp. 2d 1044 (N.D. Ill. 2013).

[16] Memorandum and Order Case 1:11-cv-08795, Document #78, filed Aug. 23, 2013 at 9.

the ground, however, were very different.[17] FHFA next argued that the City of Chicago ordinance made FHFA subject to fines it is legally shielded from paying. In addition, it claimed it was likely to incur such fines because the city's maintenance requirements were more stringent than FHFA's. It is true that federal law protects FHFA, when acting in its role as conservator, from these fines. The maintenance of property, however, seems to be the responsibility of Fannie Mae and Freddie Mac as servicers, and not FHFA in its duty as conservator. As such, their actions or inactions in maintaining properties should not be afforded FHFA protections.[18] However, the courts have agreed with FHFA.[19] FHFA, Fannie Mae and Freddie Mac (the latter two because of the continued conservator relationship) have been found not responsible for paying these registration fees.

FHFA has not altered its position that local governments cannot exercise any authority over Fannie Mae or Freddie Mac relating to maintenance of the properties they own.[20] In the end, FHFA reached a settlement with the City of Chicago. It has agreed to voluntarily register its properties, without paying the fee. Ultimately, though, there remains no reliable way to require Fannie Mae or Freddie Mac to maintain their abandoned properties. Further, there is ample evidence from across the country that they do not maintain them, particularly in minority neighborhoods.[21] Instead, the federal government, through FHFA, has dumped the responsibility back on the neighbors and communities where the abandoned properties are located. Most communities are still grappling with the mess.

When FHFA has tried to secure and maintain properties, it has not always done so responsibly. One of FHFA's largest contracts is with a company known as Safeguard Properties. Complaints began to mount at the height of the crisis that Safeguard was locking homeowners out of their properties illegally.[22] In 2015, the Illinois attorney general reached a million-dollar settlement with the company.[23] Safeguard continues to deny any wrongdoing, but the issue points to yet another area where the solution has become the problem. The standard mortgage contract contains a clause that permits lenders to secure a mortgaged property if it is

---

[17] See, *The Banks Are Back: Our Neighborhoods Are Not: Discrimination in the Maintenance and Marketing of REO Properties*, NAT'L. FAIR HOUSING ALLIANCE (Apr. 4, 2012), https://national fairhousing.org/wp-content/uploads/2017/04/Banks-are-Back-Final-12.3.2012.pdf;   GAO-12–34, *supra* note 10, at 61; *Zip Code Inequality*, *supra* note 9, at 9.

[18] Summers, *supra* note 3, at 281.

[19] Memorandum Opinion and Order, Judge Thomas M. Durkin, Fed. Housing Fin. Agency v. City of Chi.

[20] See, Matthew Connelly, *Rejecting Federal Preferences: Why Courts Should Not Exempt Fannie Mae and Freddie Mac Properties from Cities' Vacant Properties and Registration Ordinances*, 49 WASH. U. J. L. POL'Y 181 (2015).

[21] See, *supra* note 17.

[22] Andrew Martin, *In a Sign of Foreclosure Flaws, Suits Claim Break-Ins by Banks*, N.Y. TIMES, Dec. 21, 2010.

[23] Michelle Jarboe, *Safeguard Properties Calls $1 Million Settlement with Illinois AG "an Amicable Resolution*," THE PLAIN DEALER, June 15, 2015.

abandoned by the owner. This right includes "enter[ing] the Property to make repairs, change locks, replace or board up doors and windows, drain water from pipes, eliminate building or other code violations or dangerous conditions, and have utilities turned on or off."[24] The issue, however, is that servicers seem to have a problem determining who has really abandoned the property and who has not. We have had several clients who were illegally locked out of their homes.[25]

Mrs. Bonnie Miller was just one client whose home was illegally broken into by the servicer. Before the death of her spouse, Mrs. Miller had never lived alone. After her husband passed away, she started spending weekends at her daughter's home. One weekend she returned to find the locks on her house changed and everything in the house removed. There was a note from her mortgage company on the door. Mrs. Miller was not in foreclosure, though she had missed one recent payment. According to the company hired to secure her property, everything that was removed from the home had been taken immediately to an incinerator and destroyed. She had lost all her possessions, including all the family photos that chronicled an entire lifetime. The lender in this case ultimately settled with her financially, but she will never be able to replace what she lost emotionally. In Mrs. Miller's case the loan servicer did not understand that a home must be foreclosed on before the bank owns it or any of its contents.

Mortgage lenders have broad powers to enter a property to secure and preserve its asset. However, that power can only be exercised legally when there is a threat to the property, not simply because someone goes away for a weekend. Once a marginally legitimate practice like this becomes widespread, scam artists move into the space. At the time we were representing Mrs. Miller, we contacted the St. Joseph County Sheriff's Office, which took the position that anyone going into the house was breaking and entering, because it could no longer tell who was really authorized by the bank to enter the home. The sheriff's department had learned of groups looking for the red tags placed by the bank to signal pending foreclosure, and breaking into these home to rob the homeowners. If someone questioned them, they claimed to be from the bank.[26] This was such a common occurrence that no one objected to their activity. It had become impossible to distinguish legal break-ins from illegal ones – which really defines the problem. Society should never allow a lender to pay an agent to conduct a "legal break-in." A police officer needs a warrant

---

[24] Fannie Mae Uniform Mortgage Document (Indiana), Fannie Mae, Security interests, https://www.fanniemae.com/singlefamily/security-instruments#.

[25] *See*, Christopher K. Odinet, *Banks, Break-ins, and Bad Actors in Mortgage Foreclosures*, 83 U. of CIN. L. REV. 1155 (2015).

[26] They may have been one and the same. Jeffrey Gentes, director of Connecticut Fair Housing, gave a presentation about this issue at recent training for legal services attorneys. He has litigated these practices perhaps more than any other attorney. He has taken extensive depositions and done a lot of fact investigation. He had seen evidence of some of the subcontractors returning to homes to rob them. How widespread this practice is, we do not know. (Apr. 25, 2018 conference.)

before entering a property, yet a lender can break in, prevent you from reentering, and call it "servicing." Clearly something has gone wrong.

FHFA's unoccupied properties are not the only issue. Boston residents discovered that FHFA is also not a very good landlord. As previously mentioned, Fannie Mae and Freddie Mac do not have a good reputation for maintaining their properties. Landlords are generally required to keep homes in a habitable condition and, in some states, a failure to do so incurs fines. In Massachusetts, state law also allows a tenant to obtain statutory damages against a landlord when the rental unit does not meet these basic habitability codes.[27] When tenants attempt to exercise their rights under these statutes, Fannie Mae and Freddie Mac appear and argue successfully that they cannot be held liable for the poor conditions of their rental units because HERA shields them.[28]

FHFA cannot be held responsible for all the wrongs in the mortgage industry. However, it is a dominant player and, as such, its actions influence others in the market. At every turn, FHFA has taken a leading role in opposing reasonable solutions. FHFA could step up and put pressure on Fannie Mae and Freddie Mac to maintain properties in a safe and responsible manner. Instead, it has been an aggressive force against any commonsense solution to the abandoned property problem. The fate of Freddie Mac and Fannie Mae is one of the most important unresolved issues of the crisis.[29] Just as some declared efforts to release the conservatorship dead, another bill to do just that has been proposed.[30] While FHFA has not been popular with industry or consumer advocates, they have recently joined in a letter asking FHFA to preserve the reforms that both sides agree were beneficial to markets.

> [A]s policymakers consider options to remove the GSEs from conservatorship, retain adequate capital to support GSE operations and foster a system that relies more heavily on private capital, there is a pressing need to ensure that the existing progress is cemented rather than cast aside. Any efforts to change the role played by the GSEs must contain safeguards against higher costs or other market disruptions that reduce access to mortgage credit in both the single-family and multifamily markets. They must also include enforceable mechanisms to serve the entire market of renters and qualified homebuyers, including underserved markets and manufactured housing.[31]

---

[27] Boston Housing Authority v. Hemingway, 293 N.E.2d 831, 843–44 (Mass. 1973).

[28] Summers, supra note 3, at 296–98.

[29] Joe Light, *Fannie-Freddie Overall Plan Is Dead for Now: Senators Say*, https://www.bloomberg.com/news/articles/2018-05-23/fannie-freddie-overhaul-plan-is-dead-for-this-year-senators-say.

[30] *As Conservatorship Reaches 10th Birthday Another Overhaul Proposal for Fannie and Freddie*, MarketWatch (Sept. 7, 2018, 12:03 PM), https://www.marketwatch.com/story/as-conservatorship-reaches-10th-birthday-another-overhaul-proposal-for-fannie-and-freddie-2018-09-07.

[31] Open Letter to the administration and the Congress, September 6, 2018, https://www.mba.org/mba-newslinks/2018/september/mba-newslink-thursday-9-6-18/on-anniversary-of-gse-conservatorship-mba-trade-groups-issue-open-letter-to-administration-congress-on-gse-reform.

FHFA has defended the worst behavior in the industry in all areas of the law. In fact, Fannie Mae and Freddie Mac took a leading role in creating one of the most significant failures in the entire foreclosure crisis, the creation of the Mortgage Electronic Registration System (MERS).

MORTGAGE ELECTRONIC REGISTRATION SYSTEM (MERS)

The problem began fifteen years before the economic downturn. In 1993, the Mortgage Bankers Association of America joined with Fannie Mae and Freddie Mac as part of the InterAgency Technology Task Force and proposed the creation of a paperless registration system to facilitate the transfer of mortgage loans called the whole loan book entry.[32] This led to the creation of the Mortgage Electronic Registration System, introduced in Chapter 1. To understand the importance of MERS, one must first understand why the industry wanted to create the system. As explained previously, most mortgage notes are negotiable instruments similar to a check. The law of negotiable instruments developed over centuries of commerce and the exchange of bills of sales and notes. The law of negotiable instruments was codified as the American Negotiable Instrument Law of 1896 and later as Article 3 of the Uniform Commercial Code.[33] Obviously, these laws were developed before electronic commerce became the dominant form of commercial interaction.

The Uniform Commercial Code has very specific rules regarding who can enforce a negotiable instrument.[34] Not all mortgage notes are negotiable instruments, but most are. To foreclose when the note is a negotiable instrument, the lender needs to be in actual possession of the original note. In addition, to perfect its security interest, the lender must register the mortgage in the land records of the appropriate jurisdiction.[35] Before securitization, this was a simple process. The borrower signed a note and mortgage. The note was retained in a secure location, and the mortgage was registered in the appropriate land records office.

Fannie Mae and Freddie Mac purchased mortgages from lenders by the hundreds of thousands and bundled them into securities. Each step in the procedure requires a transfer of the note and mortgage.[36] According to the Uniform

---

[32] Phyllis K. Slesinger, *Whole Loan Book Entry: A Blueprint for the Future*, TITLE NEWS 19 (Jan. to Feb. 1994), https://www.alta.org/title-news/1994/v73i01.pdf.

[33] JAMES STEVENS ROGERS, THE END OF NEGOTIABLE INSTRUMENTS 2 (2012).

[34] §3-301 U.C.C. (2002); see, *Application of the Uniform Commercial Code to Selected Issues Relating to Mortgage Notes*, AM. L. INST. & NAT'L. CONF. OF COMMISSIONS ON UNIFORM STATE L. (Nov. 14, 2011), http://www.uniformlaws.org/Shared/Committees_Materials/PEBUCC/ PEB_Report_111411.pdf (for a comprehensive explanation of how the Uniform Commercial Code relates to mortgage instruments).

[35] *See*, Dale A. Whitman, *A Proposal for a National Registry: MERS Done Right*, 78 MO. L. REV. 1 (2013) (for an explanation of all the reasons mortgages need to be recorded).

[36] RESTATEMENT (THIRD) OF PROPERTY: MORTGAGES § 5.4(A); *see* Whitman, *supra* note 35, at 4–8 (for an explanation of the development of the "mortgage follows the note" doctrine).

Commercial Code, negotiable instruments (the notes) must be endorsed, and the actual document passed on to the new owner.[37] The accompanying mortgage must be assigned to the new owner and then refiled in the name of the new owner in the land records.[38] Millions of loans were being securitized, and thus millions of documents needed to change hands and millions of mortgages had to be recorded in the local land records. Although it is relatively inexpensive to record one mortgage, recording the millions of required documents was expensive and time consuming. MERS was created to make the process more secure and cost-effective for the industry.

The process required MERS to become the mortgagee, as "nominee" for the lender. As pointed out by the Indiana Supreme Court in *CitiMortgage v. Barabas*,[39] these are inherently contradictory terms. "Mortgagee" implies a principal or owner-ship relationship and "nominee" suggests an agent.[40] Unfortunately, the entire scheme was created without first considering the underlying legal principles. The result should have been expected: It was a mess. To make matters worse, many of the parties did not follow in practice what was outlined in theory. For example, we know of Fannie Mae's required process through a shareholder complaint.[41] Fannie Mae first required the notes to be endorsed in blank. A note endorsed in blank became bearer paper, like a check made out to "cash."[42] Whomever holds it can enforce it. "The notes would then be delivered to one of three places: the Fannie Mae storage facility in Herndon, Virginia; to one of 58 certified independent custody agents; or to the mortgage servicer."[43] Theoretically, if the servicer needed to foreclose, it could contact one of those facilities to retrieve the documents. That sounds reasonable, but there was no reliable method or system to track the notes.[44] It soon became obvious that lenders were not properly endorsing notes and MERS was not properly tracking them.[45] At first, no one noticed. Homeowners rarely had legal represen-tation and most foreclosures were by default. As the crisis wore on, however, consumer advocates began to challenge this house of cards and, as expected, it began to fall.

---

[37] U.C.C. §3–204.

[38] *Transfer and Assignment of Residential Mortgage Loans in the Secondary Mortgage Market*, (Am. Securitization Forum, White Paper Series, 2010), https://www.mersinc.org/media-room-docman/52-asf-white-paper-11-16-10/file.

[39] CitiMortgage, Inc. v. Barabas, 975 N.E.2d 805 (Ind. 2012).

[40] *See*, CitiMortgage, 975 N.E.2d at 813; *but see*, Whitman, *supra* note 35, at 41 (discussing the litigation surrounding the legal status of a nominee).

[41] Alan M. White, *Losing the Paper: Mortgage Assignments, Note Transfers and Consumer Protection*, 24 LOY. CONSUMER L. REV. 468, 474 (2012).

[42] U.C.C. § 3–205(b).

[43] White, *supra*, note 41, at 474.

[44] *Id.*

[45] *Id.* at 486–88; *see also* Christopher L. Peterson, *Two Faces: Demystifying the Mortgage Electronic Registration System's Land Title Theory*, 53 WM. MARY L. REV. 111, 126–28 (2011).

We became aware of paperwork problems with the mortgage of Elaine Simmons. Mr. and Mrs. Simmons found themselves unable to make their mortgage payments very early in the subprime crisis. Their trouble began when Mr. Simmons become ill. When he passed away, Mrs. Simmons was unable to sustain the mortgage payments and fell into foreclosure. When she came to us for help, the paperwork looked very strange. Her loan had been originated by a lender that had since gone out of business, yet the mortgage had been assigned to the current servicer just days before the foreclosure was filed. We wondered how a lender that had gone out of business years ago was able to endorse a mortgage note in the present. One inquisitive law student looked hard and long and located the woman whose name appeared on the paperwork. She had quite a story to tell. She explained that, yes, her name was on the paperwork, but she had not signed it. In fact, she had signed an affidavit explaining that the servicer had a backroom where people forged all kinds of documents and signed her name and the names of others. When presented with the affidavit, the lender dismissed the foreclosure, with prejudice. A foreclosure with prejudice cannot be refiled. Or can it? We will revisit that issue in Chapter 6.

For now, however, we need to understand how MERS was theoretically supposed to work compared to how it did. The MERS system allowed its employees to be delegated vice presidents for the lenders whose mortgages they held. When a foreclosure was necessary, the MERS employees then created mortgage assignments from the originating lender to the foreclosing lender, to allow the foreclosure to occur. This caused a wave of controversy regarding the legitimacy of the assignments, based on the legitimacy of the signers.[46] It is important to understand that the rules of the Uniform Commercial Code are very specific. A promissory note can never be assigned, it must be endorsed. An assignment of a note is a meaningless exercise under the law. MERS apparently lacked a basic knowledge of the law because it often attempted to assign the mortgage, along with the note – a legal impossibility. MERS would attempt to fix its error by adding endorsements to the notes and creating assignments of the mortgages after the fact. The practice of documenting the transfers at some point later in time is not inherently illegal, though many homeowners have been deceived by internet posts claiming otherwise. It only becomes a problem when the documents fail to comply with legal requirements or fail to match the actual transfers. In those case – and there were many – MERS was creating legally flawed documents, leaving holes in the chain of title. You will recall the Indiana attorney general's investigation discussed in Chapter 3 that discovered assignments naming the wrong originating bank.[47] A proper chain of title is important because many states require proof of an unbroken chain of

---

[46] White, *supra* note 41, at 488.
[47] *See infra* 41–48.

assignments from the originating bank to the lender attempting to foreclose.[48] Eleven states also require a chain of assignments.

Problems arose when a lender endorsed a note from one lender to another but failed to notify MERS, so MERS had no record of the transfer. When a note was sold from one lender to another, it often did not physically move the actual note from one location to another. Instead, an electronic notation was made that indicated the note had been sold from one lender to another, but the note remained in a warehouse. When a lender failed to notify MERS of a transfer, that notation was not made. When it was time to foreclose – the point at which you need the physical note – MERS was often unable to find it because it did not know who actually possessed it. Even more troubling, when it attempted to recreate the chain of title it got it wrong, because its record of transfers was inaccurate.[49]

Other issues arose when MERS signed documents as "attorney-in-fact" for a lender. An attorney-in-fact is someone appointed under a power of attorney. To be valid, the attorney-in-fact must be able to produce the underlying power of attorney. However, the servicers were rarely able to produce that required document. The few we saw during the crisis were not valid. Either they designated a different employee, or they had expired before the document in question was signed. Similarly, lenders created problems when attempting to recreate the chain of title when one of the lenders in the chain was no longer in business. Let us illustrate: Originating lender (A) sells the loan to a new lender (B), which sells it to third lender (C). The paperwork necessary to legally transfer the promissory note was not completed at the time of the sale. Lender C wants to foreclose on the loan, but to do so it needs a chain of endorsements. By this time, however, lender A has gone out of business. No one remains with the legal authority to transfer the note from lender A to lender B. Ignoring the law, servicers routinely created the missing paperwork by forging the missing authority from lender A.

Because of all these paperwork issues, MERS has been very controversial – indeed a lightning rod for the entire foreclosure crisis. We have already described the multiple instances of lost or robo-signed paperwork and shown how the presence of MERS makes zombie mortgages more likely.[50] Some loans become zombies for no other reason than a lack of paperwork needed to foreclose. In light of all the

---

[48] At common law, the mortgage follows the note so only the chain of title of the note is required. This is not true for all states. Massachusetts created a stir with its decision in US Bank v. Ibanez, 941 N.E.2d 40 (Mass. 2011). The court set aside two foreclosures because there was no complete chain of title for the mortgage as well as the note. *See,* Elizabeth Renault, *Property Title Trouble in Non-Judicial Foreclosure States: The Ibanez Time Bomb?,* 4 Wm. Mary Bus. L. Rev. 111 (2013).

[49] Whitman, *supra* note 35, at 19–22.

[50] Linda Allen, Stavros d Peristiani & Yi Tang, *Bank Delays in the Resolution of Delinquent Mortgages: The Problem of Limbo Loans,* 8 (Fordham University Schools of Business Research Paper No. 2108948, 2013), https://ssrn.com/abstract=2018948 or http://dx.doi.org/10.2139/ssrn .2018948.

controversary, the New York Federal Reserve began conversations within the industry to create a federal electronic system that will do what MERS was intended to do. The Uniform Law Commission, the authors of the Uniform Commercial Code adopted in all fifty states, is currently working on draft legislation to create an electronic system for the registration of mortgages, including revising the underlying Uniform Commercial Code.[51] Unfortunately, instead of seizing this opportunity to update a terribly antiquated legal system, the Uniform Law Commission chose to simply overlay the electronic registry on top of the existing Uniform Commercial Credit Act. The commission might have thought the legislation would be more likely to be approved if it was built upon a framework used in all fifty states. At the same time, the mortgage industry has done an abysmal job of complying with existing law, so it is hard to believe they will comply with the new provisions of an electronic registry.

Consumer groups have expressed concerns with this process, largely due to their negative experiences with MERS, which was proposed to perform the functions of the proposed electronic registry. MERS hopes to be involved in the new process, making consumer advocates even more suspicious. It seems likely the foreclosure crisis will lead to some kind of electronic mortgage registry system. This time around, the industry is focusing on building the underlying foundation before trying to build the house. Whether it will work properly or lead to a repeat of the previous crisis has yet to be seen.

DISTRESSED ASSET STABILIZATION PROGRAM (DASP)

We already discussed the problem of abandoned properties, many of which were owned by Fannie Mae and Freddie Mac. As the foreclosure crisis continued, many lenders found themselves responsible for hundreds of thousands of properties, some of which were occupied, but many of which were not. The Department of Housing and Urban Development (HUD), which also guarantees mortgages, additionally found itself in possession of many nonperforming loans. When a government-insured loan goes into foreclosure, the government picks up some, or all, of the shortfall. At the same time, servicers for GSE loans had limited options in terms of loan modification. These factors combined to create mounting losses in the mortgage guarantee programs. The best solution in the long run might have been to loosen modification standards and allow principal reductions, but FHFA chose a different path. In 2010, HUD created a pilot program to sell these nonperforming

---

[51] *See,* Committee: Electronic Registry for Residential Mortgage Notes, UNIFORM L. COMMISSION, http://www.uniformlaws.org/Committee.aspx?title=Electronic%20Registry%20for%20Residential%20Mortgage%20Notes; Committee: UCC Articles 1,3,8 and 9, Amendments, UNIFORM L. COMMISSION, http://www.uniformlaws.org/Committee.aspx?title=UCC%20Articles%201,3,%208%20and%209,%20Amendments%20to. The Uniform Law Commission is a group consisting of representative lawyers, judges and legislators who meet regularly to create uniform laws that are then presented to states to enact. The Uniform Commercial Code is their most successful product.

loans to third parties. In 2012, HUD was satisfied with the success of the pilot program and announced the creation of the Distressed Asset Stabilization Program (DASP).[52] Freddie Mac followed with a similar pilot program in 2014 and conducted its first nonperforming asset sale in 2015. Fannie Mae followed.

HUD's program was initially advertised as a way to "to give homeowners with seriously delinquent loans the chance to avoid foreclosure."[53] It allowed servicers to put loans into a pool of loans to be resold if the borrower was at least six months delinquent, had not filed bankruptcy, had exhausted all other loss mitigation procedures and had filed, but not completed, a foreclosure.[54] You will recall that at about this same time we noticed a strange phenomenon in the court records. Servicers in Indiana were going back into foreclosure cases and setting aside judgments. In several of these cases, the lender's counsel informed the court that HUD had required them to set aside the foreclosure judgments. It seems more likely that the servicer was trying to meet the requirements of DASP, so it could transfer the loan back to HUD to be included in one of the sales. Not all of HUD's nonperforming loans were included in these sales. Instead, they were concentrated in certain states, Indiana being one of them.[55] We contacted HUD to inquire about the practice of reversing completed foreclosures. We were shuffled around, told we would have to talk to legal counsel and then disconnected from the phone call. Multiple attempts to reach the legal department to ask whether HUD was advising servicers to set aside foreclosed properties to qualify for DASP went unanswered. Advocates in Cleveland, Minneapolis and other areas especially hard hit by the crisis noticed similar servicer activity. HUD has never responded to our inquiries.

HUD's reasons for creating this program sound viable, especially to those unfamiliar with what was happening on the ground. Unlike HUD, private entities are not restricted in what they can offer to homeowners by way of loan modifications. By selling these assets to private buyers at a discount, the government hoped buyers would pass those discounts on to homeowners in loan modifications that included principal reductions. As consumer advocates pointed out, however, instead of selling these loans off, HUD could have – and perhaps should have – better managed the issues that caused these loans to languish, specifically with better management of their loan servicers.[56] Existing HUD programs could have provided the needed loss

---

[52] *Fact Sheet: Distressed Asset Stabilization Program Enhancements*, DEPT. OF HOUSING & URBAN DEV. 2012, https://www.hud.gov/sites/documents/FINAL_DASP_FACT_SHEET.PDF.

[53] Prepared Remarks of Secretary Shaun Donovan at Press Conference Announcing Distressed Asset Stabilization Program June 8, 2012. (HUD Press Room Speech 06082012).

[54] U.S. DEP'T OF HOUSING & URB. DEV., HUD No. 12–096, HUD to expand sale of troubled mortgages through program designed to help avoid costly, lengthy foreclosures, (June 8, 2012), https://archives.hud.gov/news/2012/pr12-096.cfm.

[55] Geoff Walsh, *Opportunity Denied: How HUD's Note Sale Program Denied Homeowners of the Basic Benefit of Their Government-Insured Loans*, NAT'L. CONSUMER L. CTR. 10 (May 2016), https://www.nclc.org/images/pdf/pr-reports/opportunity-denied-report.pdf.

[56] *Id.* at 18.

mitigation. Servicer-caused delays were creating many of the problems. Instead, the loans were sold to private equity firms. Once they were sold, many homeowners lost the right to access loan modification programs previously associated with the loan; moreover, the new entities failed to create promised substitutes.[57] Multiple home-owners with FHA loans reported being in the midst of mediation when their loans were sold into these pools, only to have the new servicer claim it no longer was required to participate in the program because it was no longer subject to FHA regulations.[58] So much for the promise of better outcomes.

Lone Star Funds, Bayview Asset Management and Selene Residential Partners purchased the majority of notes in the HUD sales.[59] Instead of working with distressed borrowers, these entities generally foreclosed upon the loans quickly, resold them or simply abandoned them. "These firms have swarmed into troubled mortgages because they can squeeze profits from these loans by either restructuring them or by foreclosing on them and then repackaging the distressed loans into bonds that are sold to mutual funds and hedge funds."[60] Consumer groups and community organizations soon began to raise concerns about HUD's sales.[61] Many of the loans sold were on homes located in areas hit hard by the foreclosure crisis and some believed the federal government was simply dumping the costs of its crisis onto local communities.[62] The majority of the loans were sold to high-bidding entities whose interest was to make a quick profit at the expense of both homeowners and communities. Nonprofits inter-ested in stabilizing neighborhoods could not compete financially with the hedge funds and, therefore, were being outbid in the loan pools. HUD did, however, respond to some of the criticism, creating neighborhood stabilization pools that included loans in targeted geographic neighborhoods with specific requirements for loss mitigation.[63]

HUD made several other changes to the program over several years, such as requiring buyers to forestall foreclosure for a year and to evaluate loans for HAMP loss mitigation. It also created sales exclusively for not-for-profits.[64] In 2016, HUD made another round of more significant changes, finally requiring servicers to exhaust all FHA remedies before selling a loan and prohibiting lenders from

---

[57] *Id.* 18–27.

[58] *Id.* at 4.

[59] *Id.* at 37; U.S. Dept. of Housing and Urb. Dev. Fed. Housing Admin., Q. Rep. on FHA Single Family Loan Sales 8 (May 30, 2014), https://www.hud.gov/sites/documents/REPORT082814.PDF.

[60] Matthew Goldstein, *As Banks Retreat, Private Equity Rushes to Buy Troubled Home Mortgages*, N.Y. Times, Sept. 28, 2015.

[61] *See*, Sarah Edelman, Michela Zonta & Shiv Rawal, *Protecting Communities on the Road to Recovery: Why Strong Standards Are Critical for the Distressed Asset Stabilization Program*, Ctr. For Am. Progress (June 2016), https://cdn.americanprogress.org/wp-content/uploads/2016/06/27153616/CommunitiesLeftBehind-report.pdf; Walsh, *supra* note 55.

[62] *Id.* at 9.

[63] Walsh, *supra* note 55, at 10.

[64] US Dep't of Housing & Urb Announces Changes to Distressed Asset Sales Program, HUD No.15–048 (Apr. 24, 2015), https://archives.hud.gov/news/2015/pr15–048.cfm.

abandoning properties.[65] We will discuss later how HUD finally almost got it right. By the time the program was making sense, however, much of the damage had already been done to both homeowners and communities.

The results of the Fannie Mae and Freddie Mac sales were no better. The reasons for these sales mirrored those for the HUD sales. These GSEs also had very specific rules about what homeowners should be offered in terms of loss mitigation, none which included meaningful principal reductions in the communities most in need.[66] And neither Fannie Mae nor Freddie Mac was adequately policing their servicers. FHFA, now the conservator of these loans, had a statutory duty to manage them with minimal losses to taxpayers.[67] The definition of "taxpayer" seemed to be quite narrow, applying only to the federal treasury and not the overall health of communities. Like HUD, FHFA determined that the best way to manage the problem was to give it to someone else. That "someone else" has turned out to be minority communities across America.

FREDDIE MAC'S MULTIFAMILY SMALL BALANCE LOAN SECURITIZATION

The foreclosure process was completed on many of the abandoned properties, but not all the abandoned properties were the direct result of mortgage foreclosures. The crisis caused other economic stresses that resulted in abandoned properties, including tax foreclosure and the simple realization that one could no longer maintain a property. The combination of what could be called normal rates of abandonment and the accelerated rates of the crisis, left many cities with numerous abandoned properties. In addition, new housing was not being built during the crisis years. As a result of all these factors, rental housing stock has become very scarce post crisis. Beginning in 2014, Freddie Mac announced steps to help improve rental markets by expanding its loan guarantee program from single family residences to multifamily and small apartment buildings.[68] A pilot program was created three years later to

[65] US Dep't of Housing & Urb. Dev., HUD NO. 16–105, FHA Announces Most Significant Improvements to Date for DISTRESSED Asset Sales Program (June 30, 2016), https://archives.hud.gov/news/2016/pr16–105.cfm.

[66] In 2016, the GSEs did begin to offer some principal reduction programs, but they were very limited. The current one-mod loan modification program also allows for some limited principal reduction. These only became effective in 2018, so it is still too early to evaluate its success. *See*, i.e., *Principal Reduction Modification*, Fed. Housing Financial Housing (Apr. 14, 2016), https://www.fhfa.gov/Media/PublicAffairs/Pages/Principal-Reduction-Modification.aspx; *Know Your Options by Fannie Mae*, Fannie Mae, https://www.knowyouroptions.com/modify/flex-modification.

[67] FHFA Strategic Plan: Fiscal Years 2018–2022, Fed. Housing & Fin. Agency (2018), https://www.fhfa.gov/AboutUs/Reports/ReportDocuments/StratPlan_Final_1292018.pdf.

[68] Brena Swanson, *Freddie Mac Offers Small Apartment Mortgages*, Housing Wire (Oct. 9, 2014), https://www.housingwire.com/articles/31669-freddie-mac-moves-into-small-apartment-mortgages.

securitize these loans, underwritten by Freddie Mac.[69] We will return to the implications in a moment, after telling you about Marshall Welton and his company, Casas Baratas.

Mr. Welton is a real estate investor in Indianapolis, Indiana with a less-than-stellar reputation.[70] His accomplishments include being featured in a WTHR Channel 13 *Eyewitness News* broadcast entitled "Where's Our Money?"[71] At the time of the story, Mr. Welton was continuing to purchase rental property while he still owed $39,000 in unpaid property taxes on his current rental units, twenty-three of which were scheduled to be auctioned off in a tax sale. In addition, Mr. Welton failed to maintain his properties and had been cited for housing code violations "numerous times."[72] In 2004 he appeared on the "Top Ten List of Problem Property Owners" in Indianapolis and in 2007 he was again featured, but this time for his role in an alleged mortgage fraud.[73] He was later cleared of those charges. Mr. Welton allegedly also had issues with his creditors, and had been sued for nonpayment a number of times. Normally, someone with this kind of business reputation would have difficulty obtaining financing. According to the complaint filed in federal court, Welton solved that problem by creating a series of limited liability companies and using them to obtain financing in massive amounts. In a series of loans, CoreVest lent him more than $12 million. This brings us back to Freddie Mac, which recently announced that its first securitization involved partnering with CoreVest to securitize its loans into a CoreVest American Finance 2017–2 Trust Mortgage Pass-Through Certificate.[74] Mr. Welton's loans are included in this portfolio.

One of Mr. Welton's more recent businesses is called *Casas Baratas*, or "cheap houses" in English. His website is casasbaratisaqui.com (cheap houses here). According to a complaint filed in federal court in Indiana, he advertises almost exclusively on Hispanic radio and by placing signs, in Spanish, in Latino neighborhoods. Yet, the documents he asks prospective buyers to sign are entirely in English, except for a flyer explaining where to pay rent. The first document a prospective buyer signs is a one-year lease with an option to purchase. Like the other land contract schemes just discussed, the document is identified as a lease and the signer as a tenant,

[69] Jacob Gaffney, *Freddie Mac Launches Single-Family Rental Financing Pilot Program*, Housing Wire (Dec. 8, 2017), https://www.housingwire.com/articles/42042-freddie-mac-launches-single-family-rental-financing-pilot-program.

[70] The story we are about to tell appears in a complaint filed in Federal District Court in Indiana. In fairness to Mr. Welton, he does dispute the characterization of his business. Fair Housing of Central Indiana stands by their facts. We are retelling the story to illustrate a new problem that has emerged, and take no position on which of the two has the more accurate story to tell.

[71] Paul Stauder, *Where's Our Money?* (Channel 13, June 13, 2002, 11:30 PM; updated August 26, 2016, 6:30 PM), https://www.wthr.com/article/wheres-our-money.

[72] *Id.*

[73] Fair Housing Ctr of Central Ind. et al. v. Marshall Welton et al., U.S. Dist. Ct. S. Dist. Indiana, 1:18-cv-1098, Apr. 10, 2018 ¶ 31.

[74] Freddie Mac Structured Pass-Through Certificates Series FRESR 2017-SR01.

but all the duties to maintain the property, pay the taxes and provide homeowners insurance fall on the tenant. The warranty of habitability is disclaimed. If the prospective buyer makes all the payments and a nonrefundable down payment within the year, a land contract is drafted. Due to the recent nature of this business, only a few land contracts have been issued. They all have the characteristically high interest rates of land contracts. While Mr. Welton promises to provide title at the end of the land contract term, these properties have all been pledged as collateral for the CoreVest loans, making it very unlikely that a clear title will be available.[75]

Mr. Welton and CoreVest were quick to take advantage of Freddie Mac's new program; perhaps that might be good for consumers. Upon learning of the federal litigation, Freddie Mac opened an investigation into how these loans could have been included.[76] The prospective for the trust specifically prohibited any of the properties from having a lease containing "any option to purchase."[77] Perhaps this will serve as a cautionary tale encouraging the GSEs to be more careful about which business enterprises they enable. The Freddie Mac program had an honorable intent – to help ease the rental market. However, that goal is not met by enabling predatory practices. Rental markets do need assistance, but that is partially because of the GSE's failure to properly manage the tide of foreclosure. The efforts to save Wall Street have been successful, but Main Street is fast becoming a homeless shelter.

SMALL BANKS AND SMALL LOANS

"Too big to fail" is now an iconic phrase from the financial crisis.[78] It derives from the belief that some financial institutions were so large that their failure would devastate the overall economy. The Dodd-Frank Wall Street Reform and Consumer Protection Act,[79] passed in reaction to the Great Recession, was meant to address the "too big to fail" problem. While this act has been very successful in reining in many of the precrisis issues, it has created some unintended consequences. Many smaller financial institutions have been driven out of business. FHFA cannot claim all the responsibility for the results, but it does bear some of the responsibility.

As conservator of Fannie Mae and Freddie Mac, FHFA continues to buy and securitize loans. Its policies favor high value loans for borrowers with high credit scores, thereby benefiting large institutions that originate a large volume of loans with the

---

[75] Fair Housing Ctr of Central Ind. et al. v. Marshall Welton et al., U.S. Dist. Ct. S. Dist. Indiana, 1:18-cv-1098, Apr. 10, 2018.

[76] Matthew Goldstein, *Freddie Mac Examines Loan to Possible Rent-to-Own Housing Provider*, N.Y. TIMES (Apr. 27, 2018), https://www.nytimes.com/2018/04/27/business/freddie-mac-affordable-housing-rent-to-own.html.

[77] Fannie Mae, supra note 66.

[78] Yalman Onaran, *Too Big to Fail*, BLOOMBERG (Dec. 8, 2017), https://www.bloomberg.com/quicktake/big-fail.

[79] Dodd-Frank Wall Street Reform and Consumer Protection Act, Pub. L. 111-203 (2010).

intention of selling and securitizing them. After the crisis, private securitization of loans became very limited. Even now, Fannie Mae and Freddie Mac securitize the majority of mortgage loans. One of FHFA's Congressional mandates is to decrease the share of loans that Fannie Mae and Freddie Mac guarantee. It has thus increased the fees charged to banks for guaranteeing the loans, called guarantee fees.[80] Small and community banks tend to retain a larger share of their loans in house, as opposed to securitizing them. These same small banks have neither the capital to afford the higher fees, nor the market share to negotiate a discount. This has caused many small lenders to fail or be consolidated into larger, existing institutions. As a result, the banks that were "too big to fail" before the crisis are even bigger now.[81]

Fannie Mae and Freddie Mac were not just crucial to the mortgage markets because of their role in securitization. Many lending institutions were also share-holders of the companies due to a federal law that created an exemption, allowing banks to purchase their shares.[82] When the Treasury took control of Fannie Mae and Freddie Mac, it also took control of their senior preferred stock. The banks no longer received their previous dividend income and had to declare the losses of the depreciating stock value.[83] The Community Bankers of America estimated that small banks were affected most, losing almost $16 billion dollars as a result.[84] Legislation was enacted to ease the burden, but in the end, it was not enough to save many of them.[85] According to one study, the number of small banks decreased by nearly 50 percent between 1993 and 2013.[86]

The reduction in small lenders also impacted the ability of low-income borrowers to obtain financing to purchase a home. Housing counselors and community advocates began to report that some of their clients, though creditworthy, were unable to obtain financing for these small home loans. As advocates gathered to discuss the problem, it became clear that in small cities across the country (e.g.,

---

[80] "Fannie Mae and Freddie Mac guarantee the payment of principal and interest on their MBS and charges a fee for providing that guarantee. The guarantee fee (g-fee), covers projected credit losses from borrower defaults over the life of the loans, administrative costs, and a return on capital." *Guarantee Fees History*, FED. HOUSING FIN. AGENCY, https://www.fhfa.gov/Policy ProgramsResearch/Policy/Pages/Guarantee-Fees-History.aspx.

[81] Mark Gongloff, Kity Hall & Jan Diehnm, *5 Years after the Crisis, Big Banks Are Bigger than Ever (Chart)*, HUFF POST (Sept. 10, 2013, 2:40 PM, updated Dec. 6, 2017), https://www .huffingtonpost.com/2013/09/10/biggest-banks-even-bigger_n_3900363.html; Matt Egan, *Too-Big-to-Fail Banks Keep Getting Bigger*, CNN MONEY (Nov. 21, 2017, 3:43 PM), https://money .cnn.com/2017/11/21/investing/banks-too-big-to-fail-jpmorgan-bank-of-america/index.html.

[82] 12 U.S.C. §§ 1718(d).

[83] Julie Anderson Hill, *Shifting Losses: The Impact of Fannies and Freddie's Conservatorships on Commercial Banks*, 35 HAMLINE L. REV. 343, 363 (2012).

[84] *Id.*

[85] *Id.* (Explaining how the Emergency Economic Stabilization Act of 2008 allowed banks to treat losses as ordinary losses to offset income.)

[86] Hester Pierce, Ian Robinson & Thomas Stratmann, *How Are Small Banks Faring under Dodd-Frank*, 10 (Working Paper No. 14–05, Mercatus Center, George Mason U, 2014), https://www .mercatus.org/system/files/Peirce_SmallBankSurvey_v1.pdf.

South Bend, Indiana; Dayton, Ohio and Wilkes-Barre, Pennsylvania), qualified borrowers were having trouble finding lenders.[87] Small lenders historically provided most of these loans, but many of these same banks have either failed or ceased offering mortgage loans.

In many smaller towns and cities, homes valued at less than $100,000 are available for sale. In towns like South Bend, there are many homes available for sale for less than $50,000. One of the reasons homebuyers are willing to purchase homes through abusive land contracts, which we discuss in detail in Chapter 5, is the inability to finance the purchase of a low-cost home in more conventional ways. This is not a result of individual credit worthiness, but a response to lenders' reluctance to under-write small mortgage loans. Lenders claim they are unable to make small loans because of the qualified mortgage (QM) rule that went into effect in January 2014.[88] The rule is designed to limit fees, prepayment penalties and interest-only loans. Lenders are not prohibited from approving a loan outside the QM rules; it is just that if they do, they lose some of the legal protections the rule provides. Staying within the rule guidelines makes loans under $100,000 less profitable for banks to originate. The Urban Institute conducted a study of mortgage finance in 2016 to determine whether the qualified mortgage rule had reduced the credit available to low-income clients.[89] The study examined the mortgage loans before and after the QM rule went into effect. While overall there has not been a decline in lending since the implementation of the Dodd-Frank rules, the study did find a decline in loans below $100,000 in some communities.[90] The researchers also looked at loans below $50,000 and found a more significant decline.[91] There are countless reasons why this may be the case: For instance, these cheap houses may be in such poor condition that lenders do not want to provide mortgages. Lenders claim the problem was Dodd-Frank, which makes these loans too costly to originate. Whatever the reasons, these homes are now more likely to be purchased by investors or house flippers than by prospective homeowners. This has further exacerbated the growing housing crisis in America.

In 2018, Congress stepped in to address the problem. The Economic Growth, Regulatory Relief and Consumer Protection Act of 2018 allegedly did a number of things to increase consumer mortgage lending. The most significant of these was to exempt small lenders from the rules in the original Dodd-Frank legislation regarding a prospective homeowner's ability to repay the loan.[92] They thus raised the asset limit of banks to which the law applied and exempted mobile home loans entirely.

---

[87] Data on file with authors.

[88] 24 C.F.R. § 203.19 (2013).

[89] Bing Bai, Laurie Goodman & Ellen Seidman, *Has the QM Rule Made It Harder to Get a Mortgage?*, URB. INST. (Mar. 2012), https://www.urban.org/sites/default/files/publication/78266/2000640-Has-the-QM-Rule-Made-It-Harder-to-Get-a-Mortgage.pdf.

[90] *Id.* at 5–6.

[91] Data on file with authors.

[92] ECON. GROWTH, REG. RELIEF, AND CONSUMER PROTECTION ACT, Pub. L. No. 115–174 (2018).

Many consumer groups believe that these efforts, including changes that weaken necessary Dodd-Frank protections, went too far. The Center for Responsible Lending, National Community Reinvestment Coalitions and the National Consumer Law Center wrote to Congress strongly opposing the changes.[93] The fear, among other things, was that the asset limit was raised more than was necessary to assist small banks and, as a result, opened the doors for larger institutions to return to their abusive precrisis practices. It is too early to tell if they are right.

HOME AFFORDABLE MODIFICATION PROGRAM (HAMP)

Before the crisis, loss mitigation for mortgage loans was only a real possibility for those with HUD-insured loans. These borrowers had the right to meet with a counselor, obtain forbearance of their payment or a "partial claim," a form of loss mitigation that allows a portion of the loan to be placed at the end as an interest-free second mortgage, which attaches to the end of the mortgage but does not come due unless the home is sold or the owner dies. For others, however, there were no such options. Precrisis, the only loss mitigation available for those wishing to retain their homes was a repayment plan or a reinstatement. In a repayment plan, the homeowner must pay the normal monthly loan payment plus an additional amount to bring the loan current. A reinstatement is a single payment that brings the entire loan current. Clearly, neither provides a real opportunity for a homeowner experiencing financial strain.

The government's response to the crisis generally was viewed as a bailout of the financial sector, one that left the public behind.[94] And so, during the early years of the foreclosure crisis, there was mounting pressure to assist homeowners.[95] The Hope for Homeowners Act was Congress' first attempt. This abysmal failure was part of the Housing and Economic Recovery Act. The program, which ran from 2008 until September 2011,[96] was designed to allow homeowners in distress to refinance their mortgages into FHA-insured mortgages. It was voluntary and, as a result, very few lenders participated.[97] The initial estimates predicted "with only

---

[93] *Opposition to S. 2155, the So-Called "Economic Growth, Regulatory Relief, and Consumer Protection Act,"* CTR. FOR RESPONSIBLE LENDING, (May 18, 2018), https://www.responsiblelend ing.org/research-publication/opposition-s-2155-so-called-economic-growth-regulatory-relief-and-consumer.

[94] *See generally,* NEAL BAROFSKY, BAILOUT: HOW WASHINGTON ABANDONED MAIN STREET WHILE RESCUING WALL STREET (2013).

[95] *See, Civil Rights Groups Call on Congress to Assist Homeowners in Its Economic Recovery Package,* MALDEF (Aug. 30, 2008), http://www.maldef.org/news/releases/call_on_con gress_083008/index.html; *NAACP Calls for Protection for Homeowners and Foreclosure Victims in Its Economic Recovery Package,* NAACP (Sept. 25, 2008), http://www.naacp.org/latest/naacp-calls-for-protection-of-homeowners-and-foreclosure-victims-in-economic-bailout-package.

[96] 12 U.S.C. § 1715z-23 (2009).

[97] Alastair W. McFarlane, Edward Szymanoski & Kurt G. Usowski, *The Impact of the HOPE for Homeowners,* (U.S. Dep't. of House. and Urb. Dev., Working Paper # REP 08–04 Oct. 2008), https://www.huduser.gov/publications/pdf/awm_ejs_kju_rep_0804.pdf.

10,000 participants annually, the Program will generate $62 million to $355 million of net benefits to society."[98] In March 2008, Brian Sullivan of the Federal Housing Authority reported that only a single homeowner had received assistance.[99] The program had multiple flaws. Homeowners had to prove they were not at fault for their foreclosure and pay expensive closing costs, but the major flaw was that it was voluntary. Mortgage servicers had neither the staffing nor the knowledge and motivation to participate in such a program. When they did, the resulting modifications were not particularly beneficial to homeowners. As one researcher commented,

> In short, the typical voluntary modifications of 2008 were not unlike the subprime loan originations they were meant to resolve: borrowers were kept in the debt exceeding home values, and exceeding their ability to amortize, with deferrals of interest, balloon payments, and temporary low interest rates.[100]

The Obama administration created a new program, the Home Affordable Modification Program (HAMP).[101] Compared to Hope for Homeowners, HAMP was a great success, which is not to say that HAMP's results did not disappoint. One improvement over HOPE was the mandatory nature of the program. Servicers signed a contract with the Treasury Department, and once they did, there were required to evaluate all the loans they serviced for HAMP loan modifications.

HAMP's design was complicated for both servicers and homeowners. In fact, there was not one HAMP program; there were multiple programs, as well as special versions for Fannie Mae, Freddie Mac and HUD. The programs tended to be more favorable for a specific type of borrower: one who had little equity, a variable mortgage that was resetting to higher rate and, as a result, an unaffordable mortgage payment. The HAMP model followed what is called a "waterfall," a term that still makes consumer advocates shudder. The first step was to capitalize all past due interest, but not late fees. Next, the interest rate could be reduced to as low as 2 percent. Then, the lender was to extend the term of the loan out to as many as 480 months. Finally (though this step is optional), the lender can reduce the principal loan amount. This series of steps was designed to reduce the homeowner's payment to no more than 31 percent of his income.[102] Once an affordable payment was reached, no further reductions took place.

The program had several unintended consequences. A homeowner was required to make three trial payments before a permanent loan modification could be

---

[98] *Id.* at 2.

[99] Tim Manni, *No Hope in "Hope for Homeowners,"* HSH.COM (Mar. 26, 2009), https://www.hsh.com/blog/2009/03/no-hope-in-hope-for-homeowners.

[100] Alan White, Deleveraging the American Homeowner: The Failure of 2008 Voluntary Mortgage Contract Modifications, 20 (2009), http://ssrn.com/abstract=1325534.

[101] U.S. Dep't of Treas., Making Home Affordable, https://www.treasury.gov/initiatives/financial-stability/TARP-Programs/housing/mha/Pages/default.aspx.

[102] FANNIE MAE, MAKING HOMES AFFORDABLE PROGRAM: HANDBOOK FOR SERVICERS ON NON-GSE LOANS, VERSION 5.2, 111–16, https://www.hmpadmin.com/portal/programs/docs/hamp_servicer/mhahandbook_52.pdf.

offered. None of the terms of the final modification were disclosed before the borrower was required to accept the trial modification. As a result, more than a few homeowners were unpleasantly surprised to discover that their new principal loan amount far exceeded the value of their home. Others found themselves facing large balloon payments at the end of their modified loan.

The Net Present Value (NPV) test was a key part of the waterfall.[103] This was an evaluation of whether foreclosing on the property was a better investment than a loan modification for the lender. Early in the program, servicers were permitted to add their own "risk premium" to the Freddie Mac discount rate in order to estimate the cash flow of a loan. Treasury found that these rates varied incredibly and were decreasing the number of qualifying homeowners.[104] The program never considered the harm foreclosures cause and lenders' interests were given priority over those of homeowners, communities and even investors. A single foreclosure can decrease the value of neighboring homes. By failing to stem foreclosures, HAMP allowed the industry to depress overall housing values with each subsequent foreclosure.[105]

This program endured much criticism from lenders and consumers alike. An early test of the viability of a loan modification program came in 2010 when a group of investors sued Countrywide, trying to force it to buy back loans that were being modified. State attorneys general had sued Countrywide for alleged predatory practices and the settlement they reached required Countrywide to modify the affected loans.[106] The case was eventually dismissed on procedural grounds, and although some had predicted a wave of such lawsuits, it never came. Loan modification as a way to deal with foreclosure has moved from the impossible to the common – so much so that Wells Fargo has recently been accused of modifying homeowners' loans even when they made no such request.[107]

HAMP had other problems worth discussing. It was conceived in the shadow of the realization that too many loans, popularly referred to as "liar loans," had been underwritten with little or fraudulent income documentation. In response, the program required double, and sometimes triple verification of every source of income or expense. Homeowners were asked to submit voluminous paperwork to be considered for a loan modification.[108] As already explained, it was often lost in

[103] *Id.* at 125–30.
[104] Off. of the Spec. Inspector Gen. for the Troubled Asset Relief Program, the Net Present Value Test's Impact on the Home Affordabile Modification Program, 7–9 (June 18, 2012), https://www.sigtarp.gov/Audit%20Reports/NPV_Report.pdf.
[105] Daniel Hartley, The Effect of Foreclosures on Nearby Housing Prices: Supply or Dis-Amenity?, 49 Regional Sci. & Urb. Econ. 108, 116 (2014).
[106] Greenwich Fin. Servs. Distressed Mtge. Fund 3, LLC v. Greenwich Fin. Servs. Distressed Mtge. Fund 3, LLC, 2010 N.Y. Misc. LEXIS 6820 (N.Y. Sup. Ct. 2010)
[107] Matt Egan, *New Wells Fargo Scandal Over Modifying mortgages without Authorization*, CNN (June 15, 2017), https://money.cnn.com/2017/06/15/investing/wells-fargo-mortgage-modification-lawsuit/index.html.
[108] FHFA financed an effort to create a Uniform Law through the Uniform Law Commission. Judith Fox was involved throughout the process. In multiple conversations with FHFA's

transit. The request for duplicate forms of verification was difficult for our clients who were often unbanked and, therefore, were operating largely in a cash society. Although there was one official application form for the HAMP program (the RMA), servicers often required borrowers to fill out their own, often duplicative, form. Sometimes, as in Indiana, the court mediation program introduced a third form.

These forms often conflicted in ways that made them difficult to complete in a consistent manner. The different questions asked by the different forms sometimes made the homeowner appear to be hiding income or expenses. For instance, one form would specifically ask for credit card payments, loans and utility payments, but not cell phone payments. Most people did not think of their cell phones as a "utility" so they failed to mention it. The second form would then ask for all monthly expenses, including cell phone payments. When the cell phone was listed on the second form but not the first, the modification would be rejected for fraud. One mediator in Indiana told us that a lender had rejected a loan modification because a two dollar video rental had appeared on the homeowner's bank statement but was not listed in the budget as a monthly expense. The mediator was quite horrified by the lender's inability to grasp that this was not a recurring monthly expense. Banks had an abysmal record when it came to properly handling applications for loan modifications during the life of the Making Homes Affordable Program.[109]

As the crisis wore on, the typical borrower needing assistance changed. Many were unemployed. HAMP at first did not allow, then did allow, and then disallowed again, any consideration of unemployment income. The model did not address the needs of borrowers who fell behind because of unemployment or illness, but later became reemployed. If a borrower could afford her payment at the time she sought assistance, she was denied. The problem with this analysis is that she had past-due amounts that had accumulated, which she could not afford to repay in one lump sum. Banks will not accept any payment from defaulting borrowers unless they include all arrears. Logically, borrowers who can make ongoing payments – but just cannot catch up with payments they were unable to make when jobless – should receive help. These were exactly the borrowers HAMP did not assist, yet these were the borrowers most likely to sustain a loan modification.

Recognizing this shortfall in its program, the federal government created the Hardest Hit Funds, which were intended to help the many people otherwise unable to access HAMP.[110] Money was provided countrywide to certain counties that had suffered high numbers of foreclosures. The funds could be used to assist borrowers whose main reason for falling behind was unemployment. States were permitted to

corporate counsel, Alford Pollard, he indicated that homeowners only needed to provide "one piece of paper" to obtain a loan modification. It was not clear whether FHFA was ignorant of the processes it created or chose to pretend that it was.

[109] Adam J. Levitin & Tara Twomey, *Mortgage Servicing*, 28 YALE J. REG. 1, 2 (2011).

[110] U.S. DEP'T OF TREAS., HARDEST HIT FUNDS: PROGRAM PURPOSE AND OVERVIEW, https://www.treasury.gov/initiatives/financial-stability/TARP-Programs/housing/hhf/Pages/default.aspx.

structure their programs according to the needs they perceived in their own states. Indiana, for instance, used some of the money to repay arrearages for homeowners who were in foreclosure because of a job loss, but could now afford payments. Nineteen states, including Indiana and New Jersey, received funding.[111] In addition to these governmental programs, lenders developed in-house, proprietary, loss-mitigation programs. These were available to homeowners whose servicer was not participating in HAMP or who failed to qualify even if their servicer was participating.

The Making Homes Affordable Program has come to an end, but homeowners still in HAMP modifications fear issues may linger. The standard HAMP loan modification lowered interest rates to as low as 2 percent, but those rates adjusted upwards after five years. Additionally, HAMP consisted of many different, although related, programs. HAMP Tier 1 was introduced in 2009 and HAMP Tier 2 in 2012. There were programs to assist in refinancing, short sales and forbearance during periods of unemployment. In many ways, this was a revolutionary idea. Investors, the ultimate owners of mortgage-backed securitized trusts, were being asked to rewrite millions of loans. Such a large-scale project is bound to have hiccups, and HAMP was no exception.

Nonetheless, HAMP continued throughout the entirety of the Obama administration. The program performance report for the third quarter of 2017 concluded that it gave more than 2.9 million homeowners some level of assistance. HAMP's legacy, however, may be more psychological than practical. As the program was coming to an end, the Mortgage Bankers Association formed a task force to formulate a successor to HAMP and called it the One Mod.[112] Soon after, Fannie Mae and Freddie Mac created their own similar version called the Flex Mod, designed to reduce a homeowner's loan payments by 20 percent. The trial modification can be approved without requiring any documentation of income.[113] Governmental loans (VA, FHA, USDA) are handled differently, as they will reset at prevailing market rates. During the crisis, the loans in need of modification nearly always had higher interest rates than those currently available. Loan modifications hence nearly always resulted in a lower interest rate. This is no longer the case. As rates have risen, loan modifications can result in a homeowner being offered a new loan with a new payment higher than the original payment – the one the

---

[111] U.S. Dep't of Treas., State Expense Allocations, https://www.treasury.gov/initiatives/financial-stability/TARP-Programs/housing/hhf/Documents/Program%20Allocations%201.31.18.pdf.

[112] *"One Mod:" Principles for Post-HAMP Loan Modifications*, Mortg. Bankers Ass'n (Sept. 2016), on file with the authors.

[113] Fannie Mae, Lender Letter, LL-2016–06, (Dec. 14, 2016), https://www.fanniemae.com/content/announcement/ll1606.pdf; Freddie Mac, Freddie Mac Flex Modification Servicer Frequently Asked Questions (July 2017), http://www.freddiemac.com/singlefamily/service/pdf/Flex_Mod_FAQ.pdf.

homeowner was unable to afford.[114] Recently, as part of Indiana's mortgage loan facilitation program, we have begun to see examples of loan modification offers that raise interest rates and payment amounts.[115] This appears especially common for HUD loans.

Previously modified loans are reappearing in foreclosure for a variety of reasons. The interest rates on HAMP Tier I loans reset to higher rates every few years, sometimes resulting in unaffordable payments. The interest rates on more than 80 percent of the HAMP Tier 1 loans will soon reset again – for some loans the third or fourth reset. The program assumed a homeowner could only afford a housing payment less than 31 percent of his income. Over the last thirty years, American workers have experienced stagnating wages.[116] It was not logical to create a program that assumes homeowners who had been given an affordable payment would somehow be able to afford a higher payment a few years later. These modifications were unsustainable by design, perhaps because the designers had no knowledge of the economic realities of the intended beneficiaries. So far, the interest rate resets have been small, and current evidence suggests they are not causing a significant number of loans to default.[117] It will be a few years before the success of this program can be fully analyzed. Hopefully, that analysis will occur before we are in the midst of our next housing crisis.

HOME AFFORDABLE REFINANCE PROGRAM (HARP)

The Home Affordable Refinance Program (HARP)[118] has received much less attention than HAMP, but many believe it has been much more successful. HARP was created in 2009 as a way to enable homeowners who owed more on their mortgage than the home was worth, to refinance into affordable mortgages. To be eligible, the loan had to be owned by Fannie Mae or Freddie Mac. While that covered a large percentage of mortgages, it did not cover all of our clients' mortgages. Some of the worst predatory loans were not part of Fannie or Freddie's portfolio. Unfortunately,

---

[114] Laurie Goodman, Karen Kauna, Allanna McCargo & Todd Hilll, *Governmental Loan Modifications: What Happens When Interest Rates Rise?*, Urb. Inst. (Jan. 2018), https://www.urban .org/sites/default/files/publication/95671/government-loan-modifications_2.pdf.

[115] Judith Fox is a facilitator as part of the Indiana Mortgage Foreclosure facilitation program. In recent months we have seen an increase in loan modification offers that actually raise homeowner payments.

[116] *See generally*, Lawrence Mishel, Elise Gould & Josh Bivens, *Wage Stagnation in Nine Charts*, Econ. Policy Inst. (Jan. 6. 2015), https://www.epi.org/files/2013/wage-stagnation-in-nine-charts .pdf.

[117] U.S. Dep't of Treas., Making Home Affordable: Program Performance Rep. Through the Third Q. oF 2017, Treas. Dept., https://www.treasury.gov/initiatives/financialstability/ reports/Documents/3Q17%20MHA%20Report%20Final.pdf.

[118] *See*, HARP, https://www.harp.gov/about; Fed. Housing Fin. Agency, Refinance Rep., Second Quarter 2018, https://www.fhfa.gov/AboutUs/Reports/ReportDocuments/Refi_2Q 2018.pdf.

the program also excluded option arm loans, some of the most notorious of the loan products and, ironically, those most in need of refinancing. These loans were almost exclusively in privately securitized funds and not guaranteed by the GSEs.[119]

Like HAMP, the program was tweaked throughout the crisis to make it more effective. The program also continued a year longer than HAMP, which expired in December 2017, while HARP expired in December 2018. HARP offered significant advantages to those who did qualify for the program. Many underwater homeowners cannot obtain a loan to refinance because they are underwater. With HARP, that did not matter. At one point you could not be underwater more than 125 percent of the value of the home, but these limits were lifted early in the program. The loans did not require underwriting, so homeowners did not experience the back and forth paperwork nightmares of HAMP. In addition, there were no fees attached with the rewrites.[120]

Since its inception, slightly less than 3.5 million homes have been refinanced through the program. More than 400,000 of those refinances were for homes whose mortgages were now for more than 125 percent of the value of the home.[121] The delinquency rate of borrowers refinancing through this program has been consistently lower than the rate of those who were eligible, but did not participate.[122] This would seem to be evidence to support continuing the program beyond the crisis. Instead, it is scheduled to end now that the crisis is perceived to be over. It is consistent with all the interventions that, instead of creating long-term policies to prevent a new housing crisis, we create programs only in reaction to a crisis, and long after the problem has mushroomed. Creating a new program takes time and money. Time lost in a housing crisis results in homes needlessly lost to foreclosure.

THE CONSUMER FINANCIAL PROTECTION BUREAU

We now come to the single most important impact of the financial crisis for homeowners and non-homeowners alike – the creation of the Consumer Financial Protection Bureau (CFPB). This independent federal agency was created by Title X of the Consumer Financial Protection Act of 2010.[123] Before the crisis, multiple agencies, including the Federal Reserve, Office of the Comptroller of the Currency (OCC) and the Office of Thrift Management, had authority to regulate financial institutions. Unfortunately, none considered the interests of consumers, or had regulatory authority over nonbank financial entities. Nonbank entities such as

---

[119] Mark Green, *Why HARP Isn't Working*, Forbes (Oct. 17, 2012), https://www.forbes.com/sites/moneybuilder/2012/10/17/why-harp-isnt-working/#586368bd3443.

[120] HARP, *supra* note 118 at 1.

[121] *Id.* at 3.

[122] *Id.* at 8.

[123] Dodd-Frank Wall Street Reform and Consumer Protection Act, Pub. L. 11–203§ 1001 (2009).

Countrywide and Ameriquest had been increasing their market share in the run-up to the crisis and played an important role in creating it. Yet, they had no federal regulator. The CFPB stepped into this void.

There is no middle ground when it comes to the CFPB. Consumer advocates and the Democrats love it and the Republican Party hates it.[124] The CFPB was the brainchild of Senator Elizabeth Warren, who conceived of the bureau while she was still a Harvard Law School professor. Consumer advocates had hoped she would be the agency's first director. She proved to be too controversial and Richard Cordray became the agency director in her stead. Under Director Cordray's leadership the agency moved aggressively to address not only the issues that caused the crisis, but also many of the lingering afteraffects.

The Consumer Financial Protection Bureau responded to the numerous servicing issues by enacting regulations that specify how servicers must interact with their customers.[125] These rules were intended to provide a framework for servicers to use when responding to borrower requests and complaints, maintaining and providing accurate information, helping borrowers in avoiding unnecessary costs and, when necessary, assisting with foreclosure loss mitigation. Despite these regulations, the CFPB continued to receive hundreds of complaints about mortgage servicers each month.[126] The regulations do not require lenders to offer any specific loan modification program; lenders are instead required to reach out to homeowners before foreclosure and, if they have a modification program, to comply with certain rules when a customer applies for it. Behavioral economists suggest that the presence of a required process can actually change behavior by moving an organization from passivity into action.[127] In the case of servicers, having a process to evaluate a loss mitigation package seems to have moved the industry from the status quo of not considering loss mitigation to a new norm of loss mitigation.[128] It is yet to be seen if this change is permanent. We are already beginning to see some back-sliding in

---

[124] *See*, Chris Arnold, *Trump Administration Plans to Defang Consumer Watchdog*, NPR (Feb. 12, 2018, 5:11 AM), https://www.npr.org/2018/02/12/584980698/trump-administration-to-defang-consumer-protection-watchdog; Alan Rappeport, *Mick Mulvaney Calls for 'Humility' from Consumer Financial Protection Bureau*, N.Y. TIMES (Jan. 23, 2018), https://www.nytimes.com/2018/01/23/us/politics/mick-mulvaney-consumer-financial-protection-bureau.html; Michael Grunwald, *Mulvaney Requests No Funding for Consumer Financial Protection Bureau*, POLITICO (Jan. 18, 2018, 9:00 AM), https://www.politico.com/story/2018/01/18/mulvaney-funding-consumer-bureau-cordray-345495.

[125] CONSUMER FIN. PROT. BUREAU, CFPB PROVIDES GUIDANCE ON MORTGAGE SERVICING RULES (Oct. 15, 2013), https://www.consumerfinance.gov/about-us/newsroom/cfpb-provides-guidance-on-mortgage-servicing-rules.

[126] *See*, i.e., CONSUMER FIN. PROTECTION BUREAU, MONTHLY COMPLAINT REP., VOL. 19 (Jan. 2017), https://files.consumerfinance.gov/f/documents/201701_cfpb_Monthly-Complaint-Report.pdf.

[127] *See generally*, Michael Collins & Carly Urban, *The Dark Side of Sunshine: Regulatory Oversight and Status Quo Bias*, 107 J. ECON. BEHAV. ORG. 1, 16 (2014).

[128] *Id.* at 8–9.

attention to loss mitigation application. While most of the remnants of the financial crisis have been negative, the servicing regulations are among one of the few positives.

The bureau was also very responsive to the issues faced by specific subsets of borrowers. One such set is known as the "successors in interest."[129] A successor in interest is someone whose ownership interest in a property has changed due to divorce or death of the primary loan holder. This most commonly occurs when one spouse is the co-owner on the house, but not an obligor under the note. When the obligating spouse dies, the surviving spouse is left to try to sort out the mortgage. The Garn-St. Germain Act, a federal statute, prohibits banks from automatically putting a loan into default because the borrower has died.[130] (If one spouse dies and the other simply continues paying the mortgage, nothing really has changed.) Unfortunately, complications often arise. Take for example, the story of Melissa Samuels. Her husband, George, always took care of paying the bills and, as far as she knew, the mortgage. A truck driver who spent much time on the road, he suffered a fatal heart attack. When it came time to make the next month's mortgage payment, the bank refused to tell Melissa the status of the mortgage or the payment amount because the loan was solely in George's name. Shortly afterwards, she received foreclosure paperwork. Her husband had stopped paying the mortgage months earlier. The bank refused to allow her to apply for a loan modification – again because the loan was in George's name. After failed negotiations and threats of a lawsuit failed, we filed a complaint to the CFPB. Melissa was finally able to assume the loan, bring it current and begin making payments.

The Consumer Financial Protection Bureau's intervention has been particularly valuable for successors-in-interest. It expanded the definition of this term beyond spouses, to children and other relatives who may have inherited property upon the death of the homeowner. Even more importantly, it includes divorced spouses as well.[131] The rule also provides a set of steps that a servicer must undertake to identify and communicate with the successor-in-interest. And, most significantly, it must provide successors-in-interest with the same loss mitigation offerings as the original borrower.[132] This is not to say that all problems have disappeared for successors-in-interest. It always takes time for the industry to catch up to regulations. At the same time, the regulations provide a framework that has survived the crisis and has the potential to become a permanent part of mortgage lending.

In a set of regulations interpreting the Real Estate Settlement Procedures Act (RESPA), the bureau tackled "force-placed insurance," a persistent problem that

---

[129] Consumer Fin. Prot. Bureau, CFPB Bull. No. 2013–12, Implementation Guidance for Certain Mortgage Servicing Rules, Oct. 15, 2013.

[130] 12 U.S.C. §1701j-3 (2006).

[131] 12 C.F.R. § 1026.2(a)(27)(i) (2016).

[132] 12 C.F.R. § 1024.38 (2016).

forced many unsuspecting homeowners into foreclosure during the crisis.[133] Force-placed insurance is exactly what the name suggests. It is insurance placed on a loan, without borrower permission, because the homeowners are thought to have failed to purchase their own homeowners' insurance. The insurance covers damage and loss to the property, though not its contents. The lender, not the homeowner, is the beneficiary. There is nothing theoretically wrong with force-placed insurance. However, servicers frequently purchase insurance that is many times costlier than what borrowers could have bought on their own. Often, servicers reap additional profits from the purchase because the insurance company has a close corporate relationship to the servicer. During the crisis, many homeowners – including a sizeable number of our clients – found force-placed insurance on their loans, despite having purchased their own policy. The cost of the force-placed insurance was added to their escrow account, increasing their monthly payments and sending them into foreclosure. Errors were not corrected, and refunds not issued, despite requests made to the servicer. The new rules require the servicer to inform homeowners before force-placing insurance on a loan, giving them the opportunity to send proof of the existing insurance. The servicer is required to refund any premiums paid in error.[134]

The CFPB also enacted multiple regulations aimed at preventing another lending crisis. Most significant of these was the "know before you owe" regulations.[135] A recurring narrative during the run up to the crisis was that of a homeowner who signed documents he or she failed to understand. As mentioned previously, closings were occurring so quickly in some cities that closing agents sometimes refused to allow borrowers to read the loan paperwork. The regulations required lenders to accurately disclose to borrowers what their loan payments would be. This is especially important for variable-rate loans, which make it very hard for homeowners to calculate the possible range of mortgage payments they have agreed to. The traditional loan documents only gave the payment for the initial (often the lowest) interest rate. The new rules require disclosure of the current payment, but also of the payments that would be required as the interest rate increases. The theory behind these disclosures is that a homeowner will be less likely to agree to a loan if the mortgage could increase to an unaffordable amount. Many consumer law regulations are based on the idea that, by disclosing crucial terms and other information, they are enabling a consumer to make rational decisions.

This assumption, however, is being challenged by both traditional economists and emerging behavioral economics theorists.[136] People tend to have an optimistic view of their prospects. So, for example, they look at a payment increase and

[133] 12 C.F.R. § 1024.37.

[134] *Id.*

[135] CONSUMER FIN. PROTECTION BUREAU, KNOW BEFORE YOU OWE/ MORTGAGE, https://www .consumerfinance.gov/know-before-you-owe.

[136] *See also*, George Loewenstein, Cass R. Sunstein & Russsell Golman, *Disclosure: Psychology Changes Everything*, 6 ANNUAL REV. ECON. 391 (2014).

convince themselves that, when it falls due, they will be earning more money. Such optimism does not always mirror reality. Besides, disclosure does not stop those whose intent is to defraud. True consumer protection requires a combination of disclosure and enforcement. The "know before you owe" rules will, therefore, only make a long-term difference if they are combined with vigorous supervision and enforcement. Unfortunately, the current direction of the CFPB suggests a lack of commitment to either.

Director Cordray resigned as the director of the CFPB soon after Donald Trump was elected President. Trump installed Mick Mulvaney, one of the bureau's harshest critics, as acting director.[137] One of Mr. Mulvaney's first acts was to "freeze hiring, rulemaking and regulatory actions for 30 days."[138] The thirty days now seems never-ending. His second decision was to change the agency's mission.[139] He inserted therein the language "by regularly identifying and addressing outdated, unnecessary, or unduly burdensome regulations."[140] Needless to say, outdated and unnecessary regulations did not cause the financial crisis. In fact, the agency has been a lifeline for many consumers. We have already discussed the servicing regulations. These alone make the CFPB a much-needed source of relief for consumers.

A series of other actions followed, including dismantling the fair housing unit and shifting the focus of the bureau away from consumers. Acting Director Mulvaney even changed the name from Consumer Financial Protection Bureau to the Bureau of Consumer Financial Protection, emphasizing the bureaucracy over the consumer. Part of the law creating the CFPB required the director to create a Consumer Advisory Board (CAB) and meet with them at least twice a year. Acting Director Mulvaney canceled the February and June meetings with the CAB and then dismantled the entire group, firing all twenty-five members. (One of us was a member until that June 2018 mass firing.) The CAB's purpose was to meet regularly, advise the bureau on what was happening in the marketplace, and consult with it on issues that impact consumers. It was working very well in the view of both consumer groups and industry.[141] The bureau gave a number of inconsistent and

---

[137] Interview with Rep. Mick Mulvaney (calls CFPB a "sick joke"), https://www.youtube.com/watch?v=RaVeNafdyVA.

[138] Gillian B. White, *Mick Mulvaney Is Quickly Deregulating the Financial Industry*, THE ATLANTIC (Jan. 5, 2018), https://www.theatlantic.com/business/archive/2018/01/cfpb-gop-trump/549755.

[139] Gillian B. White, *The CFPB's New Mission*, THE ATLANTIC (Jan. 25, 2018), https://www.theatlantic.com/business/archive/2018/01/cfpb-trump-mulvaney/551504.

[140] *Id.*

[141] Op-ed, Kathleen Engel & Judith Fox, *Mick Mulvaney Fired Us for Advocating for Consumers*, CNN (June 14, 2018), https://www.cnn.com/2018/06/08/opinions/mick-mulvaney-doing-the-financial-sectors-dirty-work-by-abolishing-cab/index.html; Joanne Needleman, *A Proper Goodbye for the Consumer Advisory Board*, INSIDEARM (June 11, 2018), https://www.insidearm.com/news/00044044-proper-goodbye-consumer-advisory-board; Arjan Schutte, *I Was on the CFPB's Consumer Advisory Board. Until Mulvaney Fired Me*, AM. BANKER (June 12, 2018), https://www.americanbanker.com/opinion/i-was-on-the-cfpbs-consumer-advisory-board-until-mulvaney-fired-

ever-changing reasons for the change, including its desire to make the group more diverse.

Prior to June 2018, the Charter for the Consumer Advisory Board called for membership of "no fewer than sixteen members" all serving staggered, three-year terms drawn from

> consumer protection, financial services, community development, fair lending and civil rights, and consumer financial products or services and representatives of depository institutions that primarily serve underserved communities, and represen- tatives of communities that have been significantly impacted by higher-priced mortgage loans, and seek representation of the interests of covered persons and consumers, without regard to party affiliation.[142]

The new charter creates one-year terms for six members, all appointed by the "Regional Reserve Bank Presidents."[143] This, apparently, makes the group more diverse? In addition, the new director eliminated two other advisory boards, the Credit Union Advisory Counsel and Community Bank Advisory Counsel, neither of which was statutorily mandated and neither of which has been reconsti- tuted to date.

One of the more interesting, and decidedly less convincing reasons given for the changes, was that they were called for in the recent responses for Requests for Information (RFI) on Consumer Engagement.[144] The bureau had previously issued many RFIs, a procedure that calls for comments from the public within a specified, statutory period. We will revisit the large numbers of RFIs issued under Mr. Mulvaney in a moment. Relevant to this conversation, the deadline to submit comments pursuant to the RFIs blamed for the decision occurred on May 29, 2018, mere days before the decision to disband the advisory boards was announced on June 6, and months after the previous meetings had been canceled. In addition, a review of those responses demonstrates that there was no call to disband the CAB anywhere in them.[145] When this was pointed out, Mr. Welcher, the bureau's spokesman, admitted as much, adding that, "[I]n the final review, nothing changed

me?utm_campaign=daily%20briefing-jun%2013%202018&utm_medium=email&utm_source= newsletter&eid=4855d71cb83bafbbeb8260c003ba590e&bxid=5a7cb577fc2383ac778b50cb.

[142] Consumer Fin. Protection Bureau Consumer Advisory Board, https://files.consumerfi nance.gov/f/1209_cfpb_cabcharter.pdf.

[143] Bureau of Consumer Fin. Protection, Charter of the Consumer Advisory Board, https://s3.amazonaws.com/files.consumerfinance.gov/f/documents/bcfp_cab_charter-amend ment_2018.pdf. (By the time the new charter came out, Acting Director Mulvaney had changed the name of the agency to deemphasize "consumer" in favor of "bureau.")

[144] Bureau of Consumer Fin. Protection, Request for Information Regarding Bureau External Engagement, Docket No. CFPB-2018–0005 (Feb. 21, 2018), https://files.consumer finance.gov/f/documents/cfpb_rfi_external-engagements_022018.pdf.

[145] CFPB, Request for Information Regarding Bureau External Engagement, public comments, https://www.consumerfinance.gov/policy-compliance/notice-opportunities-com ment/archive-closed/request-information-regarding-bureau-external-engagements.

from the direction we were headed."[146] In other words, the bureau planned to dismantle the advisory boards and hoped the RFIs would give justification for this action. When they did not, Mr. Mulvaney proceeded anyway.

It is clearly impossible at this point to determine what other changes are being contemplated at the CFPB. (Mr. Mulvaney renamed the CFPB the BCFP, placing the bureau and its attending bureaucracy before the consumer.) However, the numerous Requests for Information – thirteen between January and April 2018 – gives us some suggestion.[147] They ask for input on everything from how the bureau should supervise companies within its jurisdiction to whether it should eliminate existing laws that protect consumers. What emerges is a blueprint for a plan to decimate the bureau to benefit big business at the expense of consumers. While enforcement appears to be reengaging, consumer restitution – a significant hallmark of past enforcement actions – is missing. Under Director Cordray, $11.8 billion was returned to consumers wronged by the financial industry.[148] None of the enforcement actions to date under Acting Director Mulvaney include reimbursements for consumers. Again, the entire focus of the agency has become one of protecting business from consumers. Of all federal governmental actions in the wake of the crisis, the CFPB has been one of the most important to consumers. The bureau has given them a voice – a voice they are now in danger of losing.

Seth Frotman, assisting director and student loan ombudsman at the CFPB, captured the sentiment perfectly in his letter of resignation. He explained that the bureau under Mick Mulvaney had "abandoned the very consumers it is tasked by Congress with protecting." Instead, he accuses Mr. Mulvaney of using "the Bureau to serve the wishes of the most powerful financial companies in America." He goes on to conclude,

> [t]he American Dream is under siege, told through the heart wrenching stories of individuals caught in a system rigged to favor the most powerful financial interests. For seven years, the Consumer Financial Protection Bureau fought to ensure these families received a fair shake as they strived for the American Dream. Sadly, the damage you [Mick Mulvaney] have done to the Bureau betrays these families and sacrifices the financial futures of millions of Americans in communities across the country.[149]

---

[146] June 6, 2018 call with current members of the Consumer Advisory Board, the Credit Union Advisory Board and the Community Lender's Advisory Board.

[147] CFPB, *supra* note 144.

[148] Lucinda Shen, *Donald Trump Is Targeting an Agency That Has Recovered $11.8 Billion for Consumers*, Fortune (Jan. 27, 2017, http://fortune.com/2017/01/27/donald-trump-cfpb-consumer-protection-financial-bureau-elizabeth-warren.

[149] Resignation letter of Seth Frotman, Aug. 27, 2018, https://www.nclc.org/images/pdf/student_loans/Frotman_Letter.pdf.

5

Rethinking *Home*: Housing Post-Crisis

The house of everyman is to him as a castle and fortresse,
as well as his defense against injury and violence, as his repose.

Judge, Sir Edward Coke

Judge Coke's famous metaphor simplified over the years to "your home is your castle," reminds us of the importance of home throughout our history. *Home*, however, is not synonymous with *housing* or even *property*. This distinction has been absent from the property theory debates raging among scholars for decades. These debates run parallel to similar discussions in the social sciences about the meaning of *home* that fail to acknowledge the legal landscape in which they operate.[1] Before we discuss the changing housing landscape, it is important to briefly consider how to reconcile the legal views of property with the social science view of *home*.

Traditional property theorists viewed property from two perspectives: (1) as in Judge Coke's formulation that peoples' homes are their castles and something over which they hold domain and (2) as a thing, a commodity and an investment in a marketplace.[2] These theories developed in tandem. Recently, however, the view of property changed from that of a single monolithic whole to a "bundle of rights."[3] Legal theory has continued to evolve and this topic has sparked considerable debate.[4] Professor Henry E. Smith expanded the concept of a bundle of rights to

---

[1] Shelley Mallett, *Understanding Home: A Critical Review of the Literature*, 52 Soc. Rev. 62 (2004).

[2] Joseph William Singer, *The Ownership Society and Takings of Property, Castles, Investments, and Just Obligations*, 30 Harv. Envtl L. Rev. 309, 314–16 (2006).

[3] Jane B. Baron, *Rescuing the Bundle-of-Rights Metaphor in Property Law*, 82 U. Cin. L. Rev. 57, 58–9 (2013).

[4] *See, i.e., Id.*; Singer, *supra* note 2; Henry E. Smith, *Property as the Law of Things*, 125 Harv. L. Rev. 1691 (2012).

conceive of property not relating to a *thing*, but "a law of modular things."[5] According to him, property theory is a theory of relationships and the management of information. His and many similar theories of property are heavily influenced by economic theory, and particularly cost-benefit analysis. But, as Professor Joseph W. Singer points out, property is more than "the allocation of scarce resources, the management of complex information, or the coordination of land use among competing users."[6] A comprehensive theory of property requires "normative judgments that cannot be addressed by an economic cost-benefit analysis or a laser-like focus on the information costs of the alternative solutions. Rather, we are confronted with a choice among values."[7] In the end, he argues – and we agree – that property is "not merely the law of things. Property is the law of democracy."[8] Rather than choose sides in this debate, we would like to broaden the scope of discussion. What, then, does it mean in a democratic society when people may be able to find "housing" but, so few can find a "home"?

At this point, the debate about the meaning of *home* becomes relevant. Outside the constraints of legal scholarship, a multidisciplinary debate has also been taking place around the meaning of *home*.[9] Lorna Fox's *Conceptualising Home: Theories, Laws and Policies* is an attempt to introduce the concept of *home* to the world of property law.[10] *Home* is much more than simply a place to lay your head. In fact, you can have housing but still be *homeless*. Researchers have found that "shelter is not the only significant attribute of a home." The idea of *home* encompasses a range of psychological and social concepts.[11] It helps form our identity, our family structure and even our place in the social order. The loss of a *home* is therefore so much more than the loss of housing. Many lost both during the crisis, but it is that struggle to regain *home* that plagues us still. For example, Tamilynn Willoughby, whose story of her lender's abuse of mortgage mediation is chronicled in Chapter 2, generally has a place to stay these days (though she did live in her car for a couple of weeks last year), but she does not have a home – her small oceanfront home was mistakenly sold and then razed, making way for a large new house, years ago. Ms. Willoughby sometimes stays with family in another state, sometimes rents a room weekly and other times couch-surfs at various friends' homes. Needless to say, she is yearning for a real home again.

---

[5] Smith, *supra* note 4, at 1700–1.
[6] Joseph William Singer, *Property as the Law of Democracy*, 63 DUKE L. J. 1287, 1299 (2014).
[7] *Id.* at 1332.
[8] *Id.* at 1335.
[9] *See*, Mallet supra 1.
[10] LORNA FOX, CONCEPTUALISING HOME: THEORIES, LAWS AND POLICIES (2007), chapter 6 is especially relevant to this debate.
[11] Lorna Fox, *The Meaning of Home: A Chimerical Concept or a Legal Challenge*, 29 J. L. SOC'Y, 580, 591 (2002).

THE CHANGING DEMOGRAPHICS OF HOMEOWNERSHIP

It is not surprising that the number of people who own their home would have decreased in the aftermath of a foreclosure crisis. It is impossible to know for certain exactly how many of those who lost a home in the Great Recession were home-owners as opposed to investors. Researchers at the Urban Institute estimate that the owner-occupied homes lost between 2007 and 2015 caused the overall rate of homeownership to drop by 3.3 percentage points.[12] It is the best estimate we have found. A few have been able to rejoin the housing market, but many others seem wary of reentering a market that let them down so significantly in their recent memory. Tighter credit standards have made it difficult for many to obtain a mortgage. This has been exacerbated by the mounting student loan debt many prospective buyers have accumulated.[13] Of greater concern is the apparent lack of interest in home ownership among millennials, those born between 1981 and 1996. In 2004, 43 percent of individuals under thirty-five owned their own home. That number was just 35 percent in 2014. Millennials were especially hard-hit by the Great Recession, but even millennials who can afford to buy are not doing so at the same rate as previous generations. They are also not forming households at the same rate.[14] Largely as a result of this, the number of "new household formation[s] fell from about 1.5 million households per year from 1997–2007 to around 500,000 per year from 2017–2010."[15] In 2016, millennials made up the largest share of the labor force, those either working or looking for work.[16] They also have the highest unemployment rate of any cohort, averaging 12.8 percent since 2000 compared to an average of 4.8 percent for all others.[17] This group is more educated than previous generations, but also has significantly higher student loan debt. The high cost of housing, combined with the burden of student loan debt, is keeping most millen-nials out of the housing market.[18] Ironically, these factors also are driving up rental costs, making renting unaffordable.

---

[12] Laurie S. Goodman & Christopher Mayer, *Homeownership and the American Dream*, 32 J. ECON. PERSP. 31, 35 (2018).

[13] *Id.* at 42.

[14] Scott Berridge, *Millennials after the Great Recession*, BUREAU OF LABOR STATISTICS (Sept. 2014), https://www.bls.gov/opub/mlr/2014/beyond-bls/millennials-after-the-great-reces sion.htm.

[15] Jeff Larrimore, Jenny Schuetz & Samuel Dodini, *What Are the Perceived Barriers to Home-ownership for Young Adults?* (Board of Governors for the Fed. Res., Fin. and Econ. Discussion Series 2016–021), 1 http://dx.doi.org/10.17016/FEDS.2016.021.

[16] Richard Fry, *Millennials Are the Largest Generation in the U.S. Labor Force*, PEW RES. CTR (Apr. 11, 2018), http://www.pewresearch.org/fact-tank/2018/04/11/millennials-largest-generation-us-labor-force.

[17] Jill Mislinski, *Millennials and the Labor Force: A Look at the Trends*, ADVISOR PERSP., https://www.advisorperspectives.com/dshort/updates/2018/10/10/millennials-and-the-labor-force-a-look-at-the-trends.

[18] Larrimore, *supra* note 15, at 17–8.

The drop in homeownership since the crisis is not evenly distributed across demographic groups. Homeownership rates for African Americans have decreased more than for Asians and whites since the crisis.[19]

[B]lack households lost ground over ... [the last thirty years], with their home-ownership rate of 43.1 percent in 2017 standing 2.7 percentage points below the 1987 level. Moreover, the black homeownership rate is also 6.6 percentage points below its mid-2000s peak, considerably more than the 5.0 percentage point difference for Asians, 3.4 percentage point difference for Hispanics, and 3.7 percentage point difference for whites. Taken together, these trends mean that while the Hispanic-white and Asian-white homeownership gaps have narrowed somewhat over the past three decades, the black-white gap has widened substantially.[20]

While these statistics are unsurprising, given that predatory subprime loan products were aimed at these neighborhoods, the disparity remains even when corrected for income. The rate of homeowners with a high school diploma or less has also seen a significant decline, relative to those with a college degree. In 1985 there was little difference in rates of homeownership between these two cohorts. In 2015, 71.4 percent of college-educated Americans owned their home compared to only 48.6 percent of those with a high school diploma or less.[21] Now, ten years out from the crisis, this appears to be less of a blip in the statistics and more like a new reality in the housing market. The growing wage gap has become the growing housing gap. At the same time, it may not all be bad news. Increases in homeownership prior to 2005 may have been artificially high. The growth was fueled by predatory, subprime products and a public policy that believed everyone should own their own home, but without the supports needed to sustain those homes.[22]

Many people discovered the negatives of owning a home during the crisis. Some homeowners who lost their jobs were unable to relocate when they could not sell their homes. Others, like Susie Simmons, whose full story we will tell in the next chapter, gave up and left anyway, abandoning their property to the bank. The length of time people stayed in their jobs increased during the crisis, suggesting that it prevented some who had hoped to switch to higher-paying jobs from doing so.[23]

We are beginning to see a shift in attitudes away from the need to own a house, to the need to find a *home*. A home is a safe, stable place to make a life. Americans still believe that home stability increases the safety and economic well-being of a community, but in a change from years past, a majority also believes that renters

[19] Goodman, *supra* note 12, at 35.

[20] *The State of the Nation's Housing 2018*, JOINT CTR FOR HOUSING STUD. OF HARVARD U. 19–20 (2008), http://www.jchs.harvard.edu/sites/default/files/Harvard_JCHS_State_of_the_Nations_Housing_2018.pdf.

[21] Goodman, *supra* note 12, at 37.

[22] *Id.* at 41.

[23] *The State of American Jobs*, PEW RES. CTR. 19 (Oct. 6, 2016), http://www.pewsocialtrends.org/2016/10/06/1-changes-in-the-american-workplace.

can be as stable and successful as homeowners.[24] In a survey completed just as the crisis was winding down, healthy majorities saw homeownership as a risky investment, both from the standpoint of wealth building and because it was perceived that lenders are quick to foreclose.[25] Yet, studies have consistently found that most Americans would like to eventually own a home, even when acknowledging that economically, it may never be possible.[26] We need to be better innovators and look at alternative ways to secure housing that include homeownership, but not exclusively. It may be too early to determine if this trend away from homeownership is permanent or a short-term remnant of the crisis. Recently, home purchase demand has begun to grow again.[27] For most of our clients, though, homeownership is now a faraway dream, and even, for some, the return of a recurring nightmare.

Lurking in the background of these issues is the dwindling of much-needed new home construction.[28] On the materials side, lumber and construction costs have increased, and fewer construction workers are in the market to be hired.[29] Not only that, but new homes have become considerably bigger over the years, increasing the cost of starter homes.[30] Tightening credit and underwriting standards after the recession have also contributed to the inability of many to buy, rather than rent. Although lenders should have restricted access to credit before the housing bust, instead they seem to have overreacted to the crisis afterwards by limiting mortgage credit availability to only those with pristine credit reports and stellar credit scores.[31]

---

[24] *How Housing Matters: Americans' Attitudes Transformed by the Housing Crisis & Changing Lifestyles: A Report of Findings Based on a National Survey Among Adults*, JOHN D. AND KATHERINE T. MCARTHUR FOUNDATION (Apr. 3, 2013), 3–4, 13, https://www.macfound.org/media/files/HHM_Hart_report_2013.pdf.

[25] *Id.* at 10.

[26] Goodman, supra note 12, at 42.

[27] *The State of the Nation's Housing, supra* note 20, at 2–3: "After a decade of soaring rental demand, US households are edging their way back into the homebuyer market. Growth in the number of renter households slowed from 850,000 annually on average in 2005–2015 to just 220,000 in 2015–2017, while the number of owner households rose 710,000 annually on average in the past two years. This reversal lifted the national homeownership rate to 63.9 percent last year."

[28] Herb Weisbaum, *Supply of Affordable Homes Expected to Shrink*, NBC NEWS (Feb. 21, 2017), https://www.nbcnews.com/business/real-estate/supply-affordable-homes-expected-shrink-n723536.

[29] See, *The State of the Nation's Housing, supra* note 20, at 9 (citing four issues constraining home construction:

(1) shortage of skilled workers, (2) the cost of building materials has risen, (3) developed land has become scarcer, and (4) local zoning and other land use regulations.

[30] *See Id.* at 8: "[E]ntry-level housing still accounts for a small share of new construction. Only 163,000 small single-family homes were completed in 2016, or 22 percent of single-family construction — down significantly from the 33 percent share averaged in 1999–2007 ... Modest-sized homes are considerably more affordable for first-time and middle-market buyers. According to the Survey of Construction, the median price for a small home sold in 2016 was $191,700."

[31] See, Maximiliano Dvorkin, Hannah Shell, *Why Did Loan Growth Stay Negative So Long after the Recession?*, ON THE ECON. BLOG (Jan. 11, 2016), https://www.stlouisfed.org/on-the-econ omy/2016/january/negative-loan-growth-great-recession.

Many of those rejected for credit in recent years because of, for example, self-employment, are readily able to make monthly mortgage payments out of savings.

Worsening the shortage of homes for sale is that investors have purchased over five million single-family homes, often at foreclosure sales or as REO stock, and converted them to rentals.[32] Many of these have been DASP sales, with investors buying hundreds of homes at once. Originally, most of these investors were hedge funds, but smaller investors have now entered the market. For instance, REO inventory has been returning to market in places like New Jersey, increasing the supply of existing homes for sale, but many are being purchased by both large and small investors who intend to rent them out.[33] One result has been that the single-family rental market has exploded in recent years. It seems unlikely that the newly rented homes will ever reenter the market for owner-occupied purchases, further decreasing supply. The phenomenon is especially acute in the lower third of the market.[34] Pent-up demand on the home purchase side then converts to increased demand for rentals.

THE AFFORDABILITY CRISIS IN RENTALS

As mentioned, while communities battle urban blight, a second housing crisis has emerged: Rental prices have soared across the country, reducing housing options and increasing inequality and gentrification. There is a relationship between the large number of foreclosures and these rent hikes (though many other factors come into play as well). The influx of new renters – many of them foreclosed upon homeowners – into the rental market has increased the demand for rental housing, helping to drive up rents. As we learned, fewer consumers have chosen to purchase a home, again increasing the demand for rentals. Both millennials and aging baby boomers have also shown an increasing preference for inner-city living, in close

---

[32] Aaron Terrazas, *Rising Single-Family Rentals Dampening Home Sales*, ZILLOW RES. (Dec. 12, 2017), https://www.zillow.com/research/single-family-rentals-bottom-17595.

> Zillow and Census data suggest that between 2006 and 2017, about 5.4 million single family homes transitioned from the owner-occupied to the rental stock. Among these homes, 2.4 million (45 percent) were homes in the bottom third of the housing market by home value, 1.8 million (33 percent) were in the middle third, and 1.2 million (22 percent) were in the top third of the housing market ... Assuming that about 5 percent of homes typically sell in a given year (roughly in line with historical norms), this would imply that the growth in single-family home rentals over the past decade have lowered annual home sales by about 270,000 units, or about 5 percent of the 5.4 million units that have sold in a typical recent year. This includes about 121,000 units in the most affordable third of the market and 59,000 in the most expensive third of the market. [citation omitted]

[33] Melanie Grayce West, *Why New Jersey's Soaring Foreclosures Are Good for the Housing Market*, WALL ST. J. (Mar. 5, 2018), https://www.wsj.com/articles/why-new-jerseys-soaring-fore closures-are-good-for-the-housing-market-1520082000.

[34] According to the Harvard Joint Center for Housing 2018 report, "Lower-cost homes are especially scarce. Virtually all of the 88 metros with data available had more homes for sale in the top third of the market by price than in the bottom third." *Supra* note 20, at 4.

proximity to services. This has helped drive gentrification and, as a result, much of the new construction consists of "luxury" apartments with granite countertops and stainless-steel appliances, open floorplans, easy access to transportation and high rents. One has only to drive around metropolitan areas like Atlanta and New York to see these new complexes springing up like mushrooms after a heavy rain.[35] These all combine to create a mismatch between renters in need of housing and the available housing, creating a market that is growing more stratified and unequal.[36]

The supply side of safe, affordable housing has been shrinking for years, long before the current crisis.[37] In fact, it is estimated that nearly 13 percent of the supply of affordable housing has been lost since 2001, and we did not have an adequate supply even then.[38] The federal government first became concerned with affordable rental markets during the Great Depression; thus the Housing Act of 1937 created the Section 8 Program. This is a voucher program and is still a valuable asset for our clients. The vouchers allow the tenant to rent a property on the open market. A tenant pays 30 percent of her income in rent and HUD pays the remainder. The property must pass an inspection proving it meets minimal habitability standards, a serious problem in low-income housing. This inspection requirement discourages some landlords from participating in the voluntary program. Congressional budget cuts in the midst of the crisis have exacerbated the problem. Section 8 vouchers, already in short supply, were reduced even further. Today, there are simply not enough vouchers to meet demand, and in city after city you will find online posts informing would-be tenants when new Section 8 vouchers will be available. Anywhere you look, the waiting lists to obtain a Section 8 voucher are years long, and the funding continues to decrease. At one point, Newark's waitlist was over twenty years long, but lately, it has been closed most of the time, occasionally opening for a few days before shutting again.[39]

After the Great Depression, the federal government continued to create programs ranging from rental supports to subsidized housing projects. The real boom in

---

[35] *See, The State of the Nation's Housing, supra* note 20, at 4: "[M]ultifamily construction ramped up quickly after the crash as rental demand surged. From a low of 109,000 units in 2009, construction of multifamily units peaked at 397,000 in 2015 and accounted for more than half the gains in housing starts over that period. However, the multifamily construction wave is now moderating."

[36] *See,* Susan Lund, Asheet Mehta, James Manyika & Diana Goldstein, A *Decade after the Global Financial Crisis: What Has (and Hasn't) Changed?,* MCKINSEY GLOBAL INST. BRIEFING (Sept. 2018), https://www.mckinsey.com/industries/financial-services/our-insights/a-decade-after-the-global-financial-crisis-what-has-and-hasnt-changed. [S]ky-high urban housing prices are contributing to other issues, including shortages of affordable housing options, strains on household budgets, reduced mobility and growing inequality of wealth.

[37] Mechele Dickerson, The Myth of Homeownership and Why Homeownership Is Not Alwaysa Good Thing, 84 Ind. L. J. 189, 233 (2009).

[38] Andrea J. Boyack, Equitably Housing (Almost) Half a Nation of Renters, 64 Buffalo L. Rev.109, 117 (2017).

[39] *See,* i.e., Newark, NJ Housing Authority, AFFORDABLE HOUSING ONLINE, https://affordablehousingonline.com/housing-authority/New-Jersey/Newark-Housing-Authority/NJ002.

construction came with the passage of the Housing Act of 1968, one of the goals of which was to build six million low-income rental units.[40] The federal government began to move away from direct rental assistance in the 1970s and between 1976 and 2000, HUD's housing assistance budget decreased by more than half.[41] Prior to 1995, the government had had a rule of replacing each low-income housing unit that was lost, but "between the mid 1990s and 2010, approximately 200,000 public housing units" were demolished, with only 50,000 built to replace them.[42] The move away from low-income housing was bipartisan. In fact, during the Clinton administration no funding was allocated for public housing construction.

Even before the crisis, the number of available subsidized housing rental units was low. But the crisis exacerbated the problem, both because the number of available properties was reduced by foreclosures, and because prospective renters – many of whom were former homeowners – had less than pristine credit. Most people misunderstand subsidies and governmental housing, believing that housing is available for anyone who is poor. Actually, applicants can be disqualified for bad credit, criminal history or the criminal history of a family member. Therefore, even if a displaced homeowner is lucky enough to live in a community with available public housing, he may be disqualified because of a previous foreclosure or other financial hardship.

The federal government has, for all practical purposes, abandoned the building of low-income housing to the private market. Some communities have reacted to this gap by requiring developers to create affordable housing, the results of which have been mixed.[43] New York City, for instance, offered tax abatements to developers who included a certain number of affordable units in their building projects. Yet, the "poor door" controversy in New York City is perhaps the most well-known example of the problems that can arise. A developer had created fifty-five affordable units in its luxury apartment building. The tenants of these units were required to enter at the rear of the building, or the "poor door" as the press named it. The other tenants entered in the front to be greeted in the spacious lobby by a round-the-clock doorman. The poor tenants had no dishwashers, no light fixtures in their bedrooms or living rooms and were forbidden to use any of the amenities reserved for their

[40] Alexander von Hoffman, *To Preserve Affordable Housing in the United States: A Policy History* (Working Paper, the Harvard Joint Center for Housing Studies, Mar. 2016), http://www.jchs .harvard.edu/sites/default/files/von_hoffman_to_preserve_affordable_housing_april16.pdf.

[41] *Changing Priorities: The Federal Budget and Housing Assistance, 1976–2002*, NAT. LOW INCOME HOUSING COALITION (May 2001), https://www.innovations.harvard.edu/sites/default/files/ nlihc_changing_priorities.pdf.

[42] Advocates Guide 2017, NAT. LOW INCOME HOUSING COALITION 4–8, http://nlihc.org/sites/ default/files/2017_Advocates-Guide.pdf.

[43] For instance, New Jersey's *Mount Laurel* mandate to create a fair share of affordable housing in each municipality has been successful for recipients, but problems remain. *Cf.* Editorial, *The Mount Laurel Doctrine*, N.Y. TIMES (Jan. 28, 2013) (referencing study by Princeton sociologist Douglas Massey documenting the success of the mandate).

wealthier neighbors, including a spacious outdoor courtyard, two gyms, a bowling alley and a movie theater.[44] Subsidized tenants are thus reminded every day of how unwelcome they really are. Basically, landlords are uninterested in affordable housing because they can profit more from renting at market rates.

The epidemic of high rents has reached crisis proportions across America.[45] In 2016, nearly 43 million Americans were renters, 9.3 million more than in 2004.[46] Interestingly, this jump is not driven by young families, as has been the pattern historically. The largest increase in renters has been among baby boomers, those born between 1946 and 1964.[47] This suggests, but does not prove, that the foreclosure crisis contributed to the increase because this is the same demographic that was most likely to own, and then lose, a home during the crisis. Increasingly, Americans are what has come to be known as "rent burdened," which is defined as paying more than 30 percent of one's income on rent. The number of rent burdened Americans increased 19 percent between 2001 and 2015, to 38 percent. The number of severely rent burdened Americans – those spending more than 50 percent of their income on rent – increased 42 percent over that same period, to 17 percent of all renters. As with homeownership, the statistics are not evenly distributed across demographic groups. In 2015, nearly half of all African Americans were rent burdened compared to a third of white Americans.

Rent burdened individuals suffer in many ways. Let us illustrate with some statistics for South Bend, where approximately 40 percent of the population was rent-burdened in 2016. The median monthly income is $2,091.66 and the median rent is $710, or 34 percent of gross income.[48] If we adjust that income to net income, the burden increases, but for the sake of illustration we will stay with the gross income figures. Below are expenses for a family of four living in St. Joseph County, Indiana, prepared by the ALICE project.[49]

---

[44] Melkorka Licea, *'Poor Door' Tenants of Luxury Tower Reveal the Apartheid Within*, N.Y. Post (Jan. 17, 2016), https://nypost.com/2016/01/17/poor-door-tenants-reveal-luxury-towers-financial-apartheid.

[45] *See, i.e,.* Michael Hobbes, *America's Housing Crisis Is Spreading to Smaller Cities*, HUFF POST (May 8, 2018), https://www.huffingtonpost.com/entry/housing-crisis-small-cities-boise_us_5ae878f7e4b055fd7fcfceeo; Joel Kotkin, *Rising Rents Are Stressing Out Tenants and Heightening America's Housing Crisis*, FORBES (Oct. 19, 2017), https://www.forbes.com/sites/joelkotkin/2017/10/19/rising-rents-us-housing-crisis/#1d71aaf01ef5; Bryce Covert, *The Deep, Uniquely American Roots of Our Affordable-Housing Crisis*, THE NAT. (May 24, 2018), https://www.thenation.com/article/give-us-shelter.

[46] *American Families Face Growing Rent Burden*, PEW CHARITABLE TRUST FOUND. 5 (Apr. 2018), https://www.pewtrusts.org/-/media/assets/2018/04/rent-burden_report_v2.pdf.

[47] Id. at 5.

[48] Eviction Lab, https://evictionlab.org/map/#/2016?geography=cities&bounds=-86.522,41.588, -86.03,41.77&locations=1871000,-86.276,41.679; U.S. Census Bureau, South Bend, Indiana, https://www.census.gov/quickfacts/fact/table/southbendcityindiana/HSG860216#viewtop.

[49] Asset Limited, Income Constrained, Employed, Nov. 2014, 204 https://iprc.iu.edu/spf/docs/United %20Way%20ALICE%20Report%20by%20County.pdf. ALICE is a project of United Ways across

Income:	$2,091.66
Rent:	$ 710.00
Food:	$ 500.00
Taxes:	$ 241.00
Health Care:	$ 518.00
Transportation:	$ 681.00
	$ −558.34

As you can see, our typical family of four is $558.34 in the red, without paying any miscellaneous expenses, let alone utilities or an unexpected flat tire. What happens to most of these families? They join the mounting number of people being evicted across the country.

As Matthew Desmond has so eloquently warned us, both with his award-winning book, *Evicted*, and now in the accompanying research project, evictionlab.org, we have an eviction crisis in America. According to Professor Desmond, more people were evicted in 2016 than were foreclosed on during the height of the Great Recession.[50] As staggering as that is, the data that evictionlab.org has collected is incomplete. They are looking only at those evictions that actually come into court, and only evictions relating to rental properties. They are not counting people who simply move when the landlord asks, or who get locked out or otherwise illegally removed from a home. Evictionlab.org's numbers do not include people evicted due to tax or mortgage foreclosure. If you could find a way to count all the evictions – perhaps an impossible feat – everyone agrees the numbers would be much larger. Yet, this crisis is receiving very little attention.

South Bend, Indiana ranks eighteenth in the country for its number of evictions among cities of more than 100,000 residents, and Indiana has the distinction of having three cities in the top twenty. Indiana's laws are very unfriendly to tenants. As a result, it is exceedingly easy to abuse tenants and exceedingly difficult for tenants to defend themselves from an eviction. Weak landlord-tenant laws and the lack of legal representation are major barriers to housing stability. A stark example of this can be seen in the difference between eviction rates in South Bend, a location with weak tenant protections, and Newark, a community with strong landlord tenant laws. The two locations have comparable rates of poverty. Newark has a much higher percentage of renters, 78 percent compared to South Bend's 41 percent, yet the rate of evictions in South Bend is more than 60 percent higher than in Newark.

Landlords – especially commercial landlords of large apartment buildings – have a lot of lobbying power, making the passage of tenant-friendly legislation a serious

---

the country. The project measures the actual cost of basic needs in communities. The most recent figures are from 2014, making them a bit older than the income and rental data.

[50] Conference Call with Michael Desmond on the launch of evictionlab.org.

challenge. In some ways, this may be the fault of advocates – including us – who have failed to educate legislators on the many negative consequences of housing instability. We know that involuntary moves cause a number of issues ranging from bad health outcomes to poor performance in school.[51] In addition, evictions cost local economies in unpaid taxes and utilities, increased health care costs and costs related to social services. Perhaps if cities realized the costs of eviction – similar to those of foreclosure – policymakers would be more inclined to tackle the issue.

An equally vexing problem is the condition of many of the so-called affordable rental units our clients are often forced to live in because they can't find an alternative. (Those who can double up with family do so, but then apartments become both overcrowded and substandard.) In 2015, the Joint Center on Housing reported that "one in seven affordable housing units (renting for less than $650 a month) is physically inadequate."[52] We have had multiple clients whose ceilings collapsed on everything from the bathroom shower to the child's playroom. We have had clients whose walls were black with mold. One landlord removed the furnace from a home and sold it, making the temperature inside so cold that the liquid detergent froze on the counter. Another landlord – angry that his tenants had banded together to report the conditions in the property – shut off all the water for a month during the hottest part of the summer. In Indiana, tenants are not permitted to withhold rent in these situations. They are permitted to go to court to request a court order. In this case, they were able to obtain a court order, but the landlord ignored it and the judge inquired "why don't you just move?" The housing code inspectors became involved, but in the end the housing court judge placed a "vacate and seal" order on the unit due to the unhealthy conditions. The landlord got exactly what he wanted – he evicted the tenants illegally when he could not evict them legally – and the tenants were rendered homeless. Housing code officers are required to report to child protective services if housing conditions present health hazards to children living in the house, creating a further disincentive for tenants to report such conditions. Tenants are then faced with the awful choice of asserting their rights, and possibly becoming homeless or having their children placed in foster care, or shutting up and enduring the conditions. All too many choose the latter.

THE RESURGENCE OF CONTRACT BUYING

As people become desperate for any way to find housing, predatory practices have risen. Some of these are not so much new, but rather reinventions of old predatory products. In the 1950s and early 1960s, African Americans moved north in large

---

[51] Brett Theodos & Sara McTarnaghan, Claudia Coulton, *Family Residential Instability: What Can States and Localities Do?*, URBAN INST. 7–8 (May 2018), https://www.urban.org/sites/default/files/publication/98286/family_residential_instability_what_can_states_and_localities_do_1.pdf.

[52] *Id.* at 4.

numbers, both to escape the violence in the south and to take advantage of the manufacturing boom that offered a middle-class life. Many found themselves unable to purchase homes because of either the racially restrictive covenants or the financial service industry's practice of of redlining minority neighborhoods. Beryl Satter, in *Family Properties*, chronicles how many of these desperate families became victims of predatory rent-to-own contracts. In Chicago, a young seminarian named Jack Macnamara organized these families into the Contract Buyers League. They held rental strikes and, in the end, were able to renegotiate many of these contracts into affordable mortgages.[53]

In 2016, Jack Macnamara contacted us. Now an elderly man, he was resurrecting the Contract Buyers League and researching the reemergence of predatory land sales contracts. The practice had returned to Chicago and – as we soon learned – to many other parts of the country. Once again, the federal government was largely to blame. As mentioned in the previous chapter, the GSEs sought to reduce their backlog of nonperforming loans by selling them in auction. Between 2010 and 2014, Harbour Portfolio was the largest purchaser of properties from Fannie Mae, but not the only one.[54] Many of these loans were purchased by other hedge funds and venture capitalists. A large proportion of these homes were already abandoned at the time of the sale and many were uninhabitable. Instead of improving them, Harbour resold the properties to unsuspecting, mostly minority buyers in ways designed to get around existing consumer protections.[55] Many of the properties were sold with disguised land contracts, much like those sparking the original formation of the Contract Buyers League nearly fifty years earlier.

Contracts for the sale of real property go by many names, including "rent-to-own," "conditional land sale contracts" and "land contracts." They differ from mortgages in very significant ways. When a prospective homeowner buys a house by way of a mortgage, she owns the home, subject to the mortgage lien. If she subsequently

---

[53] BERYL SATTER, FAMILY PROPERTIES (2010); *see also* Richard Rothstein, The Color of Law: A Forgotten History of How Our Government Segregated America 97-997); (Introduction)

[54] Chuck Collins, *Private Equity: The New Neighborhood Loan Sharks: Veterans of the Contract Buyers League Hit the Doors Again*, THE AM. PROSPECT (July 11, 2017), http://prospect.org/article/private-equity-new-neighborhood-loan-sharks.

[55] *Id. See also*, Matthew Goldstein & Alexandra Stevenson, *Market for Fixer-Uppers Traps Low-Income Buyers*, N.Y. TIMES (Feb. 20, 2016), https://www.nytimes.com/2016/02/21/business/deal book/market-for-fixer-uppers-traps-low-income-buyers.html; Matthew Goldstein & Alexandria Stevenson, *Cincinnati Sues Seller of Foreclosed Homes, Claiming Predatory Behavior*, N.Y. TIMES (Apr. 20, 2017), https://www.nytimes.com/2017/04/20/business/dealbook/cincinnati-sues-harbour-seller-foreclosed-homes.html; Sarah Mancini & Margot Saunders, *Land Installment Contracts: The Newest Wave of Predatory Home Lending Threatening Communities of Color*, FED. RES. BANK OF BOSTON (Apr. 13, 2017), https://www.bostonfed.org/publications/commu nities-and-banking/2017/spring/land-installment-contracts-newest-wave-of-predatory-home-lend ing-threatening-communities-of-color.aspx; Alan Semuels, *A House You Can Buy, but Never Own*, THE ATLANTIC (Apr. 10, 2018), https://www.theatlantic.com/business/archive/2018/04/rent-to-own-redlining/557588.

defaults on the mortgage, she can cure the default. If the homeowner cannot cure the default, the home must be foreclosed on and sold. The homeowner is entitled to any equity in the property above the sale price. In contrast, a land contract purchaser does not own the home until every payment has been made and the owner transfers the title.[56] In the early years of a land contract, a default results in a forfeiture and summary eviction. The buyer loses the value of any equity and any repairs. In certain states, including Indiana and New Jersey, homeowners at some point are deemed to have enough equity that the law presumes the land contract to have become an equitable mortgage. If there is a default after this point, the seller would need to foreclose on the home as if it were a mortgage. Land contracts can be an effective way for a homeowner who is unable to obtain a mortgage to purchase a home. Unfortunately, they are all too often predatory products that do not result in homeownership.

In reselling its properties, Harbour Portfolio and others created a product that combines aspects of a lease agreement with those of a land contract. The prospective buyer is renting the property for a period of time after which, if she continues to make payments, she becomes an actual buyer. The properties are sold "as is," a euphemism for uninhabitable. Many contain a clause like this provision from a Kaja Holdings contract:

> the VENDOR transfers the said property to the VENDEE in strictly "AS IS" condition and the VENDEE is solely responsible for bringing the building and premises to a habitable condition within a reasonable period of time not exceeding THREE (3) months and maintaining the property in good state of repair during the term of this agreement.[57]

Some contracts even go so far as to forbid the prospective tenant from living in the home she is allegedly renting.[58] Every rental contract comes with an implied warranty of habitability. These contracts attempt to waive that responsibility by claiming the buyer is not a tenant, but a buyer.

But is she? The contracts require the tenant/buyer to pay all the property taxes, provide homeowners insurance and make all repairs to the property. These are the duties of an owner, not a tenant. A large, nonrefundable deposit, similar to a home buyer's down payment, is a common feature of these products; here, though, is where the similarities end. Unlike a mortgage payment, only a portion of the

---

[56] *See,* Jeremiah Battle, Sarah Mancini, Margot Sanders & Odette Williamson, *Toxic Transactions: How Land Installment Contracts One Again Threaten Communities of Color,* NAT'L CONSUMER L. CTR., July 2016; Alexandra Matthew Goldstein & Alexandra Stevenson, *Market for Fixer-Uppers Traps Low-Income Buyers,* N.Y. TIMES (Feb. 21, 2016), https://www.nytimes.com/2016/02/21/business/dealbook/market-for-fixer-uppers-traps-low-income-buyers.html.

[57] Document identification: 01611130014, recorded in Lorain County, Ohio.

[58] Horne et al. v. Harbour Portfolio et al., Case 1:17-CV-954-RWS, United States District Court, Northern District of Georgia.

contract payments are initially applied to the sale price, and those are often subject to conditions that make a sale unlikely to occur. If one payment is late, the buyer/tenant can be evicted quickly and easily. The implied warranty of habitability is explicitly waived, something not permitted in a rental agreement. The hallmark of these contracts is that they attempt to vest the seller with all the benefits of home-ownership, while placing all the burdens on the buyer. Likewise, the so-called tenant has none of the advantages, but all the disadvantages of tenancy.[59]

These contracts have become very controversial, prompting both investigations and litigation.[60] Advocates have alleged that Harbour Portfolio and other similar entities have seriously inflated the selling prices of homes. For instance, an unsuspecting Georgia buyer purchased one of these homes for $52,425 only three weeks after Harbour Portfolio had bought it from Fannie Mae for $15,543. Another homeowner was charged $34,500 for a property purchased for $10,467.[61] The documents the buyers receive are very confusing. For instance, many of these sellers use the standard HUD-1, a document used to disclose the costs of a mortgage transaction. It uses the word "mortgage" throughout even though this is not a mortgage. Letters are sent congratulating buyers on their home purchase, while at the same time disclaiming that the transaction is a sale, and reaffirming the buyers' obligations to make all repairs. The contracts routinely include mandatory arbitration clauses, something not permitted in a mortgage transaction.

FHFA's role in the sales has been one of the most troubling aspects of these cases.[62] History seems destined to repeat itself. Minority groups have long been prevented from purchasing homes due to the redlining encouraged by the federal government. During the subprime lending boom, the same previously redlined neighborhoods were targeted for subprime loans, or reverse redlining. When those homes fell into foreclosure, the government did little to help homeowners save them. As a result, these communities were soon full of nonperforming loans and abandoned properties. The federal government stepped in again, this time to sell the properties to hedge funds and speculators. These homes, now largely in deplorable conditions, are being resold in abusive rent-to-own contracts.

Numerous lawsuits have been filed, claiming these contracts disproportionately impact minority neighborhoods and therefore violate the Fair Housing Act.[63] While

---

[59] Matthew Goldstein & Alexandra Stevenson, *'Contract for Lease' Lender Gets Federal Scrutiny*, N.Y.TIMES (May 10, 2016), https://www.nytimes.com/2016/05/11/business/dealbook/contract-for-deed-lending-gets-federal-scrutiny.html.

[60] Matthew Goldstein, *States Acting to Protect Buyers of Seller-Financed Homes*, N.Y. TIMES (Oct. 3, 2017), https://www.nytimes.com/2017/10/03/business/states-acting-to-protect-buyers-of-seller-financed-homes.html.

[61] Horne et al. v. Harbour Portfolio et al., Case 1:17-CV-954-RWS, United States District Court, Northern District of Georgia, at 34.

[62] *See*, SATTER, *supra* note 53 and Rothstein, at 97–99.

[63] Demarkus R. Horne & Jackie Brown v. Harbor Portfolio VIII, LP et al., File 1:17-cv-954-RWS, (1:2017:cv:00954, (Northern District Georgia)); Espinoza, Kamano, Martinez & Tejada

none of the cases has been completely resolved, efforts by Harbour to have them dismissed have failed. In theory, at least, the courts acknowledge that the Fair Housing Act does apply. These sellers target minority groups, most commonly African Americans and Hispanics. Harbour Portfolio is only one of many players in this market. As a result of all the controversy, several states have adopted or are considering legislation to protect consumers from this type of transaction.[64] The Consumer Financial Protection Bureau initiated an investigation into Harbour Portfolio and took the aggressive step of suing in federal court when it failed to comply with an investigatory subpoena.[65] While the CFPB won its court case, it may, in the end, lose the war.[66] Once President Trump appointed Mick Mulvaney acting director of the bureau, investigations seemed to come to a halt. The fair housing unit of the CFPB was neutered.[67] It seems that any action on these predatory products will be left to the states and consumer advocates. On a more positive note, the outcry from community organizations and housing advocates has prompted the GSEs to stop selling nonperforming loans to entities engaging in these practices.[68] Still, for the victims, this result was too little, too late.

HOMELESSNESS IN AMERICA

Finally, policymakers' continued denial of the housing crisis may well make America not the land of homeowners, but the land of the homeless. Each year, during the last week of January, shelters and other organizations are asked to take a count of the homeless population in America. In 2017, American homelessness increased for the first time in seven years, a circumstance caused mainly by a 9 percent increase in the number of people living on the streets in major cities.[69] Roughly one-third of the homeless are families with children.[70] More tragically, children under the age of

v. Rainbow Realty et al., File 1:17-cv-1782, (Fair Housing Center of Central Indiana v. Rainbow Realty Group, No. 1:17-cv-01782-RLM-TAB (Southern District of Indiana)); City of Cincinnati v. Vision Property Management, docket A170256, Hamilton County Court of Common Pleas; State of Wisconsin v. Vision Properties et al., Circuit Court, Case 17-CX-003.

[64] Illinois recently passed the public law 100–0416. Michigan and Ohio are currently debating legislation.

[65] Matthew Goldstein, *Consumer Agency Seeks to Hold South Carolina Company in Contempt*, N.Y. TIMES (June 21, 2017), https://www.nytimes.com/2017/06/21/business/consumer-agency-seeks-to-hold-south-carolina-company-in-contempt.html.

[66] Court order of Feb. 15, 2017, C.F.P.B. v. Harbour Portfolio et al., Case No. 26–141833.

[67] Acting Director Mulvaney also changed the name of the organization from the Consumer Financial Protection Bureau to the Bureau of Consumer Financial Protection. We use the historic name throughout as it is the name most recognized.

[68] Matthew Goldstein & Alexandra Stevenson, *After Complaints Fannie Mae Will Stop Selling Homes to Vision Property*, N.Y. TIMES (May 23, 2017), https://www.nytimes.com/2017/05/23/business/dealbook/after-complaints-fannie-mae-will-stop-selling-homes-to-vision-property.html.

[69] DEP'T HOUSING AND URBAN DEV., THE 2017 ANNUAL HOMELESS ASSESSMENT REP. (AHAR) TO CONGRESS, PART I 22 (Dec. 2017), https://www.hudexchange.info/resources/documents/2017-AHAR-Part-1.pdf.

[70] *Id.* at 1.

eighteen constitute 59 percent of the homeless population.[71] Housing instability has serious implications for children in terms of their development, health and ability to learn.[72]

Another serious development is the criminalization of homelessness.[73] Many well-intentioned local governments try to make their communities appear more attractive and their residents more secure by hiding the homeless. One way to do so is by criminalizing what is seen as aberrant homelessness behavior. In a recent survey of nearly 200 cities, The National Law Center on Homelessness and Poverty reported that 73 percent banned begging, 53 percent banned lying down in public spaces and 43 percent banned sleeping in a vehicle.[74] As a result of these and other similar ordinances and regulations, homeless individuals – especially single men – are more likely to end up in the criminal justice system. Once there, they are less likely to have money for bail or the ability to be released back into the community. This criminalization of what is essentially a social problem – America's lack of affordable housing – and not a personal failure, is a serious miscarriage of justice.

We are seeing a post-crisis America that is increasingly segregated into the haves and the have-nots. The growing income gaps are reflected in homeownership gaps. While gentrified, higher-income areas of America have largely recovered, many other communities have not. Many of our clients have given up on the American dream because it is simply no longer possible. Major investments in affordable housing, changes in how we approach code enforcement, renewed vigilance against predatory practices and a redoubled effort to assist – not punish – homelessness are all essential to solving this conundrum. Sadly, in this moment in history, with America divided against itself and bitter partisan bickering consuming the nation, action on any of these issues seems unlikely.

---

[71] *Id.* at 32.

[72] Megan Sandel, Richard Sheward, Stephanie Ettinger de Cuba, Sharon M. Coleman, Bebra A. Frank, Mariana Chilton, Maureen Black, Timothy Heeren, Justin Pasquariello, Patrick Casey, Eduardo Ochoa & Diana Cuts, *Unstable Housing and Caregiver and Child Health in Renter Families*, 141 Pediatrics 1, (Feb. 2018), http://pediatrics.aappublications.org/content/pediatrics/141/2/e20172199.full.pdf; Martha Galvez & Jessica Luna, *Homelessness and Housing Instability: The Impact on Educational Outcomes*, URBAN INST. (Dec. 2014), https://tacomahousing.net/sites/default/files/print_pdf/Education/Urban%20Institute%20THA%20Homelessness%20and%20Education%202014-12-22.pdf.

[73] *See,* Karen Dolan with Jodi L. Car, *The Poor Get Prison: The Alarming Spread of the Criminalization of Poverty*, INSTITUTE FOR POLICY STUDIES, https://ips-dc.org/wp-content/uploads/2015/03/IPS-The-Poor-Get-Prison-Final.pdf; Sarah McKenzie Prather, *The Criminalization of Homelessness* 12 (UNLV Theses, Dissertations, Professional Papers, and Capstones, 2010), https://digatalscholarship.unlv.edu/thesesdissertations/12.

[74] Prather, *supra* note 73, at 24.

6

Foreclosure or a More Sustainable Mortgage?

Applying established law ... has become more problematic as courts address
the problems the financial services industry has created for itself.[1]

Maine Supreme Court

You have now seen how housing finance policy made it more difficult for some to
obtain and maintain a sustainable mortgage, despite the many available properties
for purchase. When those loans became delinquent, help was slow in coming. Loss
mitigation does not always work, especially when it fails to lower monthly payments.
In the end, many homeowners faced the final crisis – the foreclosure process itself.
This process is complex and very stressful for all parties involved. Loan servicers are
still not well trained to understand procedures in different states and even in
different jurisdictions within states. In this chapter we take a closer look at the
foreclosure process itself, its benefits and its harms. But first we need to glance at
how our foreclosure laws have developed over time.

BRIEF HISTORY OF MORTGAGE LAW

As was explained earlier, every modern mortgage loan consists of two distinct
documents: the promissory note recording the debt and the security instrument
defining the security (collateral). While notes have been standardized, the security
documents and the law surrounding enforcement of those documents have not.
Like most American law, mortgage law first developed in England, where the lender
held title to the property until the mortgage was paid. This "title theory" of
mortgages was adopted in the colonies and some of the earliest areas of the United
States. Under this theory, if a borrower defaults on the loan, the lender can take
possession of the property with no legal process because the lender essentially

---

[1] M&T Bank v. Lawrence F. Plaisted, Aug. 16, 2018, 2018 ME 121

already owns the property. This is known as "strict foreclosure" and is still part of the legal structure in certain situations in some states.

To further complicate matters, early American settlers also brought with them the concept of "equity of redemption," which developed in early seventeenth-century English law. The equity of redemption provided a means for chancery courts – or courts of equity – to soften the blow of default. Instead of the lender immediately taking possession of the property, the equity of redemption gives the borrower the right to reclaim it by paying what is owed. Foreclosure law developed as a legal process through which lenders could eliminate this right of redemption by "foreclosing" it. Foreclosure, which required a judicial process, marked the move from strict foreclosure to judicial foreclosure. New York was the first state to recognize this new process.[2]

As the colonies moved away from English rule, they also began to drift from strict adherence to these English legal doctrines. In 1828, New York again led the way, becoming the first state to develop a competing theory of mortgages known as the "lien theory." In lien-theory states, ownership vests with the borrower, subject to defaulting on the mortgage.[3] As a result, in case of a default, there must be some process beyond possession to allow the lender to take ownership of the security interest because the buyer, not the lender, owns the home. These new legal theories required new documentation. Two distinct documents developed to explain the relationship between the security interest and the debt: the mortgage and the deed of trust. In states that use deeds of trust, ownership is vested in a third party, the trustee, until the mortgage is paid. Mortgages typically only create a lien and not a title to the property.

In response to these changes, lenders did what lenders do when they are attempting to circumvent new laws they do not like – they appealed to their lawyers. The lawyers then developed the "power of sale" clause. These clauses in loan documents allow a sale after default without any judicial process. At first, courts were unwilling to enforce these clauses. However, in 1827, in *Newman v. Jackson*, the United States Supreme Court recognized the validity of "due on sale" clauses. The nonjudicial foreclosure was born: A lender simply has to provide notice and retake the property. In some states, Texas for example, it can happen in as little as a week or two.

Other minor changes occurred over time, leaving us with a hodgepodge of law and practices across the country. Generally, if the collateral document is a mortgage, it is a lien-theory state and judicial foreclosure is required. Indiana and New Jersey, where most of the people discussed in this book live, fall into this category. These

[2] Harold C. Vaughan, *Reform of Mortgage Foreclosure Procedure: Possibilities Suggested by Honeyman v. Jacobs*, 88 U. PA. L. REV. 957, 960 (1940).

[3] Andra Ghent, *The Historical Origins of America's Mortgage Laws*, RESEARCH INSTITUTE FOR HOUSING AM. SPECIAL REP. 1, Oct. 19, 2012.

states tend to be older and closer to the east than the west coast, but not always. In title-theory states, the security instrument is a deed of trust. These are generally nonjudicial states, like Arizona, where the lender simply must notify the homeowner of default. The process can be very swift.

Before you get too comfortable with these clearly defined categories, however, it is important to note that they are not always so clear. For instance, Massachusetts is a title-theory, nonjudicial state, but it uses a mortgage and not a deed in trust. Maryland is a lien-theory state that uses a mortgage but allows both judicial and nonjudicial foreclosure. Currently, most states are considered nonjudicial, but lenders can choose to use a judicial process. Anyone examining a foreclosure situation must know the underlying foreclosure theories and documents used in that state. Decisions and processes from one state may have little or no bearing on another state. The largest mortgage lenders operate at a national level with staff trained to handle paying customers and the occasional default. But the national foreclosure crisis suddenly required staff members to understand all the documents and procedures of different states. Foreclosing attorneys were suddenly faced with thousands of cases, most of which involved securitized mortgage pools. Neither group understood the complexities of the laws and the varying systems. To put it bluntly, they made a mess of things.

THE HARMS OF FORECLOSURE

Despite the growing evidence that foreclosure causes great harm to both consumers and their communities, the mortgage industry still advocates quick nonjudicial foreclosure with minimal due process for homeowners. It offers several justifications for this position. Some older studies have shown that judicial foreclosure makes credit more expensive in some areas. However, recent evidence suggests that the securitization of mortgage loans eliminated any such pricing differential. Securitization allows lenders to spread their costs across loans, but it also allows them to spread costs across jurisdictions. Some researchers have found that lenders mitigate the possible increased costs of judicial foreclosure by securitizing a higher percentage of their loans in those jurisdictions. In fact, more recent evidence suggests that in judicial states mortgage interest rates are marginally lower than in nonjudicial states.[4] In the end, in today's highly securitized mortgage market, it does not appear that judicial foreclosure is driving up borrowers' costs in comparison to states with nonjudicial foreclosure.

---

[4] David M. Harrison & Michael J. Seiler, *The Paradox of Judicial Foreclosure: Collateral Value Uncertainty and Mortgage Rates*, J Real Estate Fin. Econ. 24, 33 (2014), http://ssrn.com/abstract+2234639. The study used loan data from 26,892 applicants from 2011 in both judicial and nonjudicial states.

Another common argument for nonjudicial foreclosure is based on the study previously mentioned. Karen Pence looked at home loans originating in 1994 and 1995 from counties bordering state lines, where one county was in a judicial foreclosure state and the other in a nonjudicial state.[5] This credible study examined approved mortgage applications in an attempt to ascertain if state law affects a consumer's ability to obtain a mortgage.[6] The findings from 1995 "estimate that loan sizes are 3 percent to 7 percent smaller in states that require judicial foreclosure processes."[7] Despite the study's age, we have been at many events, including legislative hearings, where it was cited as proof that judicial foreclosure harms home buyers by limiting the size of available mortgages. This is one of the dangers of research. Its conclusions are contingent on the veracity of the underlying assumptions made and the details of exactly what was being tested, but those details are often lost in translation. There are several important things to remember about this study and its conclusions. Pence's conclusions were likely accurate when the research was completed, but they offer nothing in the way of explanation for the market today. In fact, recent attempts to duplicate these results show that securitization has smoothed out the differences.[8] Loans are no longer smaller in judicial states. One explanation offered is that the securitization machine operating in the pre-crisis period lacked or ignored an understanding of the differing foreclosure systems. This fact, however, is not cited by industry lobbyists.

The real reason the industry favors nonjudicial foreclosure is relatively simple and consistent: It is cheaper for the lender.[9] Looking simply at process costs, judicial foreclosure is more expensive than nonjudicial foreclosure. What business would not prefer a money-saving process? However, the lender is not the only stakeholder in this transaction. When comparing a nonjudicial to a judicial foreclosure, the former may well be cheaper for the lender, but that is the wrong comparison. The proper comparison to make is not between the costs of nonjudicial versus judicial foreclosure but between the cost of foreclosing on a home versus not foreclosing on the home. The lender's costs should not be the only costs considered. Instead, we should be looking at costs to the lender, the homeowner, the neighbors, the municipality and all other affected entities. When looking at foreclosure from this perspective, the costs of foreclosing as opposed to not foreclosing are substantial.

---

[5] Pence, Karen Pence, Foreclosing on Opportunity: State Laws and Mortgage Credit, 88 Rev. of Econ. & Statistics 177, 179 (2006).

[6] *Id.* at 177. She controls for several factors that might affect her results, such as the census characteristics of the residents, property tax and age of housing stock, just to name a few. *Id.* at 179.

[7] Pence, *supra* note 5, at 180.

[8] Mian, Atif Mian, Amir Sufi & Francesco Trebbi, Foreclosures, House Prices, and the Real Economy, 70 J. of Fin. 2587, 2591, (Dec. 2015).

[9] *See,* Brian Ciochette, *Loss Characteristics of Commercial Mortgage Foreclosure,* 14 REAL ESTATE FIN. 53 (1997); Cem Demiroglu, Evan Dudley & Christopher James, *State Foreclosure Laws and the Incidents of Mortgage Default,* 57 J. L. ECON., 280, 228 (2014); Anthony Pennington-Cross, *Subprime and Prime Mortgages: Loss Distributions,* (Office of the Fed. Housing Enterprise Oversight, Working Paper, #03–1, 2004).

In one common area of research, industry and consumer advocates agree. Studies conducted both before and after the mortgage crisis have verified that the value of properties located near a foreclosure will decrease, but specifics about the size of the decline, as well as its geographical and temporal impacts, differ slightly.[10] "A 10 percent increased in homes on the market caused by foreclosure causes house prices to fall by 4 percent."[11] The size of the price decline is larger in nonjudicial foreclosure states than in judicial foreclosure states because homes are more likely to be foreclosed in nonjudicial states. In fact, Mian, Sufi and Trebbi discovered that lenders in nonjudicial states were twice as likely to foreclose on homeowners as in judicial states, even though default rates in nonjudicial and judicial states are nearly identical.[12]

Researchers have posited several theories to explain why foreclosures depress neighboring house prices. It could be a problem of supply and demand. Theoretically, because there is no demand for property during a credit crunch, home values fall. In addition, an unusually large number of properties become available when foreclosures rise, and an oversupply of available properties flood the market. Anenberg and Kung have labeled this the "competitive effect."[13] It does seem logical that buyers have more control of negotiations and can offer lower prices when there are a lot of properties available for purchase. In addition, homeowners facing foreclosure and anxious to sell may well have to accept the price offered rather than the price preferred. For example, sellers appear to drop their asking price when a home near to them is foreclosed and sold back to the lender.[14] One thing is certain: Properties sold because of a foreclosure tend to sell for less than properties sold under normal conditions.[15] Sellers tend to be homeowners desperately trying to get out of a bad situation or lenders trying to unload an unwanted asset. Buyers of these properties are frequently investors who intend to resell the property, as opposed to prospective homeowners who intend to occupy it, a problem we will revisit in a moment.[16]

---

[10] *See*, i.e., Elliot Anenberg & Edward Kung, *Estimates of the Size and Source of Price Declines Due to Nearby Foreclosures*, 104 AM. ECON. REV. 247 (2014); Charles Calomiris, Stanley D. Longhofer & William Miles, *The Foreclosure-House Nexus: Lessons from the 2007–2008 Housing Turmoil*, 25 NAT. BUREAU OF ECON. RES., Working Paper 14294, 2008, www.nber.org/papers/w14294; John Y. Campbell, Stefano Giglio & Parag Pathak, *Forced Sales and Housing Prices*, 101 AM. ECON. REV. 2108, 2124 (2011); John Harding, Eric Rosenblatt & Vincent W. Yao, The Contagion Effect of Foreclosed Properties, 66 J. of Urb. Econ. 164, 165 (2009). Daniel Hartley, *The Effect of Foreclosures on Nearby Housing Prices: Supply or Dis-Amenity?*, 49 REGIONAL SCI. & URB. ECON. 108 (2014); Dan Immergluck & G. Smith, *The External Costs of Foreclosures on Neighborhood Property Values*, 17 HOUSING POL'Y DEBATE 57 (2006)(foreclosure within 1/8 of mile reduces the value of neighboring houses 1.1 percent); Atif Mian, *supra* note 8; Anthony Pennington-Crosse, *The Value of Foreclosed Property*, FED. RES. BANK OF ST LOUIS, Working Paper 2004-022A (2004).

[11] Mian, *supra* note 8, at 2589.

[12] *Id.* at 2588.

[13] Anenberg, *supra note* 10, at 2527.

[14] *Id.* At 2528.

[15] Campbell, *supra* note 10 (finding that homes sold in foreclosure sold for 27 percent discount).

[16] Harding, *supra note* 10, at 206.

This small pool of buyers has a different set of expectations about price and plans to buy at a discount.[17] Often, the only buyer at a foreclosure auction is the lender itself.[18]

Another plausible explanation for why foreclosures depress home values is that these properties are often under maintained and, therefore, worth less than surrounding properties.[19] Anenberg and Klug dubbed this the "disemenity effect."[20] This matches the experience of our clients, who often would like to make repairs to their homes but fear they are simply throwing money away. Before investing more money in the property, they want to be guaranteed to not lose it, something no one can promise. Other clients really want to make repairs but are struggling to come up with money to catch up on the mortgage and simply do not have the cash flow. It is foolish to repair a home and miss a mortgage payment. It is impossible to borrow money to repair a home that is in foreclosure. Even community grant funds earmarked for low-income homeowners cannot be used on a home in foreclosure. Recent evidence also suggests that homes in proximity to foreclosed homes also become under maintained, perhaps from a sense that the neighborhood is declining.

The price declines appear more stark when the neighboring home is bank owned.[21] Banks have been notorious for not taking care of their foreclosed properties, particularly in minority areas. This is well supported in the research and consistent with our experiences with clients. In June 2018, a coalition of civil rights organizations filed a federal lawsuit against Bank of America alleging that it failed to maintain foreclosed properties in thirty-seven metropolitan areas, spanning twenty-two states and the District of Columbia. This is just one of several such lawsuits filed against financial institutions in recent years.[22] All these factors combine to drive down appraisal values for other homes in the area, as appraisers take neighborhood conditions into account.[23]

The industry blames judicial foreclosure – as opposed to foreclosure generally – for depressing housing prices. This is a favorite position of researchers Kristopher

---

[17] *Id.* at 204.

[18] Debra Pogrund Stark, *Facing the Facts: An Empirical Study of Fairness and Efficiency of Foreclosures and a Proposal for Reform*, 30 U. MICH. J. L. REV. 639, 663 (1997).

[19] *See*, Anenberg, *supra* note 10, at 2550; *see also* Hartley, *supra* note 10, at 116 (finding that his findings that could be explained by oversupply); Mian, *supra* note 8, at 2589 (finding "foreclosure-induced increase in supply" depresses neighboring house prices).

[20] Anenberg, *supra* note 13, at 2527.

[21] *Id.* at 2550.

[22] National Fair Housing Alliance et al. v. Bank of America, et al, Case 1:18-cv-0919-CCB, U.S. District Court for the District of Maryland, June 26, 2018. National Fair Housing Alliance v. Fannie Mae, 4:15-cv-06969-JSW, District Court for the Northern District of California, Dec. 5, 2016; National Fair Housing Alliance v. Deutsche Bank, 1:18-cv-00839, U.S. District Court in the Northern District of Illinois, Feb. 1, 2018.

[23] Lisa Prevost, *Neighbors' Effect on Appraisals*, N.Y. TIMES (Feb. 14, 2013), http://www.nytimes.com/2013/02/17/realestate/neighbors-effect-on-appraisals.html.

Gerardi and Paul Willens who, in a series of papers with various coauthors, consistently argue against borrower protection and advocate for nonjudicial foreclosure. They believe it is the amount of time it takes to complete a foreclosure, not the foreclosure itself, that creates the well-documented negative effects to housing prices.[24] Housing prices, they posit, are depressed because houses are either stalled in the foreclosure process or are foreclosed upon (but not maintained) by the banks that own them. Many researchers posit that the negative outcomes are the result not of the foreclosure, but the lack of maintenance once foreclosure occurs.[25] Although Willens and Gerardi's description of the problem is accurate, their argument is circular because, but for the underlying foreclosure, the maintenance issues are unlikely to occur. The two cannot be separated arbitrarily, as one depends on the other. Their argument also depends on the myth that courts cause delays in foreclosure, when all the evidence points to lenders as a major cause of the delays.

Falling home prices are not the only negative effect of foreclosures. Mian, Sufi and Trebbi also found that as house prices drop, so does overall residential investment.[26] There is little incentive to invest in areas with shrinking home values. Their results are more pronounced in nonjudicial states because, as mentioned earlier, nonjudicial states have had more foreclosures relative to their default rates.[27] Interestingly, their evidence suggests that it is not only housing-related consumer spending that suffers as a result of foreclosed properties in the neighborhood. They found, for example, that auto sales from 2008 to 2010 "were 5 to 10 percent lower in non-judicial states" as compared to judicial states.[28] If consumer spending dips, so does the overall economy because consumer spending makes up a significant part of our GDP. As we have moved from a manufacturing to service economy, that portion has grown. It is easy to see how a downturn in consumer spending would cause a corresponding decline in the overall economy. Foreclosures, therefore, have far-reaching effects on the economy in general and not just on local housing prices.[29]

Research also is beginning to emerge about a broader range of foreclosure's negative effects, and many studies have found a connection between home foreclosure and deteriorating health.[30] Several have documented elevated rates of

---

[24] Kristopher Gerardi, Eric Rosenblatt, Paul S. Willen & Vincent Yao, *Foreclosure Externalities: New Evidence*, 87 J. Urb. Econ. 42, 55 (2015); John Harding, Eric Rosenblatt & Vincent W. Yao, *The Contagion Effect of Foreclosed Properties*, 66 J. Urb. Econ. 164, 177 (2009).

[25] Gerardi, *Foreclosure externalities: New Evidence* at 44.

[26] Mian, Atif Mian, Amir Sufi & Francesco Trebbi, Foreclosures, House Prices, and the Real Economy, 70 J. of Fin. 2587, 2590, (Dec. 2015).

[27] *Id.* at 2588–89.

[28] Atif Mian, Amir Sufi, and Francesco Trebbi, *Foreclosures, House Prices and the Real Economy*, 25, January 14, http://ssrn.com/abstract=1722195.

[29] Mian, *supra* note 26 at 2590.

[30] Dawn E. Alley, Jennifer Lloyd, José A. Pagán, Craig E. Pollack, Michelle Shardell & Carolyn Cannuscio, *Mortgage Delinquency and Changes in Access to Health Resources and Depressive Symptoms in a Nationally Representative Cohort of Americans Older than 50 Years*, 12 Am.

hypertension and psychiatric issues for patients involved in a foreclosure action.[31] These results hold true even when one accounts for differences in health status before the foreclosure began.[32] Several studies have even found that health problems extend beyond the homeowners to others who live in the neighborhood.[33] For instance, one study found that people living in proximity to foreclosures actually get fatter.[34] Because the foreclosure crisis hit hardest in disadvantaged communities already dealing with various social inequities, these communities are now experiencing a disproportionate number of health issues, especially mental health.[35] People struggling economically are more likely to forego medical treatment, particularly because job losses resulted in lost health insurance. This causes health issues to become more severe, often requiring more expensive emergency medical care. The lost tax revenue caused by the crisis further exacerbated the problem because it has resulted in cuts to programs that offered medical care options and other services in already hard-hit communities. In our own small foreclosure defense practices, we have seen numerous people experiencing depression, serious physical ailments and even one suicide.

The negative effects of foreclosure to overall health cannot easily be measured in dollars. Certainly it is an economic issue, but it is also an issue of basic human rights. Foreclosures make people sick, a fact completely ignored by policymakers. The medical profession, on the other hand, has gotten the message. Housing issues are particularly relevant to medical professionals because research has shown housing to be a major social determinant of good health. For instance, negative health outcomes are closely associated with evictions, whether or not they are the result of a foreclosure.[36] The rise in medical-legal partnerships is one of the more interesting

---

J. Pub. Health 2293, 2293 (Dec. 2011); Janelle Dowing, *The Health Effects of the Foreclosure Crisis and Unaffordable Housing: A Systematic Review and the Explanation of Evidence*, 162 Soc. Sci. Med. 88, 92 (2016); Jason N. Holue, *Mental Health in the Foreclosure Crisis*, 118 Soc. Sci. Med. 1 (2014); K. A. McLaughlin, A. Nandi, K. M. Keyes, M. Uddin, A. E. Aiello, S. Galea & K. C. Koenen, *Home Foreclosure and Risk of Psychiatric Morbidity during the Recent Financial Crisis*, 42 Psychol. Med. 1441 (2012); Nancy Menzel, Sheniz Moonie & Melva Thompson-Robinson, *Health Effects Associated with Foreclosures: A Secondary Analysis of Hospital Discharge Data*, ISRN Public Health, doi: 10.5402/2012/740731 (2012); Jason N. Holue, *Mental Health in the Foreclosure Crisis*, 118 Soc. Sci. Med. 1 (2014); Hugo Vásquez-Vera, Laia Palència, Ingrid Magna, Carlos Mena, Jaime Neira & Carme Borrell, *The Threat of Home Eviction and Its Effects on Health through the Equity Lend: A Systemic Review*, 175 Soc. Sci. Med. 199 (2017); Anastasia Beletsky, *Strain Drain, A Qualitative Analysis of the Impact of Mortgage Strain Recovery Strategies on Health Outcome and Behaviors* (Jan. 2015) (Yale, Masters of Public Health Theses) (on file with Yale Eli Scholars Lib. Yale).

[31] Menzel, *supra* note 30.

[32] Alley, *supra* note 30, at 2293.

[33] Dowing, *supra* note 30, at 94; *see also* Alley, *supra* note 30, Beletsky, *supra* note 30 and *Houle*, *supra* note 30.

[34] Mariana Arcaya, M. Mara Glymour, Prabal Chakrabarti, Nicholas A. Christakis, Ichiro Kawachi & S. V. Subramanian, *Effects of Proximate Foreclosed Properties on Individuals' Weight Gain in Massachusetts, 1987–2008*, Am. J. Pub. Health e50 (2013).

[35] Holue, *supra* note 30, at 6.

[36] Vásquez-Vera, *supra* note 30.

post-crisis developments.[37] The medical profession has discovered that resolving a patient's legal issues can help resolve his health issues. As a result, doctors, hospitals and clinics have reached out to the legal profession for help in dealing with the underlying legal issues that are causing their clients to become ill.[38] As one health official explained to us, all the medication in the world will not bring down a patient's blood pressure if he leaves the office and goes home to the stress of wondering when he will be evicted from his foreclosed home. Racial discrimination exacerbates the problems.[39] During the crisis, minority neighborhoods were targeted for subprime loans and, as a result suffered disproportionate numbers of foreclosures. These neighborhoods also suffered disproportionate declines in health outcomes during the crisis.[40]

Overall, foreclosure is negative for all parties involved. We are not arguing for barring foreclosures in every circumstance, or even for prolonging foreclosure timelines. But we do advocate a foreclosure policy that makes sense in the real economy and for real people, one that takes into account the harm of foreclosure to the community and not just the bottom line of the lender. We do not dispute lenders' contention that judicial foreclosure is slower than nonjudicial foreclosure. The question is whether the price society pays for that speed is worth the cost. We believe it is not. At its most fundamental level, this is about due process of law. It is hard to monetize due process and economists tend to ignore what cannot be readily reduced to dollars. At the same time, some of the consequences of foreclosure can be measured. For example, there is growing evidence that faster foreclosures result in faster overall home price declines in the market.[41] This has been especially true in the areas of concentrated foreclosures seen during the crisis. We agree that delays in an inevitable foreclosure do cause harm. However, many of the delays we saw during the crisis were not caused by judicial foreclosure or the courts, they were the fault of the lenders that either failed to have proper staffing and proper documentation of their loans, or simply walked away from the process altogether. None of this justifies removing the limited due process offered by judicial foreclosure. If anything, it speaks to the need to strengthen borrower protections.

Some of the lingering negative effects are clearly due to the large number of foreclosures we saw during the crisis – far too many homes for the industry to

---

[37] For a nice review of the literature, see Tishra Beeson, Brittany Dawn McCallister & Marsha Regenstein, *Making the Case for Medical-Legal Partnerships: A Review of the Evidence*, NAT. CTR. FOR MED. LEGAL PARTNERSHIPS (Feb. 2013).

[38] Dayna Bowen Matthews, *The Law as Healer: How Paying for Medical-Legal Partnerships Saves Lives and Money*, 11 CTR FOR HEALTH POLICY, BROOKINGS INST. (Jan. 2017), https://www .brookings.edu/wp-content/uploads/2017/01/es_20170130_medicallegal.pdf.

[39] *Id.* at 16–23.

[40] Antwan Jones, Gregory D. Squires & Cynthia Ronzio, *Foreclosure Is Not an Equal Opportunity Stressor: How Inequality Fuels the Adverse Health Implications of the Nation's Financial Crisis*, 37 J. URB. 505, 506 (2014).

[41] Mian, *supra* note 26 at 2589.

properly manage. The industry failed to keep up with the number of foreclosures during the crisis, so the claim that increasing the speed and number of foreclosures would have created fewer negative results is not credible. Moving to universal nonjudicial foreclosure would not have solved the problem either. It was the lenders after all who took steps to slow down the foreclosure process during the crisis. What we need now is a foreclosure system that can be sustained even when too many foreclosed homes swamp the market, as in the recent financial crisis. A significant example of how slowing down foreclosures during a crisis could benefit the overall economy is illustrated by one recent study that looked at the relationship between slowing down a foreclosure and employment opportunity. It discovered that people faced with foreclosure often moved quickly to find a job, but they tended to find jobs that paid less than was needed to sustain the mortgage. When foreclosures were stalled, people had longer to look and eventually found employment that allowed them to make the mortgage payments.[42] Delays in this case were better for the lender, the homeowner and the neighborhood. This study suggests that in periods of high unemployment, lenders would be better off slowing down the foreclosure process. Researchers continue to study these relationships and public policies on mortgage foreclosure need to respond in ways that allow the mortgage foreclosure process to slow down when it is truly necessary and provide for flexible alternatives that are more likely to benefit all stakeholders.

DEFICIENCY JUDGMENTS

The loss of a home is a significant negative result of any foreclosure, but it is not the only one. As we have explained, homes sold in foreclosure sales tend to sell for less than market value and sometimes for less than the amount owed on the mortgage. The difference between what is owed on the mortgage and the selling price of the home becomes a deficiency balance still owed by the borrower. After the Great Depression, policymakers became concerned with the rise in deficiency balances, and many states responded by enacting "anti-deficiency laws," which prevent lenders from collecting that difference.[43] The Depression-era laws remain in effect in many states, but many others still allow deficiency collection. During the most recent crisis, however, there were no widespread calls to limit deficiency collections. Perhaps this is because the collection of deficiency judgments in the years prior to the financial crisis had become rare. Most homeowners did not even know they had this lurking liability. Unfortunately, it became conventional wisdom for attorneys to tell their clients not to worry about deficiencies because banks did not attempt to

---

[42] Kyle F. Herkenhoff & Lee E. Ohanoan, *The Impact of Foreclosure Delay on U.S. Employment*, 38 (Nat. Bureau of Econ. Research, Working Paper 21532, 2015).

[43] Grant Nelson, *Deficiency Judgments after Real Estate Foreclosures in Missouri: Some Modest Proposals*, 47 MISSOURI L. REV. 151, 154 (1982);

collect them. The problem with the conventional wisdom – sadly – is that it is not always true.

Since our last large housing crisis, significant changes have occurred in the debt-buying market.[44] There is now a healthy market for unpaid mortgage debts. Lenders can easily sell their deficiency judgments, and they seem to be doing just that. Not surprisingly, whether or not a state allows collection of a deficiency judgment has little effect on borrowers' behavior.[45] Just as average law professors have no idea whether they live in a judicial or nonjudicial foreclosure state, average homebuyers have no idea whether they live in a state that allows deficiency judgments. Most homebuyers, if they learn this at all, discover it only when the collector comes to call. Deficiency collection can be devastating by virtue of the size of the judgments involved. An example will illustrate the problem.

This case was taken from the public record, so we have had no opportunity to talk with the family involved. It concerns a foreclosure filed in July 2010 in St. Joseph County, Indiana.[46] On February 23, 2011, the house was foreclosed on and a personal judgment for $132,706.33 was entered. The bank waited over two years before finally taking the property to sheriff's sale on July 25, 2013, nearly two and a half years later. If one were to look at this loan as part of an aggregate data set, it would appear that the foreclosure was stalled in court for three years, the time it took to go from filing to sale. However, the actual court record reveals a different narrative. It was the lender, not the court, that delayed asking for judgment and then delayed the sheriff's sale, canceling it at least once. Situations like this can be found throughout the court record and is one reason why the industry's calls for faster foreclosure are disingenuous. But we digress.

Once the sale was scheduled, the lender purchased the home at auction for $88,750, leaving a deficiency balance of nearly $44,000; or at least that is how it appeared to the homeowner. Those are the numbers in the court record and all the information the homeowner ever received, and only if she was assertive enough to ask. But $44,000 is not what the homeowner actually owed. Judgments in Indiana continue to grow at the statutory interest rate from the time of judgment – 8 percent in this case. This growth occurs even though the bank waited two years to put the property up for sale, something the homeowner had no control over and could not change even if she had tried. At the time of the sheriff's sale, a rough estimate of the accrued interest estimates the judgment to have been over $148,000.[47] The deficiency was, therefore, over $59,000 after the sale. At the time of this writing, the

---

[44] Fox, Judith Fox, Foreclosure Echo: How Abandoned Foreclosures Are Re-Entering the Market through Debt Buyers, 27 Loy. Consumer L. Rev. 25, 68–70 (2013), at 68–70.

[45] Andra C. Ghent & Marianna Kudlyak, *Recourse and Residential Mortgage Default: Evidence 1*, (Fed. Reserve Bank of Richmond, Working Paper No. 09-0R, 2011), https://ssrn.com/abstract=1432437 or http://dx.doi.org/10.2139/ssrn.1432437.

[46] GMAC v. Fisher, 71D06–1007-MF-000599, Superior Court, St. Joseph County, Indiana.

[47] The calculations are based on a yearly interest rate without compounding. The accrued interest is probably higher, as most institutions do a daily calculation and compound the interest.

judgment has increased to well over $85,000, and it continues to grow. In Indiana, a bank can attempt to collect this debt for a period of twenty years. It is easy to see that such a large debt would put most families into bankruptcy. The potential exists for all deficiency judgments entered during the crisis to go into collection, pushing families only just recovering back into financial peril. In the Notre Dame clinic, we are beginning to see deficiency collection actions. Because our clients are low income, the collectors do not often have much to collect. This is not true for the hundreds of thousands of others who once lost their jobs and homes, but have since recovered.

Most foreclosures do not result in a deficiency judgment. Unfortunately for our clients, Indiana is in the minority of states that allow collection of deficiency judgments with no limitations.[48] An almost equal number of states bar deficiency judgments for most mortgages.[49] The rest, which include New Jersey, home to many of the clients we discuss, fall somewhere in the middle.[50] Some states restrict the amount of the judgment by requiring that it be offset by the fair market value of the property, as opposed to the selling price at the foreclosure sale. Others have very short time periods in which a lender can assert a deficiency: In New Jersey, the lender has only three months from the time of foreclosure to seek a deficiency judgment. Doing so reopens the foreclosure and the foreclosure sale.[51] Such an action would present lenders with a new set of problems. It is not too surprising, therefore, that we have seen almost no deficiency actions at all in the state.

Prior to the financial crisis of 2008, it was relatively uncommon for lenders to pursue deficiency judgments, but that has changed partially due to the federal government. A 2013 audit by the Office of Inspector General chastised Fannie Mae and Freddie Mac for their lack of deficiency collections.[52] Since then, Fannie Mae has become aggressive and, according to the *Washington Post*, referred nearly 300,000 cases for further debt collection in 2013.[53] The Federal Housing Finance

---

[48] The states that have no limitation of deficiency judgments are Alabama, Delaware, Illinois, Indiana, Kentucky, Maryland, Massachusetts, Mississippi, Missouri, New Hampshire, Rhode Island, Tennessee, Virginia, West Virginia and Wyoming. They are also allowed in the District of Columbia. NAT. CONSUMER L. CTR, FORECLOSING AND MORTGAGE SERVICING §12.3.2, https://library.nclc.org/forcl/120302.

[49] *Id.* Twelve states have these rules: Alaska, Arizona, California, Hawaii, Minnesota, Montana, Nevada, North Carolina, North Dakota, Oklahoma, Oregon, and Washington.

[50] *Id.* These include Colorado, Connecticut, Georgia, Idaho, Kansas, Louisiana, Maine, Michigan, Nebraska, Nevada, New Jersey, New York, Oklahoma, Pennsylvania, South Carolina, South Dakota, Texas, Utah, Vermont, and Wisconsin.

[51] N.J. STAT. ANN §2A:50–1.

[52] FED. HOUSING FIN. AGENCY OFF. OF INSPECTOR GEN., FHFA CAN IMPROVE ITS OVERSIGHT OF FANNIE MAE'S RECOVERIES FROM BORROWERS WHO POSSES THE ABILITY TO REPAY DEFICIENCIES, AUD 2013–011 (Sept. 24, 2013), https://www.fhfaoig.gov/Content/Files/AUD-2013-011.pdf.

[53] Kimbriell Kelly, *Lenders Seek Court Action against Homeowners Years after Foreclosure*, WASH. POST (June 15, 2013), https://www.washingtonpost.com/investigations/lenders-seek-court-actions-against-homeowners-years-after-foreclosure/2013/06/15/3c6a04ce-96fc-11e2-b68f-dc5c4b47e519_story.html?utm_term=.4a60b4928ae4; *see also* Michelle Conlin, *Debt Collectors Harass*

Agency also issued an Advisory Bulletin in 2013, encouraging Fannie Mae and Freddie Mac to develop policies for collecting deficiency judgments.[54] In a January 2017 directive, servicers were told to pursue deficiencies on FHA and VA loans "if so instructed."[55] Fannie Mae claims to only target "strategic defaulters."[56] Unfortunately, there is no consistent definition of this term. The idea that large numbers of homeowners strategically defaulted, allowing their homes to be foreclosed on when they could have paid their mortgages, is not well supported.[57] The belief that large numbers of people surrendered their home for strategic reasons has created additional problems for homeowners who did not strategically default but left their homes when they thought all other options were closed and believed, incorrectly, that they had left those worries behind them. They are now being pursued for possible deficiency judgments. To make its position clear, in 2018 Fannie Mae created a webpage informing past and present borrowers that it would be referring such cases to debt collectors.[58]

FHFA's aggressive collection policy has unearthed a truly evil incarnation of deficiency collection actions – the primary mortgage insurance (PMI) collection. Homeowners are vulnerable to this action whether or not their state permits deficiency judgments. Banks place primary mortgage insurance on a home when the loan exceeds 80 percent of the equity therein. For instance, if you are purchasing a home that is valued at $100,000 with a down payment of $5,000, your lender is financing 95 percent of the purchase price. Knowing that it would not be able to collect 100 percent of the loan's value after default, the lender adds insurance. Homeowners pay the premium as part of the monthly payment, but never see the underlying policy. If the loan defaults, the insurance company pays the lender the difference between the amount of the loan and 80 percent of the home value. In this example, that amount is $15,000. The homeowner continues to pay the insurance premium until the loan balance falls below the 80 percent threshold. During and immediately after the crisis, housing prices fell rapidly in some areas. Homeowners who had just reached the stage where they could have canceled the extra PMI payment were unable to do so because their homes were now worth less than the original price. The PMI payments continued.

Americans Even after They've Lost Their Homes to Banks, HUFF POST (Dec. 4, 2014), https://www.huffingtonpost.com/2014/10/14/debt-collectors-foreclosure_n_5981622.html.

[54] Fed. Housing Fin. Agency, Management of Deficiency Balance, Advisory Bulletin 2013–15 (Sept. 16, 2013), https://www.fhfa.gov/SupervisionRegulation/AdvisoryBulletins/Pages/AB-2013-05-MANAGEMENT-OF-DEFICIENCY-BALANCES.aspx.

[55] Fannie Mae, Servicing Guideline, E-3.3–06: Pursuing a Deficiency Judgment (01/18/2017), published Feb. 15, 2017, https://www.fanniemae.com/content/guide/servicing/e/3.3/06.html.

[56] Fannie Mae, Deficiency Collections Overview (July 8, 2015), https://www.fanniemae.com/content/fact_sheet/deficiency-collections-overview.pdf.

[57] Fox, *supra* note at 26.

[58] FANNIE MAE, *Know Your Options: Don't Walk Away*, https://www.knowyouroptions.com/dontwalkaway.

United Guaranty was the primary mortgage insurer for many of the Fannie Mae loans originated during the crisis. Homeowners with Fannie Mae loans are not given a copy of the insurance policy, nor are they ever informed of its contents. Embedded in the PMI policy is a clause that allows United Guaranty to pursue collection against the homeowner for any money paid out to Fannie Mae. Before the crisis, such collection activity was unheard of. In 2015, several homeowners in the Boston area were sued by PMI insurers, and the New England Center for Investigative Reporting began an inquiry.[59] They contacted us to see if we had ever heard of these collections. At the time, the answer was "No." Exactly one day later, we got our first call from a client.

Susie Simmons had purchased a modest home in South Bend. Her mortgage was for $46,000. When the financial crisis hit, she lost her job. She tried to sell her home, but she received no offers. Eventually, she found a new job in Michigan and moved. The bank filed to foreclose, and she did not contest it. The lender obtained a judgment of slightly over $49,000. Fannie Mae repurchased the home for $22,800 in the sheriff's sale and recently resold it for a slight profit. Fannie Mae obtained a deficiency judgment against our client for $27,000 and allegedly assigned it to Guaranty. Even assuming Fannie Mae had made repairs to the property, the bank realized a profit when it resold the home for a price far exceeding the $27,000 deficiency. Despite all this, Guaranty United is suing Ms. Simmons for $9,000, the amount it claims to have paid Fannie Mae in insurance benefits. Ms. Simmons clearly did not strategically default. She did everything reasonably possible to sell the home, but she had to relocate and could not afford two mortgages. She diligently paid the insurance premiums for years. Now her best option appears to be bankruptcy, a ridiculous result for all. She has received no benefits from the premiums paid, nor was she ever really informed of the possibility of a deficiency judgment. It is hard to make the economically "rational" decision when you are not given all the necessary information.

Fannie Mae appears to realize some of the inequities in this situation, but its awareness is coming too late for our client. Fannie Mae published a guidance statement on March 14, 2018. This document instructs servicers that they can waive deficiency judgments, but only after they have contacted the mortgage insurer and obtained a waiver. If the waiver is not approved, they must notify the borrower that the insurance company may be able to pursue the deficiency after judgment.[60] Ms. Simmons may not have been able to choose another course, but we will never know because she – and others like her – were never given the information needed to

---

[59] Jennifer McKim & Jes Aloe, *Homeowners Billed for Houses Lost in* Foreclosure, Boston Globe (Jan. 18, 2015), https://www.bostonglobe.com/metro/2015/01/17/insult-injury-home-owners-get-big-bills-for-houses-already-taken-foreclosure/wSJHCbr2AQriwk2LRUHmiI/story.html.

[60] Fannie Mae *Pursuing a Deficiency Judgment, Servicing Guide E-3.3–06*: (Jan. 18, 2017), first published Mar. 14, 2018, https://www.fanniemae.com/content/guide/servicing/e/3.3/06.html.

make an informed choice. Had she known, perhaps she would have pursued an alternative such as an agreed in-rem judgment or a deed-in-lieu of foreclosure, either of which would have allowed her to give up the home without a deficiency judgment. Instead, she was surprised and shocked when a summons appeared on her door claiming she owed money to an insurance company she had never heard of on a policy she had paid for years. A successful collection action will financially ruin her.

THE RISE OF FAST-FORECLOSURE LAWS

We explained earlier how entire communities were ravaged by the crisis. Large numbers of abandoned properties accumulated and "fast-track foreclosures" were developed in response.[61] A fast-track foreclosure is a way to speed up a judicial foreclosure while preserving the judicial framework. As discussed, the mortgage industry has complained about judicial foreclosure for years. The most audacious – and frankly dishonest – claim was that judicial foreclosure is the reason so many abandoned properties appeared in cities across America. At least twice in recent years, lobbyists for the Mortgage Bankers Association made these arguments to the Indiana legislature, seeking to replace judicial with nonjudicial foreclosure. Happily both attempts failed when consumer advocates, governmental officials and even attorneys for the foreclosing banks joined forces to present the truth. (Something roughly similar happened in New Jersey as well.) Delay may contribute to the abandonment of some properties, but it is not caused by judicial foreclosure. In fact, according to a recent presentation by the National Stabilization Trust, in 2017 more than three-fourths of all abandoned properties were not in foreclosure but instead were investor owned.[62]

State legislators across the country have searched for ways to address current abandoned properties and to prevent more properties from being abandoned through the foreclosure process. Many have turned to fast-track foreclosures as the solution. As of now, fifteen states have enacted fast-track foreclosure laws, Indiana and New Jersey among them.[63] Once abandoned, homes deteriorate

---

[61] Geoffrey Walsh, *Fast Track Foreclosure Laws: Are they Headed in the Right Direction?*, NAT'L. CONSUMER L. CTR, Jan. 2014. At the time of the report, six states had enacted such laws (Illinois, Indiana, Michigan, Nevada, New Jersey, and Oklahoma). In 2016, New York and Ohio passed their own fast-track foreclosure laws. Pennsylvania has been debating, but as of the writing of this book, has not passed a law.

[62] Robert Finn, "Does Fast Track Judicial Foreclosure of Vacant Properties Fight Blight?" presentation May 2018.

[63] Indiana (IND. CODE §§ 32-30-10.6-1 to 32-30-10.6-5); Illinois (735 ILCS 5/15-1505.8); Kentucky (Ken. Rev. Stat. § 426.205); Michigan (M.C.L.§600. 3240–321); Maryland (§ 7–105.14); Nevada (Nev. Sen. Bill 278 (2013), amending Nev. Rev. Stat. 107.080 – 107.110); Ohio (R.C. § 2308.02); Oklahoma (46 Okla. Stat. § 302); New Jersey (N.J.S.A. 2A:50–73); New York (McKinney's RPAPL § 1309); Pennsylvania (69 Pa. C.S.A § 2301); South Carolina (S.C. Code Ann. § 29-3-625); Wisconsin (W.S.A. 846.102)

quickly. When enacting these laws, policymakers assumed that lenders would want to move quickly to take control of abandoned homes to stem the deterioration. They were wrong – or, more correctly – they were fooled. The real aim of industry efforts to enact these laws was not to end abandoned property, it was to end – or at least significantly diminish – judicial foreclosure. In some states these laws have included provisions that further weaken borrower protection. In Michigan and Oklahoma for instance, fast-track foreclosure is allowed even for occupied properties that are undermaintained.[64] In others, like Ohio and Indiana, provisions were added making it a criminal violation for the homeowner to damage a property in foreclosure. Consumer advocates fear that these laws will be the first steps in a movement toward universal nonjudicial foreclosure.

These laws have had no measurable effect on abandoned properties. Lenders have failed to take advantage of these expedited foreclosure procedures because they never really wanted to foreclose on these abandoned properties in the first place. Besides, in some states the process can be so cumbersome that it is actually more expensive and confusing for a lender to use the expedited process than to simply wait to file the foreclosure action in the normal way. Advocates anticipated these problems, but they still hoped these laws would encourage lenders to do what they had told state legislators they wanted to do, foreclose quickly. If the lending industry had been honest and abandoned properties were the result of a prolonged foreclosure, expediting the process should have solved the problem. It did not.

Instead of moving to foreclose on these properties quickly, the financial industry has instead moved to block efforts that would force lenders to foreclose on abandoned properties. Advocates for abandoned foreclosures were heartened by the decision of the Wisconsin Supreme Court in *Bank of New York Mellon v. Carson*, which involved a classic zombie mortgage.[65] In 2011 the homeowner fell behind on the mortgage and the bank filed to foreclose. A judgment was entered in June 2011, but the bank never sold the property. The homeowners had moved, believing the home lost. Instead, years later they found themselves facing mounting civil penalties for failing to maintain the property. The homeowners took the unusual step of obtaining legal counsel and petitioning to have the home declared abandoned, thereby forcing the lender to schedule the sale. The Wisconsin Supreme Court agreed. The homeowners finally had the means to force the lender to complete the foreclosure it had started, but the victory was short-lived. The mortgage industry moved in and successfully lobbied to have the law changed, eliminating a homeowner's ability to have a property declared abandoned. This was a significant step backwards for cities and homeowners alike, but it was not a complete loss. The new statute does provide that if the bank either fails to hold a sale within twelve months

---

[64] Walsh, *supra* note 61, at 14–15.

[65] Bank of N.Y. v. Carson, 361 Wis.2d 23 (2015). *See also* Justin Mertz, Benjamin Patrick Payne & Kail Decker, *Foreclosures in Limbo: Zombie Properties*, 22 WIS. LAWYERS (Oct. 2015).

or does not vacate its foreclosure judgment and release the lien, the homeowner can step in and ask for a sale.[66] This "use it or lose it option" is a much better way to prevent abandoned properties.

Despite the efforts of many advocacy groups, no one has been able to definitively determine whether or how often these statutes are being used. Early in the history of Indiana's fast-foreclosure law, we did a very informal email survey through the Indiana State Court Administrator. The response was small, but no judge remembered ever seeing a lender use these laws. We also informally asked attorneys at many of the major foreclosure firms whether they could remember ever being asked by a lender to expedite a foreclosure through this process. None could remember such a request. We were unable to find any appellate cases using Indiana's or any other state's fast-foreclosure statute, but again this is not surprising considering the recency of many of them. There is some indication that a few lenders in New York have used their fast-foreclosure law, but since New York has the longest foreclosure timeline in the country, lenders might have a bit more motivation.

Lenders' reluctance to use these laws is not surprising. An abandoned property is not a valuable asset as it generally must be secured and maintained, and has likely become the subject of code enforcement actions and fines. It may even have squatters to be evicted. Vandals often strip the properties of such valuables as pipes, cabinets and even aluminum siding. For many lenders, these properties are simply not worth the time, money or potential liability to be worth the effort of foreclosure. As a result, many of the abandoned properties plaguing inner city communities have been abandoned by both lenders and the owners.

TAX FORECLOSURES

Although mortgage foreclosures garnered most of the attention during the crisis, they are not the only way a home can be foreclosed. When homeowners are unable to pay property taxes, the responsible municipality has the authority to sell the property at tax sale. Homeowners are given notice and, if taxes are not paid in time, the home is sold, usually at auction. Although the process is typically explained as a sale of the property, the buyer actually purchases a tax certificate, thereby gaining the ability to foreclose on the property if the homeowners fail to redeem it in the allotted time. To do this, the homeowner must pay the taxes due plus penalties and interest. Interest rates on unpaid property taxes tend to be high: New Jersey and many other states have a particularly high rate of 18 percent a year.[67]

Even before the crisis, investors found these tax certificates to be good investments. A tax certificate has what is known as a "super-priority" lien. If the certificate

---

[66] Wisconsin Stat 846.102(3).
[67] *See, Tax Foreclosures and Tax Sales as a Redevelopment Tool*, Housing and Community Development Network of New Jersey, https://www.hcdnnj.org/tax-foreclosure-and-tax-sales.

is not redeemed, the certificate holder can gain title to the property through a tax foreclosure, wiping out any previous liens, such as the existing mortgages and code enforcement fines.[68] Municipalities consider tax sales a good way to obtain past-due taxes because investors purchasing the certificates must pay the unpaid taxes at once. As with mortgage foreclosure, the local practices of tax foreclosure can differ significantly by jurisdiction. Tax sales did not get much attention during the crisis; nonetheless, they also suffered under the strain of the financial downturn. Before the crisis, the tax certificates market was vibrant. Many an investor would purchase a tax certificate as an investment, hoping to earn interest when the homeowner redeemed it but not necessarily expecting to obtain the house. In fact, investors who did, often abandoned them. Many of the properties in question were – and are – simply not worth the cost of repairing. Some investors, primarily house-flippers, do use tax sales as a way to purchase homes at a discount in order to resell them for profit. While the market was booming, these buyers were welcome because they could take an abandoned property and put a family in it. This changed when the housing bubble burst. Buyers left the market and many investors could not profitably rehab and resell the homes they had acquired. Properties went unsold and many became and remained abandoned.[69]

When investors began leaving the market, municipalities faced a problem. There were no buyers for the tax sale properties. Indiana was one state hit hard by this phenomenon. Counties were required by state law to sell a tax sale property for the amount of taxes due, but soon found they were auctioning off properties for significantly more than they were worth. As a result, no one was buying. States took many steps to try to alleviate these problems. Many moved the sales online to increase the number of buyers. While this did work to encourage some buyers, it did not prevent those buyers from later abandoning the properties once their condition became apparent. This may well explain why so many investor-owned properties are abandoned.

Despite these efforts, many properties remained unsold. In Indiana, the state legislature intervened to create the "commissioners' sale." If a property fails to sell

---

[68] *Id.*

[69] *See*, e.g., William Flood, *Everything You Need to Know about Tax Lien and Tax Deed Investing: Junk Property*, FitSmall Business, https://fitsmallbusiness.com/tax-lien-and-tax-deed-investing. If you don't adequately research the property you are bidding on, you may end up with something that has no value and that you don't really want. That equates to not being able to get your money back out. Here's an extreme example: You invest in a tax lien for what was at one time a junkyard. The owners never redeem, so you never earn any interest. When it comes time to foreclose, you realize what you are dealing with and that there's no real likelihood you'll ever be able to resell that parcel, even if you acquire it for the amount of back taxes your winning bid represents. Since it's undesirable, you may never sell the property. In fact, that may be the reason why it ended up in tax default to begin with!

See also, blog post, *Solution: Close the Tax Sale Loophole*, Housing Policy Watch (Apr. 7, 2016), https://www.housingpolicywatch.com/legislative-and-policy/solution-close-the-tax-sale-loophole.

at a tax sale, a second sale can be held, wherein the property can be sold for less than the amount of taxes due. In fact, some sell for as little as twenty-five dollars. Another change shortens the period in which the homeowner can redeem the property after the sale from twelve to four months. These changes in some ways mirror the changes made to expedite the foreclosure process for abandoned properties. All these strategies are mean to encourage buyers and turn abandoned properties into occupied ones, thereby stabilizing neighborhoods. Additional programs (for instance, one created in South Bend), allow homeowners adjacent to vacant, but unowned lots, to acquire ownership at little or no cost. These lowered costs have helped to clear some of the properties by also providing a way for not-for-profits interested in community development to acquire real estate. Unfortunately, it has also opened the door to some bad actors.

A seemingly strange practice has developed out of the tax sale process, not just in Indiana, but across the country. Investors looking to make a quick buck are purchasing properties at tax and foreclosure auction using fictitious names or the names of companies they know are no longer operating legally. Where state law allows, a similar practice entails purchasing the property, but deliberately failing to complete the transfer of title. By so doing, unscrupulous investors and slum landlords can acquire property without incurring liability for taxes and code enforcement issues. Wisconsin is one of the states experiencing this problem and, in 2018, it began requiring buyers to verify that they had no past-due property taxes or code enforcement fines before they could bid on a property.[70] Wisconsin also prohibits qualified buyers from transferring a property to someone who would otherwise not be qualified to buy the property.[71] If such a purchaser ends up with a property, it can be forfeited back to the municipality. This sounds like a reasonable solution, but Indiana has had a similar statute for years, and it has not prevented this practice. Specifically, it failed to prevent Marshall Welton, whose story we recounted in Chapter 4, from buying multiple properties at tax sale, then renting them in deplorable condition, and it has not slowed down one of South Bend's more infamous slum landlords, Steven Kollar.[72]

Like Mr. Welton, Mr. Kollar creates multiple limited liability corporations, often failing to provide required annual reports to the secretary of state. As a result, the companies are administratively dissolved and cease to exist as legal entities. Nonetheless, Kollar continues doing business in the name of these defunct enterprises, knowing they have no real assets from which to pay fines or court judgments. We have located approximately fifteen such enterprises opened and closed by Mr. Kollar

---

[70] 2017 WI Act 339, Wis. Stat. 846.155 and 846.16 (1)(d). *See also infra* pp. 183–84 regarding these and other Milwaukee efforts to clean up the tax foreclosure process.

[71] 2017 Assembly bill 691.

[72] Caleb Bauer, *South Bend Landlord Faces Charges of Cheating Renters*, SOUTH BEND TRIB. (Sept. 9, 2018), https://www.southbendtribune.com/news/business/south-bend-landlord-faces-allegations-of-cheating-renters/article_9f163844-84fc-51ea-9770-daf208dfb461.html.

in recent years, and there are undoubtedly more. He rents these properties out in deplorable condition but avoids any liability though a series of transfers, both legal and not. Unfortunately, he is not alone. A look through the title history of some of the worst properties in St. Joseph County, Indiana, shows that it is surprisingly common among a small group of slum landlords to flip properties to each other and back again in order to avoid paying property taxes and code enforcement fines. Why is it allowed to continue? The city and county simply do not have the time and staffing to check on the backgrounds of multiple buyers, many of whom are out of state. It is a practice with little risk to those involved.

These unscrupulous landlords take advantage of unsuspecting investors and the tax foreclosure system. They are assisted by Indiana law that allows property to be held in the name of a trust, thereby hiding the true owner from creditors.[73] An example of how the transfers work to allow Mr. Kollar to avoid paying the taxes and fines he owes can be seen by reviewing the records of several properties. A good example is 1722 Dunham. In 2013, the property was deeded to 1722 Land Trust, whose address matched a company affiliated with Mr. Kollar. Between December 2016 and December 2017, several thousand dollars in unpaid fines and fees accumulated because of the unsafe condition of the property. In late 2017, an unaffiliated company purchased the property at tax sale, but Kollar continued to collect rent until the city issued a vacate and seal order in early 2018.

Sometimes, legitimate buyers become involved in these schemes without realizing it. Mr. Kollar's most recent enterprise involves a block of former foreclosures purchased in March 2018 by Pro Cap VI, a company located in New Jersey. We have no reason to believe that Pro Cap knew of Mr. Kollar's history or was in any way colluding with him. However, it found itself at the center of a recent firestorm. Before obtaining title to all the properties, Pro Cap VI apparently made an agreement to sell them to Capital Housing, a company with some affiliation with Kollar. Unlike Wisconsin, Indiana does not bar the resale of parcels from an eligible buyer (Pro Cap VI) to an ineligible buyer (Capital Housing). Mr. Kollar, on the other hand, began claiming ownership of the properties months before the sale was completed. He advertised and rented those not inhabited and demanded rent from those with existing tenants. He collected thousands of dollars in rent he was not entitled to. Many of these properties have serious habitability issues ranging from lack of working plumbing to sagging walls and collapsing floors. Because Mr. Kollar failed to complete the deal he allegedly made to Pro Cap VI, the sale was not completed as planned. He might have continued to rent out these properties had we not notified Pro Cap, which sent Koller a cease and desist letter. He then had no choice but to pay Pro Cap VI and complete the purchase, though it appears he did so by duping another set of investors. It is unclear whether he had planned to illegally collect rent as long as possible and never put the properties into his name or

<hr />

[73] Ind. Code §30-4-2-13.

to rent them until he had enough rent money to fund the purchase without involving new investors. In either case, when his plan was thwarted, Mr. Kollar retaliated against tenants who complained by shutting off their water and filing eviction actions. At a recent conference on abandoned properties, city officials across the Midwest described similar practices. Unscrupulous landlords are taking advantage of the shortage or rental properties and the ambiguities of the tax foreclosure system to cheat tenants and investors.

Tax foreclosures faced other challenges during the crisis, challenges that have lingered. A bursting housing bubble means falling home values but does not necessarily mean falling property tax bills. While municipalities are quick to raise property assessments when home prices rise, they are not so quick to do the reverse. In fact, the tendency is to increase rates as assessments drop.[74] A case study of several areas with rapidly rising and falling home prices showed that assessments continued to rise even when prices fell.[75] This reality causes real problems for struggling homeowners. Professor Bernadette Atuahene researched tax foreclosures documenting how the City of Detroit had failed to adjust taxes to correspond to falling home values. She concluded that, "between 2009 and 2015, the city assessed as many as 85 percent of Detroit homes at rates that violated Michigan law."[76] The research does not make clear whether these overcharges stemmed from a deliberate effort to increase revenue or from simple negligence. Detroit certainly was strapped for cash. In fact, in July 2013 it was forced to file for Chapter 9 bankruptcy protection.[77]

Tax foreclosures can be abusive to homeowners in other ways as well. In September 2013, the *Washington Post* investigated abuses of the tax foreclosure system in Washington, DC, publishing a series of stories on their findings. The study made clear that tax foreclosures have a disproportionate impact on the poorest neighborhoods. Roughly 30 percent of homeowners in tax foreclosure owed less than $1,000 in unpaid taxes. In one case, the homeowner owed $287 in taxes. Eight weeks later this unfortunate man lost his home to the tax sale; the investor sold it for $129,000. Companies caught breaking the laws in other states were still able to purchase more than forty homes at the DC tax sale. The situation was exacerbated by the DC tax office itself, which seems to have inadvertently sold 1,900 tax liens for homes on which property taxes were not delinquent. Many homeowners have spent years trying to fix such problems, including one "64-year-old woman [who] spent two

---

[74] Byron Lutz, Raven Malloy and Hui Shan, *The Housing Crisis and State and Local Government Tax Revenue: Five Channels*, FED. RES. BOARD OF GOVERNORS 8, Aug. 2010–49.

[75] *Id.* at 13–17.

[76] Bernadette Atuahene, *Opinion, Don't Let Detroit's Revival Rest on an Injustice*, N.Y. TIMES, July 22, 2017.

[77] Monica Davey & Mary Williams Walsh, *Billions in Debt, Detroit Tumbles Into Insolvency*, N.Y. TIMES, July 18, 2013.

years fighting to save her home in Northwest [Washington, D.C.] after the tax office erroneously charged her $8.61 in interest."[78]

The *Post* led off the series by telling the story of an elderly man suffering from dementia at the time of eviction:

> On the day Bennie Coleman lost his house, the day armed U.S. marshals came to his door and ordered him off the property, he slumped in a folding chair across the street and watched the vestiges of his 76 years hauled to the curb. Movers carted out his easy chair, his clothes, his television. Next came the things that were closest to his heart: his Marine Corps medals and photographs of his dead wife, Martha. The duplex in Northeast Washington that Coleman bought with cash two decades earlier was emptied and shuttered. By sundown, he had nowhere to go ... In 2006, he forgot to pay a $134 tax bill, prompting the city to place a lien on the home and add $183 in interest and penalties. His son paid the $317 bill in 2009, records show, but that wasn't enough. The Maryland company that had bought the lien had already gone to court to put a foreclosure in motion. To lift the lien, the company's lawyer was demanding steep legal fees and expenses— $4,999.[79]

Property taxes can drive homeowners into mortgage foreclosure. Remember the Owens's fiasco, chronicled in Chapter 2. Their foreclosure was entirely the result of a mistake in their property tax bill, caused by a computerized accounting system. A property tax bill triggers the computerized accounting program to recalculate the escrow account. An increase in taxes of $600 increases a mortgage payment by more than $50 a month. This can be enough to force some into foreclosure.

Finally, unpaid property taxes often result in reverse mortgage foreclosures. Reverse mortgages – Home Equity Conversion Mortgages (HECM) – were created by the federal government in the late 1980s to help people over the age of sixty-two retain ownership by using the equity in their homes to obtain funds for living expenses.[80] The mortgage is called "reverse" because no monthly payments are required as long as the homeowner remains alive and living in the home (though interest starts accruing immediately). Once he or she dies, though, payment is due from the estate. While reverse mortgages are salutary in theory, in practice they entail large fees and other costs, some arising because of the complex nature of these transactions. For instance, one of our clients was an elderly widow, whose husband had died a year or two before the representation. Because he had taken care of all the bills, she was unaware that having a reverse mortgage meant she still had to pay taxes and insurance even though she was not making monthly payments. A tax foreclosure action had been filed and since she had no assets, she lost her home of

---

[78] *See*, Michael Sallah, Debra Cenziper & Steven Rich, *Homes for the Taking*, WASH. POST, Sept. 8, 2013.

[79] *Id.*

[80] *See*, Jessica Guerin, *The History of the HECM: A Detailed Timeline.* THE REVERSE REV. (Oct. 2012, at 40–5), http://www.reversereview.com/magazine/spotlight-a-historical-timeline-of-the-hecm-program.html.

many years. This client was actually more fortunate than many because we were able to help her quickly obtain subsidized senior housing, but her dependent daughter was no longer able to live with her.

HOMEOWNER ASSOCIATION FORECLOSURES

Certain states (i.e., New Jersey, Florida, California and Texas) have thousands of planned communities such as homeowners associations, condominium communities and cooperative housing, all governed by community associations. How many of us have driven through these areas, noticing one gated community after another, or mile after mile of apartment buildings converted into condominiums? In these states such associations represent a significant percentage of all residential housing. On a national level, the Community Associations Institute indicates that 21.3 percent of the US population lives in communities with some type of homeowner association.[81] Condominium units are often cheaper than free-standing homes, and thus more affordable to the financially strapped, particularly when they are located in lower-income neighborhoods.

Living in a condominium comes with obligations to other owners in the complex, including maintenance of the common areas. To fund this maintenance, condominium associations impose various fees on owners. Special assessments above and beyond regular monthly assessments may be raised to fund major repairs, such as a new roof. Obviously, all residents suffer when certain owners fail to pay. For that reason, states often afford such fees special status as "super priority liens." A super-priority lienholder can foreclose on the property and have their lien paid even before a first mortgage. This has resulted in a large number of homeowners' association (HOA) foreclosures, many for small dollar amounts not usually associated with foreclosure.[82]

Many condominium buildings are in serious states of disrepair, especially in the inner city. Residents who initially felt that being a member of a community would also mean living in a building that was better maintained than rental buildings, are surprised to discover that this is not always the case. States often prohibit withholding association fees and assessments, even when tenants in those same states are permitted to escrow their rent in cases of poor maintenance.[83] Outside the bylaws,

---

[81] *See, The Community Association Factbook, National and State Statistical Review for 2016: Community Association Data,* COMMUNITY ASS'N. INST., https://www.caionline.org/About-CommunityAssociations/Statistical%20Information/2016StatsReviewFBWeb.pdf.

[82] *See,* Henry C. Walentowicz, *Assessments and Liens,* N.J. PRACTICE SERIES, CHAPTER 13 CONDOMINIUMS§ 13.36 (2018).

[83] *See,* A Country Place Condominium Assn. v. Maroeche Abdelhak (Sup. Ct. NJ, App. Div. June 6, 2017), citing N.J.S.A. 46:8B-17. For the right to withhold rent, *see* N.J.S.A., sections 2A:42–87-88; Marini v. Ireland, 265 A.2d 526 (1970).

condominium unit owners have few means to assert their rights. Residents can easily be thwarted by a single entity that possesses a majority ownership interest in the complex. We have represented a number of unit owners in these actions and are currently litigating a case involving a three-building, 100-plus unit complex in an inner-ring suburb of Newark that is in shocking condition, with constant water leakage, mold and other longstanding problems plaguing the residents.

Mortgage companies face these same issues when attempting to foreclose on a borrower who has stopped making the payments on his condominium. They may find their mortgage lien subordinated by the past-due homeowners' association dues. At the same time, if they successfully foreclose on such a property, they too become owners who must pay the fees. Many lenders have chosen to simply walk away. The homeowners association dues remain unpaid, there is no money for maintenance and the property continues to deteriorate. It is a vicious cycle.

SOME INTERNATIONAL PERSPECTIVES

Foreclosure, like the financial crisis, is a worldwide phenomenon. It may be instructive to briefly look at how several other nations – Iceland, Spain and Ireland – handled their delinquent mortgages. We look at these three partially because each one took a different approach and partially because the International Monetary Fund chronicled their successes and failures during and after the crisis. Iceland suffered significantly in the financial crisis, but it also had one of the quickest and most successful recoveries.[84] Like America, Iceland's citizens had a lot of personal debt, which combined with declining economic activity led to a foreclosure crisis. The country's initial reaction was to freeze all foreclosures, which it did for three different periods. Eventually the government required lenders to write down "qualifying mortgages to 110 percent of collateral value," followed by a second write-down of inflation-indexed mortgages. Iceland safeguarded social programs that focused on protecting the most vulnerable, as opposed to the big banks. As a result, Iceland's recovery was faster and more robust than other nations. Iceland did not bail out its large banks, instead it let them fail.[85]

Ireland presents an example of good intentions with bad results. Ireland's housing market was a classic example of boom and bust. Since its independence from Britain in the 1920s, Irish governmental policy has supported home ownership with substantial grants and other governmental lending programs. As a result, by the 1950s, 97 percent of new homeowners had received public subsidies and three-quarters of

---

[84] Garyn Tan, *The 10-Year Recovery, and Lessons from Iceland*, APPS POLICY FORUM (Jan. 15, 2018), https://www.policyforum.net/10-year-recovery-lessons-iceland.

[85] Jochen R. Andritzky, *Resolving Residential Mortgage Distress: Time to Modify?*, 10–13 (IMF Working Paper, WP/14/226).

the money had been "derived from the exchequer."[86] These housing support policies continued into the 1980s, when commercial banks took over the bulk of the financing. By then, home ownership had dropped but rates were still high, with approximately 80 percent of Irish citizens owning their own homes. The boom continued up until the financial crisis, and then the bubble burst.[87] Unlike in the United States, lenders in Ireland had little experience dealing with mortgage defaults, and personal bankruptcy was difficult, if not practically impossible.[88] Ireland reacted with several attempts to encourage lenders to develop what it titled "Mortgage Arrears Resolution Strategies."[89] The resulting procedures were not introduced until late in the crisis. As lenders were ill-equipped to perform and largely did not, the number of homeowners declined. Enthusiasm about home-ownership has dampened as well. The banks were nationalized and social services cut.[90] Ireland, as a result, has been slow to recover.

Finally, we look to Spain, which also had a housing boom, but not necessarily a homeownership boom. In fact, at the time of the crisis it had many unoccupied properties. The country's foreclosure system was very favorable to lenders and many foreclosure evictions followed. As their number rose, so did related suicides, putting pressure on the government to act.[91] Policies preventing evictions were instituted a few times in a largely unsuccessful attempt to help. The government did enact a few periods of foreclosure moratoria, which eased the suffering for a while. In the end, though, Spain was the victim of the false promise of austerity. Pressured by the International Monetary Fund and the European Union, it enacted austerity meas-ures to cut spending and social programs.[92] Spain's economic woes continue to this day.

In an interesting footnote, one Spanish family facing eviction filed a complaint with the United Nations Committee on Economic, Social and Cultural Rights. The home they were evicted from was rented, not owned, which perhaps makes the

---

[86] Michelle Norris, *From the State to the Market: Irish Home Ownership in Historical Perspective*, Mar. 14, 2017, UCD Dublin, https://www.housingagency.ie/Housing/media/Media/About%20Us/Banners/Housing-Agency-Lecture-Prof-Michelle-Norris.pdf.

[87] *Id.*

[88] Joseph Spooner, *Long Overdue: What the Belated Reform of Irish Personal Insolvency Law Tells Us about Comparative Consumer Bankruptcy*, 86 Am. Bankr. L. J. 243, 245 2012.

[89] Jochen R. Andritzky, *Resolving Residential Mortgage Distress: Time to Modify?*, 10–13 (IMF Working Paper, WP/14/226).

[90] Carmel Crimmins & Andras Gergely, *Ireland Nationalizes Anglo Irish Bank*, Reuters (Jan. 15, 2009, 6:30 PM), https://www.reuters.com/article/us-angloirish-idUSTRE50E8K620090115.

[91] Nigel Davies, *Spain Promises to Spare Needy from Eviction after* Suicides, Reuters (Nov. 12, 2012), https://www.reuters.com/article/us-spain-evictions/spain-promises-to-spare-needy-from-eviction-after-suicides-idUSBRE8AB0GY20121112.

[92] *Austerity in Spain, under Pressure from All Sides*, The Economist, Oct. 20, 2012. Austerity was the lie forced on many nations after the crisis. Portugal revolted against austerity and their economy boomed. *See*, Owen Jones, *No Alternative to Austerity? That Lie Has Now Been Nailed*, The Guardian (Aug. 24, 2017), https://www.theguardian.com/commentisfree/2017/aug/24/austerity-lie-deep-cuts-economy-portugal-socialist.

decision even more significant. In July 2017, the court found: "Evictions should not render individuals homeless. Where those affected do not have the means to acquire alternative housing, State parties must take all appropriate measures to ensure, where possible, that adequate alternative housing, resettlement or access to productive land, as the case may be, is available."[93]

Whether this decision opens possibilities for better foreclosure policy will be explored in the final chapter. For now, however, it is necessary to stress that a policy of foreclosing as quickly as possible and evicting the homeowners has not led to better outcomes for the economy or society in general. Instead, it has fueled fraudulent actors, increased poor health and sped the decline of entire neighborhoods. Countries that have helped their citizens and let the bankers pay for their own mistakes have fared better, in the end. A housing policy that prioritizes foreclosure over ownership is a bad public policy, and it has had the results bad policies often have: It has made the situation worse. Yet, the policy continues. The United States continues to believe the myth that the market will cure all and that getting homes back into the market is always a priority – even if the market is ill-prepared to handle them. Instead, we need a public policy that prioritizes its citizens and their communities, not just the banking industry.

[93] Views adopted by the Committee under the Optional Protocol to the International Covenant on Economic, *Social and Cultural Rights Regarding Communication No. 5/2105.*, 11 July 21, 2017.

7

Picking Up the Pieces and Revitalizing Neighborhoods

> Whites are moving back to Inglewood. There goes our neighborhood.
>
> Erin Aubry Kaplan, *Los Angeles Times*

Are there any signs of hope in communities decimated by foreclosure? After all, the stories recounted in this book thus far have been almost uniformly dismal tales of unremitting loss. While our work has helped save homes for some of our clients, we have sometimes only been able to help them gain the cash to start new lives as renters. Lower-income communities have become increasingly isolated, with residents observing from a distance as property values rebound in middle- and upper-middle-income areas. Moreover, in low- to moderate-income communities, gentrification is fomenting resentment as people watch their neighbors displaced by rising costs.[1] In his now famous rant about the gentrification of neighborhoods in New York City, Spike Lee expressed this frustration, often in terms a bit too colorful to reproduce here.

> I mean, they just move in the neighborhood. You just can't come in the neighborhood. I'm for democracy and letting everybody live but you gotta have some respect. You can't just come in when people have a culture that's been laid down for generations and you come in and now shit gotta change because you're here?[2]

Even small cities like South Bend, Indiana have gotten into the gentrification game. Many investors have come into the city to rehabilitate old buildings into

---

[1] Liam O'Donoghue, *Don't Call It Gentrification*, SALON, Nov. 2, 2014; Andrew Romano & Garance Franke-Eruta, *A New Generation of Anti-Gentrification Radicals Are on the March in Los Angeles – And around the Country*, HUFFINGTON POST, Mar. 5, 2018; Erin Aubry Kaplan, *Whites Are Moving to Inglewood. There Goes Our Neighborhood*, L.A. TIMES, Nov. 26, 2017.

[2] Spike Lee's gentrification rant transcript: *Fort Greene Park Is Like the Westminster Dog Show*, THE GUARDIAN (Feb. 26, 2014), https://www.theguardian.com/cities/2014/feb/26/spike-lee-gentrification-rant-transcript.

apartments and condominiums. In March 2018, investors broke ground on a $40 million condominium project, $5 million of which came from public financing.[3] The river-front properties are set to sell for $500,000, a price that may look like a bargain on either coast, but in a community with a mean income of less than $40,000 per year, they are out of reach. Millennials are moving into the downtown area and helping to fuel an economic resurgence. Restaurants are opening and people can often be seen dining al fresco, biking or strolling, sights absent over the last ten years. These are all positive developments for the city, but they have also fueled significant resentment among long-term residents who feel they have received little or no assistance as their neighborhoods struggled and now are being asked to celebrate as newcomers move into homes they and their neighbors once occupied.

Gentrification in Newark, New Jersey, is beginning to crowd out residents of a few neighborhoods, such as the Ironbound – historically a working-class Portuguese-Brazilian community – and portions of downtown. Plans for high-rise luxury apartments languished for years, only becoming realized now that the larger economy has rebounded. There is even a Whole Foods store in downtown Newark.[4] But in much of the rest of the city, neighborhoods still atrophy and vacant homes abound. Conditions may be better than they were several years ago, but the situation is still dire.[5] Can the city achieve a balance between affordability and decent housing, or between renovation and gentrification? We are not optimistic.

Newark is far from the only city whose future hangs in the balance. Hundreds of communities across America are attempting to deal with the vacant and foreclosed properties left by the foreclosure crisis and to work toward brighter futures. To be successful they need to balance the need to stimulate renewal against the needs of the existing residents, all without disrupting the character of the community. Programs vary from straightforward efforts such as Detroit Block Busters to more complex endeavors, such as land banking or renovating foreclosed homes to sell or rent as affordable housing in targeted neighborhoods. Preventive measures to keep people in their homes also are occurring. There are, for instance, programs that purchase mortgage notes in bulk and modify mortgages with significant principal write-downs. Unfortunately, these practices have led to a market for speculators as well, making it difficult for families attempting to reenter the market to distinguish the good guys from the bad. We do not yet know how successfully these efforts will

[3] Caleb Bauer, *Riverfront Development Breaks Ground at Former Wharf Site in Downtown South Bend*, SOUTH BEND TRIB. (Mar. 21, 2018), https://www.southbendtribune.com/news/local/river front-development-to-breaks-ground-in-downtown-south-bend-at/image_fd98d750-0015-54a0-9c 4f-eb16bbe01c30.html.

[4] WHOLE FOODS MARKET, https://www.wholefoodsmarket.com/stores/newark.

[5] Wallethub just named Newark the least desirable city in the country for raising a family. *See*, *The Tri-State Area Is Home to the Worst City for Raising a Family*, NBC.COM (Sept. 4, 2018), https://www.nbcnewyork.com/news/local/Tri-State-Area-Home-Worst-City-Raising-Family-Rep ort-Best-WalletHub-New-York-Jersey-Connecticut-NY-NJ-CT-Parents-Children-492409671.html.

revitalize high-foreclosure areas, given their relatively small scale and the many obstacles to their success. Scaling up is one of the main challenges we consider in this chapter.

MOVING FROM CRISIS TO RECOVERY

During the crisis, housing counselors were quite effective in reducing the incidence of foreclosures and assisting homeowners to remain in their homes. Homeowners with such assistance were more likely to get a sustainable loan modification that reduced their payments.[6] Funding for housing counselors was available through entities such as NeighborWorks, a nonprofit chartered by Congress to support community development work across the country. It administered the National Foreclosure Mitigation Counsel Program from 2007 to 2017 and continues to support smaller-scale counseling efforts.[7] Much of NeighborWorks' funding has been public, though it has also received financial support from federal settlements with banks over their predatory lending and foreclosure practices. HUD continues to provide grants to local organizations to fund housing counselors, providing $50 million to entities across the country in its most recent grant cycle.[8] A HUD study found that homeowners who worked with NeighborWorks America's prepurchase counseling are one-third less likely to become ninety or more days delinquent during the first two years than those not receiving counseling. The finding is consistent across the years, even as the mortgage market changed, and it applies equally to first-time homebuyers and repeat buyers. The effect of pre-mortgage

---

[6] Neil Mayer, Peter A. Tatian, Kenneth Temkin & Charles A. Calhoun, *National Foreclosure Mitigation Counseling Program Evaluation Final Report Rounds 1 and 2*, URBAN INST. (Dec. 2011), https://www.urban.org/sites/default/files/publication/24966/412475-National-Fore closure-Mitigation-Counseling-Program-Evaluation-Final-Report-Rounds-and-.PDF:

> *Cf.* Sumit Agarwal, Gene Amromin, Itzhak Ben-David, Souphala Chomsisengphet & Douglas Evanoff, *The Effectiveness of Mandatory Mortgage Counseling: Can One Dissuade Borrowers from Choosing Risky Mortgages?* (National Bureau of Econ. Research Working Paper 19920, Feb. 2014), http://www.nber.org/papers/w19920.pdf.

> > We explore the effects of mandatory third-party review of mortgage contracts on consumer choice—including the terms and demand for mortgage credit. Our study is based on a legislative pilot carried out by the state of Illinois in a selected set of zip codes in 2006. Mortgage applicants with low FICO scores were required to attend loan reviews by financial counselors. Applicants with high FICO scores had to attend counseling only if they chose "risky mortgages." We find that low-FICO applicants for whom counselor review was mandatory did not materially change their contract choice. Conversely, applicants who could avoid counseling by choosing less risky mortgages did so. Ironically, the ultimate goals of the legislation (e.g., better loan terms for borrowers) were only achieved among the population that was not counseled. We also find significant adjustments in lender behavior as a result of the counseling program.

[7] NEIGHBORWORKS, http://www.neighborworks.org/About-Us/What-We-Do/History.
[8] *See, HUD Awards $50 Million in Housing Counseling Grants*, HUD EXCHANGE (July 6, 2017), https://www.hudexchange.info/news/hud-awards-50-million-in-housing-counseling-grants.

counseling remains strong because it reduces the likelihood of deceptive practices and other forms of borrower manipulation.[9]

Funding was also available during the crisis for public/private initiatives facilitating support for borrowers, such as foreclosure task forces. For instance, the Newark/Essex Foreclosure Task Force operated for years under the aegis of the city and county. It primarily served to educate and coordinate activities of groups representing and advocating for homeowners facing foreclosure. These included housing counselors, lawyers, government representatives, academics and other nonprofits. It was effective in providing a forum for sharing information and getting the word out on related activities, as well as organizing joint efforts. These included having members fan out across the Upper Clinton Hill neighborhood, which was targeted for relief efforts, with a list of properties in foreclosure, along with contact information for the lender's property manager. New Jersey had recently passed the Creditor Responsibility Act, placing responsibility for maintenance of vacant properties on the lender during the foreclosure process.[10] We identified houses that appeared to be vacant and not properly maintained, and immediately called the property manager. In most cases, managers either disclaimed any responsibility for the property or seemed to have been unaware of their responsibility. Such identification and outreach can be an effective method for seeking enforcement of a new law. After a period of dormancy, the Creditor Responsibility Act is now being enforced in various areas of the state.

The Newark/Essex Foreclosure Task Force also helped renters in properties whose landlords were in foreclosure. Stephanie Greenwood, its first director, says:

> With the percent of renters so high (approximately 75 percent) in most Newark neighborhoods, the bulk of our outreach efforts actually went to trying to convince tenants that New Jersey law protected them from eviction if their landlords went through foreclosure … We were usually unable to convince renters to stay and exercise their rights. This was true because people didn't believe us, having been unlawfully evicted before, and also in many cases because the house was in such poor condition that the renter didn't want to stay. Also, understandably, many felt insecure about dealing with a bank representative as a landlord. We did, however, persuade a few families to stay, including one dramatic case of a woman packing to go to a shelter with her 8-year-old daughter the day we knocked on her door because a crooked real estate agent had threatened her with eviction and offered her money if she left right away. The State's [former] Office of the Public Advocate got involved, holding briefings and education sessions for real estate professionals on

[9] *See*, Neil S. Mayer & Kenneth Temkin, *Prepurchase Counseling Effects on Mortgage Performance*, 18 CITYSCAPE: A J. POLICY DEV. RES. 73 (2016), https://www-jstor-org.proxy.library.nd.edu/stable/pdf/26328257.pdf?refreqid=excelsior%3A9f2e82da15b2c0572e521fe94816c5c3.
[10] N.J.S.A. 46:10B-51.

the law's requirements. We also helped educate the Sheriff's office that they could not evict renters in sheriff sale homes.[11]

Additionally, the task force helped put together a successful proposal for federal Neighborhood Stabilization Program (NSP) funds, with the collaboration of various local members, including five cities, the county and several community development agencies. Congress enacted the NSP to respond to the ripple effects of the foreclosure crisis, appropriating over $6 billion between 2008 and 2010.[12] The funds were awarded to acquire and rehabilitate vacant foreclosed properties, an urgent need in the area. Given the time and costs involved in acquiring unrelated properties, the grant did achieve some successes, but not on a large scale. The major stumbling block for all programs dealing with foreclosed homes is scalability: The legal and financial situation surrounding each home is unique and often very time-consuming to untangle. Renovations present similar problems. Habitat for Humanity, a group presumably familiar to most readers, has programs in both Newark and Paterson, New Jersey. (We have volunteered for the Paterson program.) According to Stephanie Greenwood:

> Habitat for Humanity operates on a sweat equity and volunteer basis and its homes almost never go to foreclosure. The Newark Habitat has embraced a neighborhood organizing model in the last few years in an area of the West Ward [of Newark], pairing housing rehabilitation and deep affordability with traditional organizing and a critical repair program. This last [point] is so important because the occupied houses in these neighborhoods are in such awful shape. And it does no good to fix up an empty house and get a family in there if all the other houses on that block are falling down. Habitat has a good organizer on staff and seems to be having some modest success.[13]

COMMUNITY DEVELOPMENT, FINANCIAL INSTITUTIONS AND MORTGAGE ACQUISITION

Community Development Financial Institutions (CDFIs) are mission-driven organizations providing financial services to underserved, lower-income individuals and communities. They may offer affordable loans to residents, but they also renovate vacant foreclosed properties to sell or rent.[14] Some have also been purchasing distressed mortgages and/or properties and helping existing homeowners remain in

---

[11] E-mail from Stephanie Greenwood to Linda Fisher, June 22, 2018.

[12] Jonathan Spader, Alvaro Cortes, Kimberly Burnett, Larry Buron, Michael DiDomenico, Anna Jefferson, Stephen Whitlow & Jennifer Lewis Buell, *The Evaluation of the Neighborhood Stabilization Program* (HUD Office of Policy and Research, Mar. 2015), https://www.huduser.gov/publications/pdf/neighborhood_stabilization.pdf.

[13] Greenwood, *supra* note 11.

[14] *What Is a CDFI?*, Opportunity Fin. Network, https://ofn.org/what-cdfi.

their homes. Certain highly successful local efforts have involved mortgages purchased by CDFIs via the federal Distressed Assets Stabilization Program (DASP). As explained in Chapter 4, DASP has had mixed success overall, in part depending on the metric used to evaluate it. But a few CDFIs, as we detail shortly, have purchased pools of DASP mortgages and achieved workouts with borrowers.

Although a few CSFIs are for-profit institutions, the entities covered in this chapter – New Jersey Community Capital, Hogar Hispano and Boston Community Capital – are nonprofits. One model employed by these nonprofit purchasers is to:

- Purchase mortgage notes via a bulk sale, at a substantial discount, preferably within a specified geographic area (in other instances, properties themselves are purchased)
- Research each borrower's situation (for occupied properties only), identifying those most likely to be helped by a mortgage modification with principal write-down (the discounted purchase price for notes or negotiated lower mortgage principal make this possible)
- Work with the borrowers, providing counseling and improving their budgeting to enable the workout to succeed long-term
- Pursue other options if no workout is possible, which can include: a rent-to-own arrangement with the homeowner/borrower; a deed-in-lieu of foreclosure, or renovations and resale of the home

These efforts have been impeded because the distressed mortgages are generally sold in pools, not individually, and purchasing a pool takes substantial resources, as well as research to identify whether workouts are likely to succeed in each situation. Further, challenges arise because "most such groups don't have the capital structure, risk tolerance, or capacity to purchase big pools of loans and handle all the loss mitigation work."[15]

The National Community Stabilization Trust (NCST) is a national nonprofit organization that helps preserve neighborhoods primarily by restoring vacant and abandoned properties. Yet, it sometimes assists borrowers remaining in their homes. It works closely with CDFIs, including New Jersey Community Capital, in several ways:

> The Property Acquisition Programs: NCST's Property Acquisition Programs, **First Look** and the Neighborhood Stabilization Initiative (NSI), link U.S. financial institutions (sellers) to local housing providers (buyers). [NCST operates] the Neighborhood Stabilization Initiative (NSI), which spans 28 hard-hit metropolitan areas, through a partnership with the Federal Housing Finance Agency (FHFA) and Fannie Mae and Freddie Mac. **To-date, NCST has conveyed approximately**

---

[15] Jeffrey Yuen, *FHA Sends Mixed Signals to Nonprofits on Sales of Delinquent Loans*, SHELTERFORCE, July 11, 2016.

25,000 distressed properties to local housing providers across the U.S. who in turn rehabilitate these homes to improve their communities.[16]

The ReClaim Project: [NCST manages] a portfolio of highly distressed mortgages to resolve delinquencies, assist homeowners, and prepare vacant properties for productive disposition.[17]

Two CDFIs – New Jersey Community Capital (NJCC) and Hogar Hispano, founded by the National Council of La Raza – have been quite successful in keeping families in their homes and renovating neighborhoods.[18] As of August 2016:

[These two organizations] have become trailblazers as they have purchased more than 2,000 nonperforming loans from the Federal Housing Administration, government-sponsored enterprises and banks … Furthermore, because the two organizations don't have to be as profit-minded as their private equity peers, they can operate in a manner that's arguably more to the homeowners' benefit than theirs … Thus far, it appears the two nonprofits have created as many, if not more, favorable outcomes for their borrowers as the rest of the industry.[19]

NJCC's ReStart program follows the model just set forth. It began in 2012, with purchases of 261 mortgages at an FHA auction, approximately half of which were properties near Newark, and the other half of which were near Tampa, Florida. The program's primary goal is to secure modifications of homeowners' mortgage loans, including principal reduction. It has been effective because the loans are purchased at a deep discount, and the borrowers are screened and receive intensive financial counseling.[20] "By keeping homeowners in their homes and turning around properties that have already become vacant, ReStart not only creates or restores hundreds of affordable homes but stabilizes their surrounding neighborhoods, counteracting the blight and socioeconomic decline that has plagued many high-foreclosure communities."[21]

A secondary goal of NJCC is to renovate properties where loans cannot be modified into affordable housing. It thus formed the Community Asset Preservation Corporation (CAPC), which,

acquires vacant and foreclosed properties from NJCC's mortgage pools and transforms them into affordable housing … CAPC acquire[d] hundreds of loans and properties at a bulk discount with capital it secured through financial institutions,

[16] *First Look & Neighborhood Stabilization Initiative Programs*, http://www.stabilizationtrust.org/what-we-do/property-acquisition/first-look-neighborhood-stabilization-initiative-programs.

[17] *Id.*

[18] N.J. COMMUNITY CAPITAL, https://www.newjerseycommunitycapital.org/initiatives/ncc.

[19] James Passy, *Are Nonprofit Loan Buyers Really Good for the Mortgage Market?*, NATIONAL MORTGAGE NEWS (Aug. 8, 2016), https://www.newjerseycommunitycapital.org/about-us/media/are-nonprofit-loan-buyers-really-good-mortgage-market.

[20] LOWENSTEIN CTR FOR THE PUB. INTEREST, *2015 Lowenstein Pro Bono Report*, 5–6 (2015), https://www.lowenstein.com/media/3927/2015-pro-bono-report.pdf

[21] *See supra* note 16.

nonprofit community development organizations, ... investing arms of companies ... and ... grants. Eventually, hedge and other investment funds also expressed a desire to invest ... "We've modified roughly 370 mortgage loans with over $25 million in principal reduction, and we expect to modify at least 250 more in 2016," noted [NJCC President Wayne Meyer in 2015]. Through CAPC, NJCC has rehabilitated more than 350 residential units with total development costs of $75 million, and an additional 80 homes that were impacted by Hurricane Sandy. In all, NJCC has served more than 27,000 people, whether through loan modification or property redevelopment, since 2010.[22]

Ms. Greenwood mentioned an additional issue that often arises with rehabilitation efforts: "Many families that lost work found new jobs paying much less. And the public subsidy available for rehabilitated properties generally doesn't reach low enough on the income scale to meet the needs of families (typically a mother with two or more kids) to afford. So CAPC is finding it needs deeper subsidies to make its rehabbed housing affordable to families with children in the neighborhood schools in Clinton Hill, for example."[23]

Boston Community Capital (BCC), another CDFI, is also currently operating in New Jersey: "BCC works differently [than NJCC], negotiating with banks to get better terms for borrowers whose job situation has improved but whose mortgages are still onerous."[24] Rather than purchasing mortgage notes in bulk, it purchases occupied homes with underwater mortgages after careful screening of homeowners, and it negotiates with the lender to purchase the home at the current market value. BCC then resells the home at market value to the existing borrowers with an affordable mortgage.[25] While many other foreclosure mitigation efforts are funded with public monies, the SUN Initiative has been funded primarily by foundations and private investors. According to Elyse Cherry, CEO of BCC, the SUN Initiative works because it's not a charity and did not raise its initial capital through donations, but through foundations and individuals who expect a return on their investment. Having put up $10 million of its own money, SUN raised enough to make over $50 million worth of mortgages, becoming a viable business model that has provided an

[22] *2015 Lowenstein Pro Bono Report, supra* note 20.
[23] Greenwood, *supra,* note 11.
[24] Joe Tyrrell, *New Jersey Still Bogged Down in Foreclosures while Rest of Country Recovering,* N.J. SPOTLIGHT, Jan. 26, 2017; *see also* Elyse D. Cherry & Patricia Han Ratty, *Purchasing Properties from REO and Reselling to Existing Occupants: Lessons from the Field on Keeping People in Place,* FED. RESERVE BANK OF BOS., FED. RES. BANK OF CLEV. AND THE FED. RESERVE BD. 115, 116 (Sept. 1, 2010), http://www.bostoncommunitycapital.org/sites/default/files/Purchasing%20Foreclosed%20Properties%20from%20REO%20and%20Selling%20to%20Existing%20Occupants%20-%20FRB%20Sept%202010.pdf.
[25] *See,* BOS. COMMUNITY CAP., http://www.bostoncommunitycapital.org. "On average SUN Initiative borrowers benefit from: 35% reduction in mortgage principal; 38% reduction in monthly payments."

annual return to its investors of 4.25 percent. In New Jersey, the program, though small, has seen some successes:

> [Martin] Gonzalez, a contractor, moved from Jersey City because he could afford to buy a home in Elizabeth. He did well at first, but his wife got ill, and he began to lose work as the recession took hold. Meanwhile, Gonzalez said, his property value plunged to less than half what he paid. "I used all my savings account to fulfill my mortgage," and negotiated with the lender, Bank of America, for two mortgage modifications, Gonzalez said. But he fell into a common trap, the temporary modification. "It didn't work ... because both times, they raised my mortgage again," he said. As the recession eased, Gonzalez's work picked up and he was able to pay his bills, except for the looming mortgage arrears, he said. The house was going to a sheriff's sale when he received a notice ... about the SUN Program. He promptly applied to BCC, and the nonprofit opened negotiations with his bank. A "very helpful" judge agreed to stay the sheriff's sale. "The process was, Boston Community Capital met with Bank of America and ... they found a way to work together" to lower his mortgage principal closer to the home's value, Gonzalez said. "We're safe; we're happy with the new mortgage," he said. "You know what this is? It's a miracle."[26]

LAND BANKS

Land banking is the practice of aggregating parcels of land for future sale or development. According to the National Community Stabilization Trust, land banks are generally public entities "that focus on the conversion of vacant, abandoned properties into productive use. Land banking is the practice of aggregating parcels of land for future sale or development."[27] Land banks exist primarily in the eastern half of the United States, though a few have cropped up in western states.[28] Land banks have been instrumental in turning (usually foreclosed) vacant and abandoned properties into occupied housing. They have rescued tens of thousands of abandoned properties from the effects of foreclosure, helping to redeem blighted neighborhoods. The Center for Community Progress, which spearheaded the land bank movement and has provided templates and expert assistance to dozens of cities and counties around the country, further explains that state enabling statutes grant land banks special powers and the legal authority to:

- Obtain property at low or no cost through the tax foreclosure process
- Hold land tax-free

---

[26] Tyrrell, *supra* note 24.

[27] *See*, NAT. COMMUNITY STABLZATION TRUST, *Land Bank*, http://www.stabilizationtrust.org/get-involved/land-banks; https://www.communityprogress.net/land-banking-faq-pages-449.php.

[28] *See*, CTR FOR COMMUNITY PROGRESS, *Nat. Map of Land Banks & Land Banks and Land Banking Programs*, http://www.communityprogress.net/land-bank-map-pages-447.php.

- Clear title and/or extinguish back taxes
- Lease properties for temporary uses
- Negotiate sales based not only on the highest bid but also on the outcome that most closely aligns with community needs, such as workforce housing, a grocery store, or expanded recreational space[29]

Most land banks receive "deposits" of tax-foreclosed vacant properties that otherwise would deteriorate, attracting squatters and thieves who strip copper pipes and other valuable materials from buildings, bringing down neighborhood conditions and property values. The most dilapidated buildings are demolished. Hard as it may be to believe, in cities such as Detroit or Cleveland, property values have been so low that demolition costs can exceed the market value of a building.[30] In such cases, demolition of vacant structures can occur only if outside funding – whether public or private – is available.[31]

In 2005 Professor Frank Alexander authored the definitive guide to land banks, *Land Bank Authorities*. He explains therein that the movement began when St. Louis created the first land bank in 1971, followed by Cleveland, Atlanta and Flint, Michigan.[32] Created in 2002, Genesee County and Flint, Michigan combined their properties into one land bank, something enabled by legislation that permitted multiple properties subject to tax foreclosure to be treated as one massive case.[33] In 2011, Professor Alexander wrote a follow-up volume, *Land Banks and Land Banking*, which delineated various barriers to the creation and operation of a successful land bank. These barriers include the inability to transfer properties to new owners because of the title issues that arise when low-income homes are passed from one generation to another without proper legal documentation. They also include the frequent inability to locate owners of abandoned properties, a process complicated by securitization.[34]

Community land trusts differ from land banks. They are nonprofit organizations designed to ensure community stewardship of land and long-term housing affordability. The trust purchases land and maintains permanent ownership, entering into a long-term lease of the property with the homebuyers instead of a traditional sale. If the homeowner later sells, the family earns only a portion of any increased

---

[29] *Id.*

[30] *See,* Dusan Paredes & Mark Skidmore, *The Net Benefit of Demolishing Dilapidated Housing: The Case of Detroit,* 66 REGIONAL SCI. URB. ECON., 16 (2017).

[31] *See generally,* Alan Mallach, *The Empty House Next Door: Understanding and Reducing Vacancy and Hypervacancy in the United States,* LINCOLN INST. OF LAND POL'Y (2018), https://www.lincolninst.edu/sites/default/files/pubfiles/empty-house-next-door-full.pdf.

[32] Frank Alexander, *Land Bank Authorities: A Guide for the Creation and Operation of Local Land Banks,* LOCAL INCOME SUPPORT CORP. 5,6 (Apr.2005), https://www.hudexchange.info/resources/documents/LandBankAuthoritiesGuideforCreationandOperation.pdf.

[33] *Id.*

[34] Frank Alexander, *Land Banks and Land Banking,* CTR FOR COMMUNITY PROGRESS, 26–7 (2011), http://action.communityprogress.net/p/salsa/web/common/public/signup?signup_page_KEY=7641

property value; the trust retains the rest. Essentially, this model separates ownership of land and housing, facilitating affordability for future low- to moderate-income families.[35]

By contrast, land banks acquire distressed properties and sell them at affordable prices, achieving the shared goal of affordable housing. Land banks have the freedom to craft their lending programs in ways that best fit the local economy. Which model works best will depend on the situation in each area. None has gained much traction in either Indiana or New Jersey. NJCC and CAPC have formed a community land trust in Essex County (home of Newark), but it has suffered from a lack of funding and willing government partners. Despite years of efforts, Indiana has yet to afford anyone outside of Indianapolis the statutory authority to create a land bank. Indianapolis's land bank was rocked by a bribery scandal and, as a result, has really slowed down on its revitalization programs.[36] Still, other areas in the country have achieved significant progress using land banks.[37]

Land banks present challenges as well. Baltimore had an abandoned property problem even before the crisis, but it got much worse afterward. In 2002, the city launched Project 5000, an effort to acquire abandoned properties. In many ways, it was almost too successful – by 2005 the city owned over 10,000 vacant properties.[38] Baltimore sought help from state legislators and in 2008 – just in time for the crisis – the state passed Senate Bill 911, enabling the creation of a land bank.[39] Unfortunately, its administration become embroiled in City Council politics and, in the end, Baltimore was ultimately forced back into an ad hoc process called Vacants-to–Values. This allows investors to identify property, have ownership removed and then have the buildings placed into receivership. It is cumbersome and expensive.[40]

With no ability to land bank, South Bend struggled to find other ways to rehabilitate its abandoned property. In 2013, the city created a task force on abandoned property, utilizing the expertise of a recently hired law professor at Notre Dame, James Kelly. Professor Kelly was fresh from his experiences in Baltimore and took on the role of chairman.[41] The task force made several recommendations, among them

---

[35] *See, Community Land Trusts: A Primer for Local Officials*, COMMUNITY LAND TRUST PROJECT, https://community-wealth.org/sites/clone.community-wealth.org/files/downloads/paper-community .pdf.

[36] Brian Eason, *Land Bank, Hit by Scandal, Holds Back as Blight Spreads*, INDYSTAR (Nov. 30, 2015), https://www.indystar.com/story/news/investigations/2015/11/30/land-bank-hit-scandal-holds-back-blight-spreads/76330380.

[37] Stephanie Greenwood, *supra* note 11; *see*, U.S. DEPT. HOUSING AND URB. DEV., *Revitalizing Foreclosed Properties with Land Banks*, Aug. 2009.

[38] Revitalizing Foreclosed Properties at 13.

[39] *Id.* at 15.

[40] Andrew Thompson, *What Philly Should Have Learned from Baltimore about Land Banks*, PHILA. (Dec. 11, 2013), https://www.phillymag.com/news/2013/12/11/darrell-clarke-baltimore-land-bank.

[41] *Vacant and Abandoned Properties Task Force Report* (Feb. 2013), https://southbendin.gov/wp-content/uploads/2018/05/Code_FinalVATF_Report_2_red.pdf.

working to reclaim vacant properties for community use and assisting homeowners in acquiring adjacent vacant lots. The city had to find creative ways to acquire properties. It cobbled together $10 million dollars through HUD's Community Block Grants and Neighborhood Stabilization Program and Indiana's Blight Elimination funding. The initiative, dubbed "1,000 Homes in a 1000 Days," sought to acquire 1,000 abandoned homes and rehabilitate those it could, tearing down the rest.[42] In many ways the project was successful. It resolved more than 1,000 properties, but not without controversy, largely because citizens could not grasp the legal realities the city faced. While a municipality may have the authority to demolish a dilapidated home that is considered a nuisance, it cannot repair it without acquiring ownership, and ownership could not easily be acquired on some properties. Just as gentrification breeds resentment, this program caused some residents in the targeted neighborhoods to question the city's motive. Some saw it as an effort to destroy minority communities.

When the program ended, many vacant lots were left across South Bend. The city then launched its next program, the Resident Legal Assistance Program (RLAP), a collaboration between the city and the Notre Dame Clinical Law Center. Through this program, citizens and not-for-profits can obtain free legal assistance acquiring vacant lots adjacent to their properties. A potential purchaser must first acquire the tax certificate in a property tax auction and then Notre Dame handles the complicated legal steps needed to turn the tax certificate into a deed to the property.

Milwaukee, a city of approximately 600,000, is what is now called a "legacy" city, or a former industrial center that declined after industry's departure. A recent stay there confirmed for us that the city resembles other Rust Belt urban areas such as Newark, Detroit and many, many others. But it is taking a number of innovative steps to reduce the harms of foreclosure. For example, Milwaukee itself functions as its own land bank. The Wisconsin property tax foreclosure statute gives the city clean title after property tax foreclosure and as a result, the city has available a large inventory of tax-foreclosed homes as well as programs to promote the sale, rehab and occupancy of them.[43] According to Milwaukee Assistant City Attorney Gregg Hagopian, a leading voice in the efforts to alleviating property-tax foreclosure, many slumlords acquire rental properties at sheriff sales in mortgage foreclosure proceedings, and then, after milking the properties for rent, fail to pay property taxes. This is much like the activity we described previously in South Bend. The difference is, in Milwaukee, the city is following this activity and pursues tax foreclosure to acquire title.[44]

---

[42] *South Bend's Vacant and Abandoned Housing Challenge: 1,000 Homes in 1,000 Days*, PD&R EDGE, https://www.huduser.gov/portal/pdredge/pdr-edge-inpractice-011116.html.
[43] Wis. Stat. 75.521
[44] Interview with Gregg Hagopian, Aug. 22, 2018.

In addition, Hagopian successfully advocated for a new Wisconsin law that permits mortgage-foreclosed properties to be sold via online auctions. This has the potential to increase the market of buyers, promote transparency and collection of data, and end problems associated with in-person auctions, such as collusion among bidders and intimidation against bidders.[45] Many states have had online tax fore-closure auctions, but they are now moving to include mortgage foreclosures to the mix. Florida has had online mortgage foreclosure auctions since its state law was changed in 2008, and in 2016, Ohio changed its state law to allow online sheriff sales in mortgage foreclosures. These auction sites can impose controls to ensure that purchasers have sufficient funds in legitimate accounts, and to gather useful infor-mation, such as the identity of the principals behind LLC purchasers. Since online sales inherently raise the risk of impulse purchases, particularly by out-of-state buyers with no real knowledge of the building's condition or vicinity, having adequate controls is imperative. Gregg Hagopian also has successfully promoted new Wis-consin statutory authority to impose the controls, and to establish eligibility require-ments to bid as a third party at a mortgage foreclosure auction (whether the auction is conducted in person or online).[46] Effective October 1, 2018, third-party bidders will only be able to bid and purchase at a mortgage foreclosure auction if (1) they (or any entity they own or control) are not more than 120 days delinquent in paying property taxes, (2) they (or any entity they own or control) have no unsatisfied court judgments against them for noncompliance with building codes, and (3) they have a registered agent in Wisconsin (in case legal proceedings become necessary).[47]

RENOVATION INNOVATION IN DETROIT

The challenges faced by small cities like South Bend were nothing compared to those faced by larger Rust Belt cities. Most readers will be familiar with the devasta-tion wrought by foreclosure in Detroit. We have all seen dramatic news footage of dilapidated homes dotting huge swaths of vacant land that extend mile after mile to the city limits. With a fragile economy even before the crisis, the city (except for the newly burgeoning downtown) was unable to withstand the plague of foreclosures. The benefits of that downtown development have not been passed on to the city's inner-city neighborhoods. Distressingly, the African-American homeownership per-centage in Detroit – and the state of Michigan as a whole – has dropped precipit-ously. According to Mark Treskon, a research associate with the Urban Institute, while homeownership dipped three percentage points from 2000 to 2016 for whites in Michigan, it declined 10 percent for African Americans during the same period. Detroit, which prior to the crisis had "some of the highest levels of black ownership

---

[45] 2017 WI Act 208, Wis. Stat. 846.16 (1g)(b).
[46] 2017 WI Act 339, Wis. Stat. 846.155 and 846.16 (1)(d).
[47] *Id.*

in the country," could not withstand the combination of subprime lending and the loss of manufacturing jobs. As a result, according to the 2016 census data, Detroit has transformed from a city where the majority of people owned their homes, to one in which 56 percent were renters.[48]

Yet creative redevelopment efforts are under way in a number of neighborhoods, and the Detroit Land Bank has been quite active, selling over 4,000 properties since its inception in 2014. The city posts auctions for vacant homes on its newly launched website, buildingdetroit.org. These homes need extensive renovations so the site also includes a conditions report and costs of rehab for each available property. All auctions begin at $1,000. So, for example, the site is advertising the La Salle Gardens duplex, "currently up for auction [, which] could go for $1,000, but the new owners should have the money to pay for renovations, which are currently estimated at $145,869." The site also offers completed rehabilitated homes, ready to be moved into, as well as vacant lots for sale.[49]

Collaborative efforts can help leverage scarce resources. Detroit Home Mortgage (DIM), launched in 2016, works with the Detroit Land Bank and leverages support from banks, community development agencies and foundations, as well as the federal government and the Clinton Global Initiative. Together they aim to address what has been dubbed the "appraisal gap," which opens when – as now – market values are too low to interest lenders that might otherwise lend to prospective homebuyers. The program also assists purchasers who need mortgage funding for rehabilitation costs, but whose houses have been appraised too low to support the needed loans. A massive effort to increase property values has taken place:

> With Detroit Home Mortgage, banks are now able to lend to a qualified home buyer the full amount needed to purchase an already renovated home or to buy and rehabilitate a home... [Q]ualifying borrowers receive a first mortgage for the appraised value of the house (less 3.5 percent down payment) and a second mortgage of up to $75,000 to fill the gap between the appraised value and the sale price plus any renovation costs ... Today, the land bank is ... providing information on Detroit Home Mortgage as a possible option to complete the renovations for a move-in ready home.[50]

Despite the foreclosure-related blight in Detroit and the overwhelming number of blocks of boarded-up homes sandwiched between large swaths of vacant land,

---

[48] *See,* Christine MacDonald, *Black Homeownership Plunges in Michigan,* DETROIT NEWS (July 10, 2018), https://www.detroitnews.com/story/news/michigan/2018/07/10/black-home-ownership-drop-largest-michigan/767804002.

[49] Robin Runyan, *Detroit Land Bank Debuts New Website,* Jan. 29, 2018; *see also* Robyn A. Friendman, *Why Cash Deals Rule in Detroit,* WALL ST. J. (Sept. 7, 2018, at M8), https://www.wsj.com/articles/why-so-many-detroit-home-buyers-are-paying-in-cash-1536159334.

[50] Frank Altman, *Detroit Home Mortgage: Innovative Rehabilitation Financing,* Feb. 2018, https://www.occ.gov/publications/publications-by-type/other-publications-reports/cdi-newsletter/single-family-february-2018/article-4-detroit-financing.html.

other creative efforts to reclaim city neighborhoods are taking place as well. Detroit Block Busters, headed by John George, a lifelong Detroit resident,

> has facilitated approximately 182,000 volunteers to stabilize the neighborhoods in Northwest Detroit. They have painted 700, secured 400, renovated 200, and built over 100 homes since the group's inception . . . They have painted murals and built Artist Village Detroit, five city blocks that have now become a campus including Motor City Java House (run by his wife Alicia), offices, a courtyard, and an art gallery where each year "Sidewalk," an outdoor arts and culture festival, takes place on the first Saturday in August. There is even Farm City Detroit, a community garden where everything grown is given away. Two blocks east, George is partnering with a veterans' organization on the renovation of an apartment building for returning veterans.[51]

It is quite heartening to walk around Artist Village, witnessing the energy and enthusiasm of its workers and volunteers. We only wish that the project was more extensive. Another creative example of renewal is the Michigan Urban Farming Initiative, located on three acres in Detroit's North End. The founders purchased the empty plot and, using sustainable techniques, have turned it into a large garden, growing fruits and vegetables that are given away to nearby residents (addressing another inner-city problem: the food desert).[52] Although the farm obviously does not supply affordable housing, its use of the land is quite productive and helps build community.

Community building is fundamentally necessary since the foreclosure crisis decimated it in the areas we have described. Community shapes the narratives that foster a shared vision and commitment, but it also creates social capital. The eminent sociologist Robert Putnam explains, "The central idea of social capital . . . is that networks and the associated norms of reciprocity have value. They have value for the people who are in them, and they have, at least in some instances, demonstrable externalities, so that there are both public and private faces of social capital."[53] It can be extremely difficult to pick up the pieces after a crisis has destroyed dreams and cast families out of a neighborhood. A certain amount of trust building and bonding in the service of a collective goal is necessary for plans to become realities. Communities need to feel they are part of the solution, not that the solution is being imposed on them or being crafted to replace them. At the same time, community without funding cannot achieve much, so the assistance of a

---

[51] THE HUB, *Detroit Block Busters Recognized for Neighborhood Turnaround Efforts* (Nov. 7, 2017), http://www.thehubdetroit.com/detroit-blight-busters-recognized-neighborhood-turnaround-efforts. *See also* NAT. PUBLIC RADIO, *Cleaning Up with the "Motor City Blightbusters"* (July 29, 2017), https://www.npr.org/2017/07/29/540300104/cleaning-up-with-the-motor-city-blightbusters.

[52] *See*, MICH. URB. FARMING INITIATIVE, http://www.miufi.org.

[53] Robert Putnam, *Social Capital: Measurement and Consequences*, http://citeseerx.ist.psu.edu/viewdoc/download?doi=10.1.1.178.6284&rep=rep1&type=pdf.

CDFI, a collaborative effort such as Detroit Home Mortgage or governmental funding is essential.

REMAINING CONCERNS

While this chapter has given examples of successful efforts to begin attacking post-foreclosure problems, it has not highlighted the many seemingly good ideas that failed. For example, an effort was mounted earlier in the crisis to have foreclosure-bedeviled cities use their eminent domain powers to purchase borrowers' failing mortgages at the fair market value of the collateral, i.e., the home. This creative proposal from Cornell law professor Robert C. Hockett was necessitated by servicers' and lenders' refusals to work out reasonable mortgage modifications with borrowers (as we discussed earlier).[54] Nor would government agencies pressure lenders to reduce the value of a mortgage to match the market value of the property, thereby allowing borrowers to make affordable mortgage payments in line with the home's actual worth.

Advocates worked with Newark and Irvington (a neighboring town) to have these cities adopt the eminent domain proposal, which was backed by, among others, financier Steven Gluckstern of Mortgage Resolution Partners.[55] Although we were initially skeptical that a market value could be placed on the value of a distressed mortgage, it turned out that there is a market for these mortgages, providing a standard for fair compensation when mortgages are seized. But the proposal got mired down in politics when Richmond, California – where it was first proposed – was subjected to intense real estate industry lobbying and a lawsuit alleging an unconstitutional taking.[56] Although the lawsuit was dismissed, the proposal failed to pass the City Council; neither Newark nor any other city adopted it thereafter and it withered on the vine. Yet the failure of this very creative idea should not preclude other ideas that have the potential to address the lingering aftereffects of the foreclosure crisis.

Still, we must remain mindful that remediation may eventually lead to gentrification and displacement of current residents. This concern is anything but unfounded, as developers seek to take advantage of the current housing shortages and gentrification creeps into previously affordable areas across the country. Our clients often are faced with an impossible choice: rising costs in gentrifying neighborhoods on the one hand, and decreasing quality of life in neglected high-foreclosure communities on the other. We have seen many clients leave the

---

[54] Robert C. Hockett, *It Takes a Village: Municipal Condemnation Proceedings and Public/ Private Partnerships for Mortgage Loan Modification, Value Preservation, and Local Economic Recovery*, 18 STANFORD J. LAW, BUSINESS & FINANCE 2013.

[55] The company is no longer active.

[56] Alejandro Lazo, *U.S. Warns against Eminent-Domain Mortgage Seizures*, L.A. TIMES (Aug. 8, 2013), http://articles.latimes.com/2013/aug/08/business/la-fi-eminent-domain-lawsuit-20130809.

New York metropolitan area, scattering to lower-cost regions, particularly in the South. Others double up with family wherever they are welcome. This migration has hurt not only individual families, but communities as well. According to Richard Rothstein, when the many subprime mortgages eventually went into default, "lower-middle-class African American neighborhoods were devastated, and their residents, with their homes foreclosed, were forced back into low-income areas."[57] Nonetheless, some of our more fortunate clients – those who retained their homes and staved off foreclosure – have been able to improve and stabilize their lives.

---

[57] Richard Rothstein, THE COLOR OF LAW: A FORGOTTEN HISTORY OF HOW OUR GOVERNMENT SEGREGATED AMERICA 109 (2017).

8

Where Do We Go from Here?

A banker is a fellow who lends you his umbrella when the sun is shining,
but wants it back the minute it begins to rain.

Mark Twain

This book has taken you on a whirlwind tour of the mortgage foreclosure crisis and post-crisis landscape. We have provided context for what we view as the most salient issues. We have also argued policy points and supported our assertions with statistical studies. Still, the stories of individuals and families suffering at the hands of bureaucratic indifference to borrowers' plights are the narratives that most hit home. The crisis becomes more than a collection of historical statistics when viewed through the individual experiences of borrowers stuck with predatory loans, unable to get their loan servicer's attention, and agonizing as their homes gradually vanish. We hope you now better understand the full impact of the housing crisis.

The looming question remains: What can and should be done to further mitigate the ongoing consequences of the crisis and prevent the next one? We have provided diagnoses and offered limited solutions that address portions of the overall problem, but this final chapter is the place to lay out broader views of reform. Given our focus herein on mortgages and foreclosure, our reform proposals address these specific areas, rather than financial reform in general.

HOMEOWNERSHIP SINCE THE CRISIS

As recounted in Chapter 5, housing markets have changed drastically since the foreclosure crisis. Homeownership opportunities have been reduced, particularly for nonwhites and younger people. Tightened lending standards, low interest rates, the decreasing housing inventory – particularly for new construction – and the conversion of many privately owned homes to rentals have combined to cause housing prices to surge once again in many markets. The obvious result has been that fewer people can afford to buy houses, with consequences rippling outward. Areas of the country most impacted by the crisis have been the slowest to recover. As Dan Immergluck observes in his book *Preventing the Next Mortgage Crisis*, when "mortgages become overly restrictive or much less affordable in hard-hit neighborhoods, it will be even more difficult for them to recover."[1] True enough, ownership rates – particularly for African Americans and Latinos – have dropped significantly from their pre-crisis levels.

Of course, as Mechele Dickerson does in her book *Homeownership and America's Financial Underclass*, one can question whether the gains of homeownership are worth the price.[2] Professor Dickerson persuasively argues that for many people, they are not. But African Americans traditionally have invested most of their wealth in their homes, so homeownership has great value and home loss hits particularly hard.[3] Americans have tended to view their homes as more than just places to live, but as an investment as well. In losing their home to foreclosure, many also lost their only retirement savings. Now, many of our clients see no pathway back their pre-crisis level of security. Homeownership, although as desirable as ever, looks completely out of reach.

For some, ownership may still be a good option, but only if, as Dan Immergluck explains, "housing finance markets are accessible, affordable and risk-limiting."[4] The reality has caused many – especially millennials who are living longer with their parents – to rethink the possibility of homeownership. We cannot presume to decide who should buy and who should not. Consumers should, however, have that choice. Currently the American Dream of homeownership is not feasible for many, yet renting is becoming increasingly unaffordable. This needs to change.

We are in this position because of the massive numbers of foreclosures in the last decade. So what can we do now? We can take steps to mitigate the damage already sustained and learn from our mistakes before the next financial downturn, which history tells us will occur. Mortgage products that do not place all the downside risk of economic fluctuations on borrowers could go a long way. Lenders seldom bear much risk in economic downturns. In fact, many of the lenders most responsible for the last crisis are larger than ever and raking in record profits, while borrowers,

---

[1]   Dan Immergluck, PREVENTING THE NEXT MORTGAGE CRISIS: THE MELTDOWN, THE FEDERAL RESPONSE, AND THE FUTURE OF HOUSING IN AMERICA (2015) at 143.

[2]   *See*, Mechele Dickerson, HOMEOWNERSHIP AND AMERICA'S UNDERCLASS (2014).

[3]   *See*, Gillian B. White, *Not All Money Troubles Are Created Equal*, THE ATLANTIC, Apr. 21, 2016:

> A prime example of this inequality is the aftermath of the housing crisis. While whites were more likely to own homes, they were also more likely to own other assets. For black homeowners, however, houses accounted for a larger portion of their wealth. That means the recession gutted much of the black wealth there was. A report from the ACLU estimates that by 2031, white families' wealth will be about 31 percent lower because of the recession. Black families will have given up around 40 percent of their wealth.

[4]   Immergluck, *supra* note 1, at 148–49.

investors and communities are left shouldering the burden. We need to ask who is in the best position to assume or allocate the inherent risks. There are valid reasons for investors and stockholders to bear losses. They are, after all, the gamblers in this equation.

Investments by their nature rise and fall in the short term, even if they increase over the long term. And any prudent investor is playing the long game. Losses are part of the risk of investing and, therefore, should be accepted. Further, investors are typically more able to assume more of those risks than the average shareholder. On the other hand, one of the problems we faced in the last crisis was that the investors of 2008 were not the investors of 1920. In 1920, investors were generally from the wealthiest families. In 2008, municipalities, 401K plans and pension funds were heavily invested in the housing market, largely in the belief that the markets would always rise. The investors, as a result, were much more middle class and, in 2008, investment losses were spread across a wider swath of people and sectors.

We learned throughout the crisis that lenders and the investment banks they partnered with were far from honest about the quality of their investments. Therefore, it would be fair for them to bear a high percentage of the loss. As we know, that did not happen. Lawsuits have been filed to enforce representations and warranties in securitization contracts that require originating lenders to repurchase certain defaulted loans from pools. Investors have also taken a range of measures to recover their losses, but borrowers themselves have received little relief. Settlements of the national lawsuits brought by the Justice Department against Bank of America, Citigroup, Deutsche Bank and others have in general not provided much borrower aid; in some cases, settlement money went directly into state general funds for purposes entirely unrelated to lending or housing.[5] In any event, *ex ante* solutions are often preferable to *ex post* remedies, which tend not to sufficiently rectify harms.

We also need to consider other housing models. Some people do not want to own a home and others will never have enough income to buy and maintain a safe, habitable one. Yet, in many locations renting costs the same (or more) than buying. We have long known that home ownership provides social as well as economic stability. It correlates with more stable families, enhanced civic engagement, better educational achievement and increased racial interaction.[6] Entrepreneurs have been experimenting with alternative housing models for years. One very promising possibility is "limited equity homeownership,"[7] a model used by Mutual Homes, a

---

[5] *See*, Bob Egelko, *California Ordered to Restore $331 Million to Fund for Homeowners*, San Francisco Chronicle, July 11, 2018 (appellate court orders money diverted to state general fund to be used to help foreclosed homeowners). Several other states, including New Jersey, similarly deposited settlement money into their general funds, without adverse consequences.

[6] Julie D. Lawton, *Limited Equity Cooperatives: The Non-Economic Value of Homeownership*, 43 Wash.U.J.L. Pol'y 187, 196 (2013).

[7] *Id.*

flourishing scattered-site housing cooperative in South Bend.[8] In these groups of stand-alone homes, costs are based on income and the development provides services like economic counseling and home maintenance. These are the kinds of supports needed for successful lower-income homeownership.

PRIVATE MORTGAGE LENDING REFORMS

When all the dust of the last crisis settled, borrowers and their communities lost the most. It mattered little if a borrower had been tricked into a predatory loan product, bought more house than she could afford or found herself unable to pay her traditional thirty-year fixed mortgage in the overall economic downturn. All were treated the same and forced to shoulder the burden of a mortgage finance system over which they had no control. In the end, many lost their only significant investment, their home. We need a better system that recognizes the risks but also acknowledges that borrowers have little influence over the economy, while lenders can make or break the financial health of a nation and even the world, as we witnessed firsthand.

Shared Appreciation and Continuous Workout Mortgages

Reforms in mortgage instruments could help spread risks and benefits for both borrowers and lenders. Several proposals for these products are currently being suggested and a few are available in the market, but in very limited numbers. In *House of Debt*, Mian and Sufi describe a "shared appreciation mortgage," or what they have termed a "shared responsibility mortgage," as one in which "(1) the lender offers *downside* protection to the borrower, and (2) the borrower gives up *5 percent capital gain* to the lender on the upside."[9] They are only two of several who have proposed such an instrument. The underlying concept of shared appreciation mortgages is that borrowers can save on their interest rate by sharing subsequent gains in property value with lenders. That way, borrowers pay less for the property over the life of the loan, while lenders stand to profit from rising markets during the same period. The extent of the gain to each party of course depends on the percentage of appreciated value a borrower must pay to the lender. During the crisis, some risk-management experts recommended shared appreciation mortgages coupled with mortgage modifications involving principal write-downs as a potential way to mitigate moral hazard; after all, borrowers and lenders share the wealth of any later growth in home equity.[10]

---

[8] SOUTH BEND MUTUAL HOMES, http://sbheritage.org/find-home/south-bend-mutual-homes.

[9] Atif Mian & Amir Aufi, HOUSE OF DEBT: HOW THEY (AND YOU) CAUSED THE GREAT RECESSION, AND HOW TO PREVENT IT FROM HAPPENING AGAIN 171 (2015).

[10] *See*, Clifford Rossi, *Share Appreciation Mortgages Is the Answer to Moral Hazard*, AM. BANKER (Feb. 17, 2012), https://www.americanbanker.com/opinion/shared-appreciation-mortgages-is-the-answer-to-moral-hazard.

Shared appreciation mortgages have been used in the United States, but only occasionally. For instance, they represent one option for repayment of reverse mortgages. According to HUD, which sets the standards for these home equity conversion mortgages,

> [a] shared appreciation mortgage, where the borrower promises to pay the lender a percentage of the appreciation in the value of the property, in addition to the outstanding balance, when the mortgage is due and payable, is also available ... Under this type of mortgage, the borrower may have the benefit of a lower interest rate and, therefore, higher monthly or line of credit payments.[11]

By contrast, Yale economist Robert Shiller has proposed a "continuous workout mortgage" with negative equity insurance. Monthly mortgage payments decrease when necessary to prevent negative equity, which occurs when a home is underwater because the borrower owes more on the mortgage than the value of the property. This is an *ex ante* solution to unanticipated price declines during the life of the loan. The benefits to the borrower are obvious, but the lender also benefits from the reduced risk of borrower default and the expenses of mortgage workouts or foreclosure. Under this model, the lender is more likely to receive a continuous stream of payments without incurring additional transaction costs. The community benefits because the home is less likely to be foreclosed, driving down the cost of adjacent properties. The downward spiral of housing values that plagued many neighborhoods could be averted.

Both alternatives entail the allocation of downside risk between the parties but each was designed for different products: The shared appreciation (or responsibility) model was originally designed for purchase or refinance mortgages (though it is also used with reverse mortgages). By lowering the interest rate, the lender will receive less income unless the property value rises. If property values drop, the lender receives nothing, but borrower default risk is reduced. Relatedly, the continuous workout model was designed for reverse mortgages. In a reverse mortgage, the "borrower" cashes out her equity and receives monthly payments or a lump sum from the bank. This option allows the owner to receive higher monthly payments. Reverse mortgages typically come due when the homeowner dies. Therefore, the heirs may owe money if the property value has risen, but the risk is diminished if more will be owed than the house is worth. Again, borrowers are less likely to default. Both are improvements on the current situation where defaulting

---

[11] *See*, HUD document 4235.1, REV-1, section 1–7 SHARED APPRECIATION; *see also* APPENDIX 11. The shared appreciation rider explains that "[notwithstanding] anything to the contrary set forth in the Note, Borrower hereby agrees to the following:

1. At the time that the Note is due and payable or is paid in full, Borrower promises to pay Lender an additional amount of interest equal to twenty-five percent (25%) of the net appreciated value of the property, except that the total effective interest rate shall not exceed twenty percent (20%)."

borrowers – regardless of why – lose their homes while lenders face the costs of foreclosure, costs they often underestimate. In fact, the very structure of mortgage financing allocates more long-term risk to borrowers and tends to obscure longer-term risks to lenders. As British lawyer and academic Sarah Nield has observed:

> The lender's obligations in providing the loan are immediately performed and remaining contractual performance rests solely upon the borrower … over the loan term. The focus of contractual failure is thus on the borrower. Nevertheless, a lender's exposure to the failure of continued borrower performance can be mitigated in a number of ways. First, the mortgage security itself provides the lender with the ultimate protection against the risk of borrower default through an ability to repossess and sell the borrower's home. Secondly, the lender is able to transfer and spread the risk of borrower default through the process of securitisation. Lastly, exposure to increases in the lender's funding costs can be covered by the short-term nature of mortgage pricing and the lender's power to vary interest rates over which there are few legal, as opposed to market, controls. By contrast, for the borrower, the [specter] of default ensures that meeting mortgage repayments is prioritised to exercise a powerful influence on the borrower's spending habits and lifestyle choices. It has been described as the hostage function of mortgage security which captures the desperation that borrowers can experience when faced with the risk of losing their home. Lender forbearance strategies rely upon this hostage function and justify a cautious application of the ultimate sanction of repossession. The extended period of loan repayment presents an increased risk that conditions may change to jeopardise the performance of the borrower's repayment obligations. Loss of job, illness, and relationship breakdown are just three events which provide the most common cause of repayment difficulties [citations omitted].[12]

Consciously distributing risk between the parties to incorporate the likelihood of loss to both borrower and lender can result in a mortgage contract calibrated for success. But it is particularly difficult to imagine most lenders adopting the continuous workout model, since – as we have demonstrated – servicers and lenders (their principals) tend to focus more on short-term profit than on longer-term consequences of their actions.

Mortgage Insurance for Borrowers

Other methods exist to ensure that borrowers do not have to bear the lion's share of risk. These include mortgage insurance as offered in the United Kingdom (UK) and Ireland. This insurance provides coverage for borrowers, not just lenders, in contrast to the primary mortgage insurance (PMI) offered in the United States, which protects lenders and is required of borrowers making down payments of less than 20 percent.

---

[12] Sarah Nield, *Mortgage Market Review: "Hard-Wired Common Sense?,"* 3 J. CONSUMER POL'Y 139, 143 (2015).

In the United Kingdom, two types of insurance are available: Mortgage life insurance pays off the mortgage if the borrower dies and is often required by the lender, while mortgage payment protection insurance provides some coverage for illness, accident and unemployment, varying with policy terms. Those policies covering unemployment have been criticized for not providing effective or adequate coverage.[13] Ireland also provides mortgage insurance for borrowers. Property law scholar Padraic Kenna explains: "In terms of mortgage insurance – there are compulsory policies in relation to death, and some in relation to critical illness cover[age]. It is also possible to get permanent health insurance to cover loss of income through illness although this tends to be expensive."[14]

Credit insurance is available in the United States, but it is most often part of a car sale and not a home purchase. It has not, however, had a good track record. It is often forced on consumers at very high cost and then amortized out as part of the loan, increasing the cost over time because the borrower is paying interest on the already inflated cost. In addition, consumers have had a very difficult time accessing the benefit, partly because they are often not given a copy of the policy they allegedly purchased. Advocates have worked tirelessly to require full disclosure and ensure that this kind of predatory product was not mandatory. We are not recommending a resurrection of those products.

The insurance industry could conceive a properly priced policy that is paid monthly, not all at once, and amortized. A fair insurance product could reduce the number of foreclosures; after all, a large percentage involve default due to illness, unemployment or often, death. Of course, the policies would need to not only provide comprehensive coverage, but also be affordable. The insurance company's duty thus would need to flow to the homeowner, not the lender. Considering our past experiences with credit insurance, we are somewhat skeptical that the US insurance market would be interested in a fair and affordable product. At the same time, if other nations can do it, we wonder why we cannot.

Servicing Reforms

Servicing presents an ongoing problem with an extensive array of errors and other negligence still to be addressed. Servicers' primary interest, it seems, is to maximize profits, but efforts to change this system are being proposed. One possible solution is to create a legally enforceable duty for servicers to borrowers. The single point of contact rule, created by the CFPB and requiring lenders to designate a single employee to assist a borrower, was a step in the right direction, but it was soon

[13] *See*, e-mail from Sarah Nield to Linda Fisher, June 18, 2018 (on file with the author). In addition, the British government provided social security-type payments covering mortgage interest, called Support for Mortgage Interest (SMI) during the crisis; the program is now converting the subsidies into loans.

[14] *See*, e-mail from Padraic Kenna to Linda Fisher, June 18, 2018 (on file with the author).

diluted to require a single team of contact.[15] Clients continue to experience problems with their single point of contact who is perpetually unavailable and liable to change, sometimes daily, because the industry is still understaffed for the job.

It is critical that servicers adopt a single servicing platform or at least collaborate to create servicing platforms that can communicate effectively with each other. One of the main causes of errors is the lack of integration of information when a file moves from one servicer to another. Mandating a single platform might not be feasible, but regulation could be drafted that more effectively holds a lender responsible when it changes servicers and data is lost or inaccurately transferred. Financial institutions are unlikely to take meaningful steps on these issues, given their hard-line anti-regulatory stance and resistance to change. Our current anti-regulatory climate does not help.

It is crucial that we retain the rules instituted during the crisis that require a lender to work with a homeowner who is facing foreclosure.[16] Already, the Trump administration is hoping to eliminate them as a burden to business. A similar requirement for workable alternatives to foreclosure is necessary. More and more lenders require unreasonable down payments from borrowers already facing financial difficulty. Such "offers" do nothing to prevent the foreclosure, an outcome that benefits neither party.

The best possible reform – and the once least likely to occur – would allow a borrower to fire a servicer. Borrowers choose a lender, hopefully for all the right reasons: the lender's rates, service record and perhaps even institutional relationship. Yet, with a separate servicer, they soon find themselves dealing with a company they did not choose and one they cannot fire. If I am unhappy with my cable company, I can switch. You cannot change loan servicers no matter how badly they perform. This relationship has all the hallmarks of a monopoly, but no protections for borrowers. We need a system that treats servicers the way we treat other monopolies. Borrowers need not just a place to file complaints, but one with the power to effect real change. The CFPB was that agency, but the Trump administration seems determined to repeal Dodd-Frank, dismantling all its consumer protections. Consumers lose again.

POLICY CHANGES AND GOVERNMENT ASSISTANCE

Current mortgage lending practices favor lenders over borrowers, in part because the government provides backstops for lenders – bailouts, loan guarantees and the like – without giving borrowers similar protections. In the wake of the 2008 meltdown, the Bush and Obama administrations sided with financial advisers who failed to grapple with the effects of foreclosures on borrowers and, maybe more importantly, their

---

[15] *See*, 12 CFR §1024.40.
[16] 12 CFR §1024.

communities. Former Special Inspector General for TARP Neil Barofsky met with Treasury Secretary Timothy Geithner in 2009 concerning HAMP, quite an anemic program at that time. In his book *Bailout*, Barofsky claims to have attended a meeting where, "In defense of the program, Geithner finally blurted out, 'We estimate that they can handle ten million foreclosures, over time,'" referring to the banks. "This program will help foam the runway for them."[17] There was no mention of borrowers. This view of foreclosures does not appear to have changed since the crisis. The mountains of evidence of the harm that just one foreclosure – let alone the millions we experienced – causes to the health and economic well-being of borrowers and their neighbors was, and is, completely disregarded.

The Federal Housing Finance Agency (FHFA), still important in the market, could lead the way on reform. And a strong GSE policy requiring lenders to look at retention options before foreclosure could move the entire market in that direction. Fannie and Freddie also could insist on stricter standards for servicer behavior. The GSEs should get credit for the "Flex Mod" program discussed in Chapter 4. It creates a payment reduction option for borrowers having trouble with their mortgage and does not require the mountains of paperwork that bogged down the HAMP program. The recent origin of Flex Mod limits our ability to say much about its success. However, the latest report, issued in August 2018, suggests that loan modifications increased slightly with the program as compared to the same period last year. More significantly, loan modifications are happening earlier in the delinquency period.[18]

We are not seeing this model used for non-GSE loans, which still employ a variety of different programs, forms and criteria. How ironic that an industry historically advocating for uniform foreclosure laws cannot agree on a single application for mortgage foreclosure assistance. Transparency also continues to be a major problem, making it extremely difficult for customers to know and understand their options. Servicers should be required to set out the specifics of what they offer and to whom.

Although the loan servicing rules enacted by the Consumer Financial Protection Bureau – including those governing the Qualified Mortgage – have remedied some servicing problems, servicing issues continue to this day. Outside the jurisdiction of the GSEs, borrower assistance remains discretionary and, as previously mentioned, borrowers have no power to make a servicer perform. A market cannot operate efficiently when customers are forced to use a company that fails to perform yet cannot be fired. Payment and foreclosure systems would be improved if mortgage modifications become a real possibility for all borrowers, not just GSE borrowers, and if borrowers who were experiencing difficulty were not left in limbo for years.

---

[17] Neal Barofsy, Bailout: How Washington Abandoned Main Street While Rescuing Wall Street (2013), at 156.

[18] FHFA Foreclosure Prevention Report, May 2008, at 3, https://www.fhfa.gov/AboutUs/Reports/ReportDocuments/FPR_May2018.pdf.

GSEs and federal regulation can lead the way on these issues. Not only that, but it is critical that nonbank lenders themselves, as well as their servicers, be carefully regulated. Ultimately, though, state foreclosure law still plays an important role.

Unfortunately, the federal government has acted much like lenders, focusing on its short-term profits, not the overall, long-term health of the market. Many of its decisions focused primarily on the fiscal health of Fannie Mae and Freddie Mac and were designed to increase profits, with no consideration of the harm they were causing. For instance, the GSEs sold many loans through the DASP after servicers failed to modify mortgages, but by selling to investors looking for quick profits, they created more problems for communities and many borrowers now face even more onerous loan terms. These sales should come with strict requirements for maintaining properties and providing workouts for homeowners. Neighborhood groups and other community not-for-profits should have the first opportunity to buy these loans. Small efforts at improvements have been made, but they were often too little and enacted too late.

While federal efforts are those most likely to create templates for action across the country, states have been very protective of their individual state foreclosure systems. Numerous efforts to unify state law have failed, with the Uniform Home Foreclosure Procedures Act of 2015 being the most recent. State and local governments should be encouraged to take the lead in modernizing foreclosure procedures, but also in creating a system that considers the value of homeownership and the fundamental right to a home. The GSEs should not step in to prevent every effort to protect homeowners and communities, as has been their practice to date. States and municipalities need to be able to police the bad actors that the industry, especially the GSEs, have failed to regulate. Particularly now, in an era when meaningful federal action is unlikely, states and municipalities can serve as laboratories for innovation and robust foreclosure prevention and remediation programs. Foreclosure law remains a very state-specific process. State legislators need to be educated on the harms of foreclosure to their communities. Reforms must include policies that recognize alternatives to harmful foreclosure practices. The licensing of servicers, to ensure compliance with best practices, is one such step.

MORE SUPPORT FOR HOUSING COUNSELING AND NEIGHBORHOOD REVITALIZATION EFFORTS

It should come as no surprise that we see a dire need for appropriations dedicated to providing housing counseling to borrowers. Housing counselors have been invaluable in assisting borrowers in trouble, but also in catching predatory loans and loan products before homeowners agree to their terms. We often think of housing counselors only in terms of loss mitigation, but they are equally important at the front end of a home purchase. Many first-time borrowers really do not understand all the ramifications of a home purchase, especially if they come from a background where homeownership was not common. Housing counselors can nip predatory lending in the bud. Policymakers should also find ways to better utilize the knowledge base of these professionals. If you want to know who the bad guys are, your local housing counselor can tell you.

On the local level, community development financial institutions and land banks can lead the way in rehabilitating areas devastated by foreclosure. Significantly more support is needed for efforts to rehabilitate foreclosed homes – particularly vacant ones – and transform them to affordable housing. Communities need money, but we also need new legal strategies. Gaining title to abandoned properties is one of the biggest challenges. Lenders should not be able to hold onto mortgages for properties they and homeowners have long abandoned. Rehabilitating these homes creates a ripple effect that extends to neighborhoods, helping to alleviate foreclosure contagion, and ultimately expanding to entire communities. Absent such efforts, the downward spiral we have chronicled is unlikely to abate, leaving poor neighborhoods in a state of permanent calamity.

LEGAL CHANGES

The financial crisis exposed numerous flaws in our legal structures. Implementing any changes in the current, anti-government, anti-regulation environment will be difficult. In many ways, we are advocating not for the creation of completely new structures, but for retaining the positive steps that have been taken in recent years. Crucial is the vigorous enforcement of anti-discrimination and anti-predatory lending laws that could have prevented the last crisis.

The Fair Housing and Equal Credit Opportunity Acts are examples of current law intended to alleviate mortgage lending discrimination. The US Supreme Court, in *Texas Department of Housing and Community Affairs v. Inclusive Communities Project*,[19] found that the Fair Housing Act protects against disparate impact discrimination – the kind most pervasive in the run-up to the crisis. The disparate impact standard protects against a seemingly neutral action, such as soliciting a neighborhood for a predatory loan product, that has a disproportionate, negative impact on a protected minority group. After the Supreme Court ruling, HUD created a new rule to implement the decision. On June 20, 2018, HUD published a "Reconsideration of HUD's Implementation of the Fair Housing Act's Disparate Impact Standard," notice asking for comments.[20] It indicates the direction the Trump administration hopes to take on this issue. For example, it asks whether the current rule avoids "unmeritorious claims," as opposed to inquiring into whether it may have supported meritorious ones. It also asks whether the framework of the current rule only applies to practices that are "artificial, arbitrary and unnecessary," language that casts the

---

[19] 135 S.Ct. 2507, (2015).
[20] 28560 FED., REG., vol. 83 no. 119, June 20, 2018.

current rule as too burdensome. Finally, it posits the need for safe harbors.[21] All this implies a move to weaken the power of the current rule and with it the Fair Housing Act itself. This is unsurprising coming from an agency that removed the promise of housing "free from discrimination" from its mission statement just months before issuing this request for comments.[22] Clearly, the Trump administration is not committed to anti-discrimination policies. Paired with its lack of support for consumer protection, it can only mean trouble in the future, unless of course you are a predatory lender.

Similarly, the Community Reinvestment Act (CRA), which has proved its efficacy in increasing neighborhood lending, should once again be aggressively enforced.[23] The CRA allows the FDIC to review banks periodically to determine if they are meeting the needs of their communities. While it does not require banks to extend credit to non-creditworthy borrowers, it does require that lending and investment occur in all neighborhoods. All too many lending institutions appear to meet their CRA obligations by funding luncheons, as opposed to offering loans. Lending institutions need to be encouraged to open brick-and-mortar locations in low-income neighborhoods and to offer safe, affordable loans to the members of those communities. Many blamed the crisis on the CRA, claiming it forced banks to lend to unworthy borrowers.[24] Banks may be required to lend in minority neighborhoods, but they have never been required to give bad loans exclusively in minority neighborhoods or to provide worse loans to minorities, despite their credit scores. Both of these abuses occurred in the subprime loan boom that helped fuel the crisis.

Probably the most important legal changes need to happen at the state level. States need to rethink all aspects of foreclosure law, including tax foreclosure. As remnants of the old English legal system, foreclosure matters are generally considered cases "in equity" as opposed to cases "in law." Courts that sit in equity are theoretically balancing the interests of the parties to come up with a solution that is both legal – in that it complies with relevant statutes and regulations – and equitable – or fair – to both parties. The latter half of that equation has been completely lost in most jurisdictions. Virtually the only consideration courts seem to weigh is how best to maximize lenders' profits. Courts appear to bend the rules to assist lenders that cannot seem to understand and follow the legal requirements. For example, a lender that fails to provide the paperwork needed to prove its standing to

---

[21] *Id.* at 28561.

[22] Tracy Lee, *Ben Carson's Housing Department Removes Commitment to Discrimination-Free Communities from Its Mission Statement*, NEWSWEEK, Mar. 7, 2018.

[23] *See*, this statement by the Federal Financial Institutions Examination Council: "The Community Reinvestment Act (CRA), enacted by Congress in 1977 (12 U.S.C. 2901) and implemented by Regulations 12 CFR parts 25, 228, 345, and 195, is intended to encourage depository institutions to help meet the credit needs of the communities in which they operate." https://www.ffiec.gov/cra.

[24] *See*, e.g., Peter Wallison, *Hey, Barney Frank: The Government Did Cause the Housing Crisis*, THE ATLANTIC, Dec. 13, 2011.

foreclose, should not be given years to come up with the documents it should have had before initiating the foreclosure, as occurred in Ned Carey's case discussed in Chapter 3. As the Maine Supreme Court very recently pointed out in frustration, "The law, the rules of evidence, and court processes have not become more complicated in these matters. Applying established law, however, has become more problematic as courts address the problems the financial services industry has created for itself."[25] Serious problems with mortgage foreclosures continue. Unfortunately, only those who are lucky enough to live in judicial foreclosure states have a realistic chance of discovering the flaws in the lender's records.

Nonjudicial foreclosure tips the balance too far in favor of creditors. Borrowers have no ability to challenge any aspect of the foreclosure unless they hire an attorney and file an action in court, all of which must be done very quickly. Needless to say, that rarely happens. During the crisis we learned the astonishing truth that not everyone whose house is foreclosed has actually fallen behind on their mortgage payments – some borrowers in foreclosure are actually up to date with payments. One of our favorite cases to share with students is an Indiana case, *Elliott v. JP Morgan Chase*,[26] which opens with the wonderful comment, "The Kafkaesque character of this litigation is difficult to deny." And it is: The home was foreclosed and sold back to the bank. The homeowners had paid off the mortgage nearly ten years earlier, so they called upon the Indiana attorney general for assistance. The AG reached out to Chase Bank, which said it had no idea why the loan was being foreclosed because the mortgage had been paid off in 2001. Despite all this, the servicer, Ocwen, and the lawyers it hired continued to push the foreclosure and the trial judge allowed it. The Court of Appeals – acting rationally – reversed the trial court's decision.[27] Granted, this appears to be an extreme situation. We wish it were. This family had the benefit of a court process to save their home, but imagine these same facts in a nonjudicial setting.

A recent development has the potential to turn things around. In August 2018 a federal court ruled that both Fannie Mae and Freddie Mac are government entities. As such, they must comply with the Administrative Procedures Act and other federal due practice protections when foreclosing on homes.[28] This is a change from prior court decisions that had determined that, because the conservatorship over Fannie Mae and Freddie Mac is temporary, they are not federal agencies. However, considering the realities, this position has become increasingly untenable. The conservatorship is more than ten years old, with no sign of ending. By any reasonable measure, it is permanent. If this decision is upheld, all foreclosures prosecuted by Fannie Mae and Freddie Mac will have to be judicial, giving borrowers not only

[25] M&T Bank v. Lawrence F. Plaisted, Aug. 16, 2018, 2018 ME 121.
[26] 920 N.E.2d 793 (Ind. Ct. App. 2010).
[27] Id. at 794.
[28] Sisti v. Federal Housing Finance Agency, 2018 WL 3655578 (D.R.I. Aug. 2, 2018).

notice, but an opportunity to be heard. Their dominant role in the market will require states to change their laws to accommodate. Judicial foreclosure could well become the dominant means of foreclosure.[29]

HOUSING AS A HUMAN RIGHT

The crisis and its aftermath bring the need for safe, affordable housing into sharp focus, both abroad and at home. As the United Nations' Special Rapporteur on Adequate Housing explained, problems of income inequality and rising home and rental prices have been "exacerbated by the adoption of legal and institutional adjustments aimed at facilitating foreclosure."[30] The result has been a worldwide foreclosure crisis and a seeming abandonment of international agreements regarding the right to safe, affordable housing. Homelessness is on the rise as are informal housing arrangements. Many of our own clients are living temporarily with family members as they search for viable places to live.

The right to adequate housing is stated in many international treaties and declarations. For example, Article 5 of the International Convention of the Elimination of All Forms of Racial Discrimination includes housing in its platform.[31] The International Covenant of Economic, Social and Cultural Rights accords each person "the right to an adequate standard of living for himself and his family, including adequate food, clothing and housing."[32] Finally, Article 25 of the Declaration of Human Rights established that "[E]veryone has the right to a standard of living adequate for the health and well-being of himself and of his family, including food, clothing, housing and medical care and necessary social services."[33] In fact, the right to safe, affordable housing is considered by many international agreements to be the "most prominent" of the economic, social and cultural rights.[34]

---

[29] Geoff Walsh, *Fannie and Freddie Foreclosures Must Meet Constitutional Due Process Standards*, NAT. CONSUMER L. CTR (Aug. 21, 2018), https://library.nclc.org/fannie-and-freddie-foreclosures-must-meet-constitutional-due-process-standards.

[30] Raquel Rolnik, (Special Rapporteur on adequate housing) Report, U.N. Doc. A/67/286 (Aug. 10, 2012), https://www.ohchr.org/Documents/Issues/Housing/A-67-286.pdf.

[31] Int'l Convention on the Elimination of All Forms of Racial Discrimination, Adopted and opened for signature and ratification by General Assembly resolution 2106 (XX) of Dec. 21, 1965 entry into force Jan. 4, 1969, in accordance with Article 19, https://www.ohchr.org/Documents/ProfessionalInterest/cerd.pdf.

[32] Int'l Covenant on Economic, Social and Cultural Rights Adopted and opened for signature, ratification and accession by General Assembly resolution 2200A (XXI) of Dec. 16, 1966 Article 11, entry into force Jan. 3, 1976, in accordance with article 27; U.N. HUMAN RIGHTS, OFF. OF HIGH COMM, https://www.ohchr.org/en/professionalinterest/pages/cescr.aspx.

[33] Universal Declaration of Human Rights, http://www.un.org/en/udhrbook/pdf/udhr_booklet_en_web.pdf.

[34] Michael Koocek, *The Human Right to Housing in the 27 Member States of the European Union*, 7 EUROPEAN J. HOMELESSNESS 135 (Aug. 2013).

International human rights frameworks hold governments accountable to their citizens, making it "a legal obligation of States to be both a key actor and a regulator of private actors."[35] Looking at housing through this lens, as opposed to viewing it as a local or state issue, raises the discussion to a more significant level. The Special Rapporteur on Adequate Housing has identified many "factors that make a human rights framework critical to the effectiveness of housing strategies." Among these are looking at human rights problems from a wholistic perspective, seeking "to identify gaps and structural weaknesses in housing systems and programs."[36] We recognize that American politicians are loath to consider international law, let alone human rights norms, and the American judiciary for the most part agrees. At the same time, the clear social harms caused by unstable housing demand redress. A legally recognized right to housing might be the solution.

Housing policy shifted in the late 1970s, not just in the United States but in many parts of the world. Instead of looking to the state to provide and subsidize housing, the focus turned toward "unrestricted free markets and free trade."[37] HUD's budget for public housing, for instance, fell from $83 billion in 1978 to $18 billion in 1983, as the government increasingly saw privatization as the key to affordable housing.[38] While it may have taken hold during the Reagan presidency, this policy change has been bipartisan. In fact, during the Clinton administration, "no funding was allocated to public housing construction."[39] During the same period, housing prices rose dramatically and the way we looked at housing changed dramatically, transforming from "a social good into a commodity."[40] Owning property was a mark of wealth and a means of acquiring more. As such, decent housing came to be seen more as a benefit of wealth and success, and less and less as a fundamental right.

Housing as a fundamental right is based on several principles: It must be secure in its tenure and protect against eviction and other threats; it must provide basic needs for safety and comfort such as adequate heating and cooling, safe water and sanitation; it must be affordable to everyone, not just the very wealthy; it must be safe and free from structural hazards; and it must be accessible to the disabled and other vulnerable groups; finally, it must be located where the residents have access to employment, schools, health services and other essential social services.[41] In order to be effective, the right to housing must also be a "legal right subject to effective remedies."[42]

---

[35] Leilana Farha, (Special Rapporteur on adequate housing), Report, U.N. Doc. A/Hrc/37/53 (Jan. 15, 2018) at 4, https://www.placetocallhome.ca/pdfs/consultations/Report-of-the-Special-Rapporteur-Leilana-Farha-EN.pdf.

[36] *Id.*

[37] A/67/286, *supra* note 30, at 3.

[38] *Id.* at 6.

[39] *Id.*

[40] *Id.* at 5.

[41] *What Is the Human Right to Housing*, National Economic & Social Rights Initiative, Aug. 25, 2018.

[42] A/HRC/37/53, *supra* note 35, at 5.

In the wake of the foreclosure crisis, American housing policy has failed to meet the basic norms set out in international law. Evictions, for example, are viewed by the Special Rapporteur as "a gross violation of human rights" that should only occur "in the most exceptional circumstances and after all alternatives have been explored."[43] Consider nonjudicial foreclosure in light of those standards. During the crisis, thousands of homeowners lost their housing with no more process than a notice in the mail and no regard to where they would live once evicted. Unfortunately, the United States was not alone in this failure.

Many European (and other) countries claim to have taken the right to safe, affordable housing very seriously – so seriously, in fact, that it is imbedded in their constitutions. Ironically, Spain – a country that became known for its foreclosure evictions during the crisis – is one of those nations.[44] South Africa, hardly the poster child for safe, affordable housing, is another.[45] Yet, these provisions do provide a domestic legal foundation for those left homeless or facing eviction. The challenge is to take those norms and ideals and turn them into real social change, and to create a housing policy that truly respects those norms.

Foreclosure is perhaps the starkest example of the challenge. In recent years, the rights of lenders have been viewed as superior to those of homeowners. Because housing policy has been seen through the lens of economic investment and contract – not as protecting a fundamental human right – the economic rights of lenders are perceived as superior to human rights of the homeowners. We must flip this paradigm. According to South African legal scholar Reghard Brits, insofar as foreclosures are concerned,

> [T]he Constitution has had an important effect in mandating a shift in approach. The consideration of the socioeconomic circumstances of mortgagors, particularly as far as their housing rights (but also their dignity) are concerned, has led to a situation where new factors ... must henceforth be taken into account as a possible counterbalance to the mortgagee's claim. Accordingly, the social impact that foreclosure will have on the occupier and his dignity is now an important consideration, although the economic importance of giving effect to creditors' rights remains relevant as well. Perhaps the simplest way to summarise the current approach is that execution against the debtor's home must be the last resort and can no longer be the default position in foreclosure cases.[46]

---

[43] *Id.*

[44] Koocek, *supra* note 34, at 137.

[45] Section 26 provides that (1) Everyone has the right to have access to adequate housing.

> (2) The state must take reasonable legislative and other measures, within its available resources, to achieve the progressive realisation of this right.
> (3) No legislation may permit arbitrary evictions.

[46] REGHARD BRITS, REAL SECURITY LAW (2016) (section 2.5 Execution against a home, subsection 2.5.1 Judicial oversight).

Professor Brits specifically mentions mortgage modifications, arguing that the right to housing has had the salutary effect of inducing more mortgage modifications in lieu of foreclosure.[47]

Recent experiences in the United Kingdom illustrate the challenge such a balancing act will entail. The United Kingdom was a signer of the European Convention of Human Rights, Article 8, which provided a right to a home.[48] Unlike the international accords we discussed previously, this section does not place any burdens on the state to provide a home; it simply discusses protection of the home from interference. Nonetheless, interference with the home is permitted "in the interests of national security, public safety or the economic well-being of the country, for the prevention of disorder or crime, for the protection of health or morals or for the protection of the rights and freedom of others."[49] The rights of the borrower, therefore, must be weighed against the rights of the creditor to determine if the interference is justified and whether the ultimate harm to the homeowner is proportional to the harm to the creditor.[50] If a less intrusive and harmful method exists, it should be employed. Such an analysis is critical in the case of a mortgage foreclosure where loss of the home is being weighed against loss of income to the lender. We have demonstrated that lenders lose money in a foreclosure and that a loan modification could provide a steady income flow, albeit a less profitable one for the lender. Unfortunately, as Lorna Fox (no relation to the author) so eloquently describes in her book *Conceptualising Home: Theories, Laws and Policies*, that is not how courts have viewed the issues.

> The pro-creditor approach that has characterized judicial decision making in the creditor/occupier context has ensured that the commercial interests of the creditors have been given presumptive, if not automatic, priority over the home interests of the occupier. This position has, in turn, been facilitated by a combination of factors, including the under-conceptualisation of home in law and the tendency in property theory and law to treat the home as a mere capital asset.[51]

A fundamental paradigm shift is required before a borrower-friendly approach will be successful. Policymakers and the judiciary must begin to accept that "home" is

---

[47] *See,* Reghard Brits, *Compulsory Debt Reorganization in South Africa Mortgage Law: Towards a Sharing Model,* unpublished paper for presentation at the 2018 meeting of the Association of Law, Property and Society (cited with permission of the author).

[48] Lorna Fox, Conceptualizing Home: Theoriesm Laws and Policies 453 (2007). *See also, Human Rights: The European Convention,* BBC News (Sept. 29, 2000), http://news.bbc.co.uk/2/hi/uk_news/948143.stm.

[49] Fox, *supra* note 48, at 453.

[50] *Id.* at 480.

[51] *Id.* at 519.

much more than a commodity. We will not try to explain here what it took an entire book for Lorna Fox to explore. Suffice it to say that "home" is a complex combination of asset, identity, physical space and social and cultural identity.[52] Until we recognize this, the balance between the creditor and the homeowner will always tip in favor of the creditor.

[52] *Id. at* 131–80.

Conclusion

We have short memories. The dust from the last crisis has not yet settled and our policymakers have all but forgotten those still struggling to regain all they lost. Effective social policy is not made during the boom or the bust, but during periods of relatively stability – like now. This is the time to act. We must strengthen and safeguard the protections gained as part of the crisis. These include the protections of the Dodd-Frank legislation and the resulting rules created by the CFPB. It is also necessary to maintain the CFPB as an agency that protects consumers, not as one that addresses "unduly burdensome regulation."[1] We need a real commitment to improving servicer performance by eliminating those that cannot perform. Standard forms and communicating platforms are a priority, especially if lenders continue to change servicers as often as most people change shoes. Regulation of nonbank lenders similarly must be robust. Innovative products that spread the risk of falling home prices and the benefits of rising ones need to be made available to the public.

Finally, and perhaps most important, we need to completely rethink foreclosure. A home is far more than an asset. It occupies a much more significant place in the minds of the residents and contributes to the economic and social stability of a community. Foreclosure law needs to take this complexity into account. Loan modifications and temporary forbearance can save a home from foreclosure, but in most cases lenders must be coerced into taking this reasonable step. A rational housing policy must provide not only the minimum due process rights that judicial foreclosure affords, but also all the creative solutions that equity allows. If we face the next crisis with the same emphasis on protecting the creditor and not the community, we will get the same results. In fact, when the next crisis comes, we may still be feeling the reverberations of the 2008 foreclosure echo.

---

[1] *Mulvaney Makes Change to CFPB Mission Statement*, CU Today (Jan. 10, 2018, 8:17 PM), https://www.cutoday.info/Fresh-Today/Mulvaney-Makes-Change-To-CFPB-Mission-Statement.

Index

FASKEN LEARNING RESOURCE CENTER

9000090012

KF
697
.F6
F57
2019

Fisher, Linda E., 1953-
author.
The foreclosure echo : how
the hardest hit have been
left out of the economic